# VOLTAIRE AND SENSIBILITY

*Voltaire*

## AND SENSIBILITY
*R. S. Ridgway*

McGILL–QUEEN'S UNIVERSITY PRESS

MONTREAL AND LONDON 1973

This book has been published with the help of
a grant from the Humanities Research Council
of Canada using funds provided by the Canada
Council.

© McGill–Queen's University Press 1973
International Standard Book Number 0 7735 0130 4
Library of Congress Catalog Card Number 72–94539
Legal Deposit 2nd quarter 1973

Design by Allan Harrison
Printed in England by William Clowes & Sons, Limited
London, Beccles and Colchester

'*Malheur aux cœurs durs! Dieu bénira les âmes tendres. Il y a je ne sais quoi de réprouvé à être insensible; aussi s^{te} Thérèse définissait elle le diable, le malheureux qui ne sait point aimer*' (Best. D2062).

'*. . .qui ne sçait point haïr ne sçait point aimer*' (Best. 8812).

# CONTENTS

# ACKNOWLEDGEMENTS

My thanks are due to a number of persons and institutions; in particular, to the Canada Council, which provided me with a substantial research grant; to the University of Saskatchewan; to Dr. Theodore Besterman, for permission to use the facilities of the Institut et Musée Voltaire, and to the friendly and efficient staff of the Institut; to the editors of *Eighteenth-Century Studies* for permission to include excerpts from my article on 'Voltaire as an Actor'; to librarians in Canada, France, and Switzerland, and especially to the staff of the Murray Memorial Library of the University of Saskatchewan, of the Bibliothèque Nationale in Paris, and of the Bibliothèque Publique et Universitaire de Genève; above all, to my understanding wife and children.

# LIST OF ABBREVIATIONS

*AUMLA*:    *Journal of the Australian Universities Language and Literature Association.*

Best.:    *Voltaire's Correspondence*, ed. Theodore Besterman (Geneva, 1953–1965). The number identifies the letter to which reference is made; preceded by the letter D, it refers to the definitive edition of the *Correspondence* (Geneva, 1968–).

*FR*:    *The French Review*

*M*:    *Œuvres complètes de Voltaire*, nouvelle édition, ed. Louis Moland (Paris, 1877–82).

*MLN*:    *Modern Language Notes.*

*MLQ*:    *Modern Language Quarterly.*

*MP*:    *Modern Philology.*

Pléiade:    Bibliothèque de la Pléiade.

*PMLA*:    *Publications of the Modern Language Association.*

*RCC*:    *Revue des Cours et Conférences.*

*RHL*:    *Revue d'Histoire Littéraire de la France.*

*RLC*:    *Revue de Littérature comparée.*

*RR*:    *Romanic Review.*

*SV*:    *Studies on Voltaire and the Eighteenth Century.* (Institut et Musée Voltaire, Geneva).

# INTRODUCTION

Sensibility, according to the *Encyclopédie*, is the 'disposition tendre & délicate de l'ame, qui la rend facile à être émue, à être touchée'. From this simple dictionary definition, the Chevalier de Jaucourt, author of the article in question, proceeds to formulate a number of principles which underlie much of the thought and literature of the eighteenth century:

La *sensibilité* d'ame . . . donne une sorte de sagacité sur les choses honnêtes, & va plus loin que la pénétration de l'esprit seul. Les ames sensibles peuvent par vivacité tomber dans des fautes que les hommes à procédés ne commettroient pas; mais elles l'emportent de beaucoup par la quantité des biens qu'elles produisent. Les ames *sensibles* ont plus d'existence que les autres: les biens & les maux se multiplient à leur égard. La réflexion peut faire l'homme de probité; mais la *sensibilité* fait l'homme vertueux. La *sensibilité* est la mere de l'humanité, de la générosité; elle sert le mérite, secourt l'esprit, & entraîne la persuasion à sa suite.

Implied in this statement, as in many other contemporary texts dealing with the same subject, is the notion that man's feelings and natural impulses are basically good. Sensibility engenders a superior kind of moral wisdom which the mind by itself cannot attain. *L'homme sensible*, although more vulnerable than others, possesses one great advantage: whatever errors he may fall into, he is necessarily virtuous.

A more extensive discussion appeared in Mistelet's book on the subject published in 1777. Here two types of sensibility are distinguished: one—'la Sensibilité physique'—which is common to all men, since everyone has senses and passions,

1

and a more refined form—'la Sensibilité de l'ame ou de sentiment'—which is confined to an élite:

> La Sensibilité physique est, sans contredit, le premier principe des passions; c'est le pinceau qui forme, à grands traits, l'esquisse du tableau; mais la Sensibilité de l'ame le perfectionne: elle en est le coloris, vif, animé, touchant; elle adoucit les traits trop rudes, & acheve de former ceux qui n'étoient qu'ébauchés.
>
> C'est de la Sensibilité physique que naît la Sensibilité du sentiment; mais l'une fait mouvoir tous les hommes, & l'autre n'étend son pouvoir que sur un petit nombre. La premiere est la source des besoins primitifs; la seconde, celle des besoins du cœur.[1]

The author is concerned only with the second, which is 'true' sensibility. Right reason, he maintains, is virtually non-existent without it. A mere abstract reasoner would be 'un être privé de ce tact sûr & délicat, de ce sentiment qui nous identifie avec nos semblables' (p. 6). Reason and sensibility, when allied in harmonious proportions, produce the man of genius and the virtuous man.[2] According to Mistelet, although sensibility activates the passions, the result is beneficial providing a balance is maintained, for 'de ce choc à peu près égal, de cet équilibre entre tant de sentiments divers, naît la vertu. Que la Raison l'éclaire et la dirige, le grand homme est formé' (p. 7).

*L'homme sensible*, being naturally benevolent, attempts to increase general happiness; he therefore supports the principle of equality and attacks abuses and injustice. Since sensibility is so closely related to virtue, its development should form part of the educational process and *drames sensibles* conveying a serious moral lesson should be encouraged.

It is notable that although Jaucourt and Mistelet, in common with most eighteenth-century writers, postulate the superiority of the heart over the intellect, these are not thought of as being in conflict. For Mistelet, sensibility is not

---

1. Mistelet, *De la Sensibilité par rapport aux drames, aux romans et à l'éducation* (Paris, 1777), p. 5.
2. 'L'alliage de la Raison et de la Sensibilité fait l'homme de génie, l'homme vertueux' (p. 6).

the antithesis of reason, but of egoism and frivolity (p. 28), and the opposite of the man of feeling is the fop or courtier, 'car le propre de la Sensibilité est de nous inspirer le dégoût de la frivolité, de la coquetterie' (pp. 45–46).

If to these definitions is added the idea of immediacy of moral and esthetic judgment,[3] the main features of what might be called a philosophy of sensibility emerge. Feelings and instincts provide a reliable and immediate guide to truth, beauty, and virtue. While all men are governed to some extent by their passions, which are the source of both good and evil in human conduct, the truly admirable person is the rare individual who has learned to combine deep feeling with reason in the service of humanity. *L'homme sensible* is not necessarily happier than other men, since unusual sensitivity implies suffering and his impulsiveness is likely to lead him into difficulty, but he lives more intensely and his ultimate satisfactions are greater. Pleasure, virtue, and sensibility are thus closely associated.

The term *bienfaisance*, coined by the abbé de Saint-Pierre, was almost synonymous with *vertu*, the difference being that the latter often retained something of the original Roman sense and had stronger overtones of manliness and good citizenship. It was also very close in meaning to another favourite word, *humanité*, defined in the 1771 edition of the *Dictionnaire de Trévoux* as 'l'intérêt que les hommes prennent au sort de leurs semblables, en considération seulement de leur simple qualité d'hommes et sans leur être unis par les liens du sang, de l'amour ou de l'amitié'.[4]

*Bienfaisance* was not, of course, a new idea. It bears an obvious resemblance, on the one hand to the Epicurean

3. Enthusiastically celebrated by Hannah More in *Sacred Dramas . . . To which is added Sensibility, a Poem* (London, 1782), p. 282:

> Sweet sensibility! thou keen delight!
> Thou hasty moral! sudden sense of right!
> Thou untaught goodness! Virtue's precious seed!
> Thou sweet precursor of the gen'rous deed!
> Beauty's quick relish! Reason's radiant morn,
> Which dawns soft light before Reflexion's born.

4. See Paul Vernière, 'L'Idée d'humanité au XVIII<sup>e</sup> siècle', *Studium Generale*, 15 (1962), 171–179.

principle that the greatest good is pleasure and the greatest pleasure is derived from making others happy, and on the other to Christian charity, but with the all-important difference that whereas, in the Christian view, man is required by religion to go against his own nature in order to practise virtue, *bienfaisance* is a natural impulse common to all men whose instincts have not been perverted. Its universality was often demonstrated by pointing to the fact that, however corrupt we may be, we are always moved by the contemplation of magnanimous acts.[5]

The whole of the eighteenth century seemed to catch the enthusiasm of the abbé de Saint-Pierre, who suggested that the teaching of *bienfaisance* was the most important duty of the state and that it should be a prominent feature of education, public life, and art, especially the theatre. Few books were written which did not profess to have as their aim the inculcation of benevolence.[6] Even the authors of 'romans libertins' felt compelled to state that they were just as much concerned with teaching virtue as anyone else. In fact, for a supposedly dissolute age, the eighteenth century was remarkably prolific in moral tracts and pious exhortations. Sentimental rhetoric was much more common than dry humour. Hundreds of works of the imagination—tragedies, comedies, *drames, contes moraux, romans sensibles,* philosophical poems—appealed to the sensibility of the public by presenting the spectacle of unusual acts of 'grandeur d'âme', self-sacrifice, and humanity. Humbler manifestations of benevolence in private life, such as friendship, marital harmony, and the bourgeois virtues of family affection, were common themes.

The philosophy of *bienfaisance* was expounded in a number of works dealing with ethics. Thémiseul de Saint-Hyacinthe, in a collection of articles in favour of sensibility

5. The most obvious link between the Christian ethic and eighteenth-century *bienfaisance* is Fénelon, who vigorously promoted the idea even though he did not use the term.

6. Loaisel de Tréogate summed up the general attitude: 'Dans quelque genre que l'on écrive, on doit avoir pour objet de contribuer, au moins en quelque chose, au bien public' (Preface to *Dolbreuse* [Amsterdam, 1783], p. v).

published in 1736, affirmed that all men are born with the same instincts to do good, the accomplishment of which is invariably rewarded by a feeling of pleasure. His definition of a 'true Christian' is reminiscent of Voltaire's *Alzire*: 'Il a appris de JESUS-CHRIST que toute la Loi est comprise dans l'amour de Dieu et du prochain, et il n'envisage rien que sa raison n'avance et que son cœur n'agrée dans des mouvemens de bienveillance pour ses semblables, et dans la soumission aux volontés d'un Etre souverainement sage.'[7] The same year, similar ideas were put forward by Levesque de Pouilly in his *Théorie des sentimens agréables*,[8] the chapter headings of which clearly indicate the drift of his argument: 'Il y a un agrément attaché à tous les mouvemens du cœur, que la haine & la crainte n'empoisonnent pas'; 'Les loix du sentiment annoncent une Intelligence bien-faisante'; 'Du bonheur attaché à la vertu'; 'Où l'on prouve que la Philosophie morale est à la portée de tous les hommes'. Antoine Pecquet, in his *Parallèle du coeur, de l'esprit et du bon sens* (Paris, 1740), unhesitatingly gave first place to sentiment, which is essential for human happiness (p. 28) and which 'seul persuade et persuade solidement' (p. 31). Madame Du Châtelet also argued that feeling is primary and added: 'Je doute qu'il y ait un sentiment plus délicieux que celui qu'on éprouve quand on vient de faire une action vertueuse et qui mérite l'estime des honnêtes gens.'[9] The aim of philosophy, according to Diderot, is to reinforce this pleasurable instinct and thus unite men by the practice of mutual *bienfaisance*.[10]

By the mid-century, *bienfaisance* was beginning to assume the proportions of a collective obsession. Innumerable treatises identified happiness with the practice of virtue.[11]

7. *Recueil de divers écrits* . . . (Paris, 1736), pp. 219–220.
8. (Geneva, 1747), pp. 10–12. See also p. 58: 'Nous portons en nous-même un germe de bienveillance, toujours prêt à se développer en faveur de l'humanité & de la vertu, dès qu'une passion contraire n'y met point d'obstacle.'
9. 'Réflexions sur le bonheur' in *Lettres inédites de Mme la M^{ise} Du Chastelet à M. le comte d'Argental* (Paris, 1806), p. 350.
10. *Œuvres complètes*, ed. J. Assézat (Paris, 1875), III, 210.
11. See Robert Mauzi, *L'Idée du bonheur au XVIII^e siècle* (Paris, 1967), pp. 601–613.

King Stanislas entitled his works *Œuvres du philosophe bienfaisant*. 'Voulez-vous savoir', he asked, 'ma passion dominante, & qui seule pourroit faire mon parfait bonheur? Cette passion, c'est de rendre, s'il m'étoit possible, tous les mortels heureux.'[12] After 1776, the *Mercure* regularly published information on good actions for the edification of its readers. Dagues de Clairfontaine provided the same service for the years 1715 to 1774 in *Bienfaisance française*, a curious collection of biographies and anecdotes amounting to public recognition of 'good deeds', from instances of magnanimity, courage, and loyalty among the great to banal accounts of family affection.[13]

One can detect in this book, as in several others of the period, a strong current of slightly hysterical patriotism.[14] In the prerevolutionary era, *bienfaisance* came to be associated more and more clearly with civic duty and words like *vertu, citoyen, patrie* acquired a similar emotive force. Chastellux looked forward to a time when 'Les Gens de Lettres deviendront patriotes; & les Sçavans, citoyens. Une correspondance générale s'établissant parmi les esprits, l'amour de l'humanité sera le ralliement commun qui réunira les gens du monde, les gens de lettres, les Sçavans et les Artistes.'[15]

The emphasis on *bienfaisance*, and particularly the idea of recording acts beneficial to the state or mankind in general, inevitably led to the cult of the 'great man,' no longer a military hero or, necessarily, a member of the aristocracy, but a man who had proved himself most useful to his fellow-citizens by setting an example of enlightened and virtuous conduct. In the words of Dagues de Clairfontaine, 'Le fondement de cette espèce de culte, c'est la gloire que les grands hommes répandent sur l'humanité qu'ils honorent, et le besoin que nous avons de ces êtres supérieurs pour

12. *Œuvres du philosophe bienfaisant* (Paris, 1763), I, 282.
13. Dagues de Clairfontaine, *Bienfaisance française ou Mémoires pour servir à l'histoire de ce siècle* (Paris, 1778).
14. e.g. 'La vertu est naturelle à tous les cœurs Français; ils n'ambitionnent d'autre récompense que celle de faire le bien' (II, 399).
15. F. J. de Chastellux, *De la félicité publique ou Considérations sur le sort des hommes* (Amsterdam, 1772), II, 75.

suppléer à notre foiblesse; mais si, né parmi nous, ou fixé par choix dans notre patrie, il a servi l'Etat par ses talens, s'il l'a éclairé par ses lumières, s'il l'a orné par ses vertus, alors la reconnoissance nous fait un devoir sacré de ce tribut de vénération et d'amour.'[16]

The evidence provided by the rare opponents of the cult of *bienfaisance* merely confirms its predominance. Boismont criticized it from an orthodox Christian point of view as a facile form of religion whose devotees were largely hypocrites. Whether one was genuinely *bienfaisant* or not, it was necessary to pay lip-service to the ideal: 'Comme le dictionnaire moral est abrégé! L'honnêteté, la droiture, l'intégrité, tous ces mots si vieux, qui inquiètent et désolent la nature, sont heureusement remplacés par ceux de *bienfaisance* et d'*humanité*; avec ces deux mots on fait de tout; de la gloire, de la réputation, de la justice. On peut corrompre, tourmenter, calomnier, voler la moitié du genre humain; pourvu que de belles tirades ou un petit acte bien public atteste qu'on s'occupe du bonheur de l'autre moitié, tout est bien.'[17] After perusing some of the more extreme examples of virtuous euphoria, it is difficult not to sympathize to some extent with the critics. Eighteenth-century writers, not excluding some of the greatest, were in the habit of proclaiming their own virtue and benevolence in extravagant terms. Lachrymose self-righteousness was one of the least attractive characteristics of the age.[18]

The widely held belief in the benevolence principle helped to foster the development of primitivism. If man is inclined to good when he follows his unperverted instincts, then primitive man, being closer to nature, is more likely to be virtuous than the European city-dweller—a theory which

16. Dagues de Clairfontaine, *Bienfaisance française*, II, 9–10.

17. Abbé N. T. de Boismont, *Lettres secrettes sur l'état actuel de la Religion et du Clergé de France* (1781), p. 3.

18. As one example among many, Formey, in his *Souvenirs d'un citoyen* (Berlin, 1789), after announcing that 'La bienveillance & la bienfaisance ont été constamment les principes de ma conduite' (I, vi), added: 'Je disois une fois au Roi: *on n'emporte de ce monde que le bien qu'on y a fait. . . .* J'ai eu du regret de n'avoir pas ajouté: *c'est-là l'évangile que j'ai toujours prêché, & c'est ce qui doit rendre l'evangile respectable, comme une doctrine de bienfaisance*' (I, xi).

seemed to be supported by the facts, that is, by the reports of missionaries and travellers.[19] It was quickly realized that contemporary social ills could be effectively attacked by comparing them with an idealized picture of primitive life. But no eighteenth-century writer—certainly not Rousseau— seriously advocated a return to the 'state of nature' and the abandonment of the advantages of civilization. Terms such as the 'noble savage' and 'luxury' have tended to obscure the unity of the Enlightenment by implying total opposition between out-and-out primitivists on the one hand and defenders of every manifestation of civilization on the other. Eighteenth-century primitivism was more often concerned with finding a balance between nature and culture. It was generally recognized, as Shaftesbury had pointed out, that man's instinct is to form societies, and that the development of society is therefore 'natural'. Thus it was possible to combine a moderate form of primitivism with the apparently contradictory idea of progress through the advancement of knowledge, and to attack certain features of contemporary society—excessive refinement, self-indulgence, hypocritical politeness, lack of seriousness and moral fibre—without condemning the whole concept of civilization.

Literature inevitably reflects the prevailing intellectual climate. One important consequence was the appearance of a form of emotionalism—completely foreign to the classical masterpieces of the seventeenth century—which equated sensibility with virtue. The aim of the serious writer was to give pleasure and at the same time to further morality by arousing the maximum amount of virtuous emotion.[20] Since the concept of *bienfaisance* as a natural instinct for good,

19. e.g. *Dialogues de M. le baron de Lahontan et d'un sauvage* (1704); Lafitau, *Mœurs des sauvages américains comparées aux mœurs des premiers temps* (1724); Charlevoix, *Histoire de la Nouvelle-France* (1744).

20. In *L'an 2240, rêve s'il en fut jamais* (Amsterdam, 1771), Louis Sébastien Mercier speaks of a new breed of writers: 'Tous les hommes éprouvent le besoin d'être émus, attendris; c'est le plaisir le plus vif que l'âme puisse goûter. C'est à eux que l'Etat a confié le soin de développer ce principe des vertus. En peignant des tableaux majestueux, attendrissans, terribles, ils rendent les hommes plus susceptibles de tendresse, & les disposent en perfectionnant leur sensibilité à toutes les grandes qualités dont elle est l'origine' (p. 226).

present to some extent in all men, logically implied the suppression of totally depraved characters, emphasis was placed on the innocent victims of misfortune. The plays and novels of the eighteenth century were full of misunderstandings, mistaken identities, and improbable combinations of circumstances whereby virtue was put to the test. The important thing in the theatre was not to analyze passion or to show the deeper significance of the action, but to engage and direct the sympathies of the audience. A good tragedy was one which caused the spectators to weep copiously, and by the mid-century the same was true of comedy. Under the influence of optimism, there was a strong tendency to idealize characters and to play down the role of the will. The true man of feeling was an uncomplicated individual, blissfully free from inner conflict. Hence the unreal psychology and the improbable paragons of eighteenth-century melodrama.

The doctrine of *bienfaisance* also implied the necessity for a moral aim. This was by no means a new idea; it was, in fact, a commonplace of classical theory; but again there was a shift of emphasis, from poetic justice and fear of divine punishment to compassion aroused by the spectacle of virtue in distress. To quote Fontenelle, 'La plus grande utilité du théâtre est de rendre la vertu aimable aux hommes, de les accoutumer à s'intéresser pour elle, de donner ce pli à leur cœur, de leur proposer de grands exemples de fermeté et de courage dans leurs malheurs, de fortifier par là et d'élever leurs sentimens.'[21]

Certain expressions, such as 'vertu', 'sensible', 'respectable', 'humanité', 'généreux', 'cœur', acquired a special emotive force. Chief among these was the word 'nature', which contained an extraordinarily complex variety of meanings: 'Nature signifie également la force productive, la collection des êtres produits, les formes primitives et non altérées par l'industrie humaine, l'amour filial, la tendresse paternelle, la vie innocente que menaient les premiers habitants de la terre, et cette inspiration sûre, indépendante

21. *Œuvres complètes*, ed. G. B. Depping (Paris, 1818), III, 17–18.

des conventions sociales, qui nous avertit, nous guide, quand nous voulons l'écouter, et qui est la conscience véritable.'[22]

Nature also meant simply external nature, particularly landscapes which were not the obvious product of human intervention. Primitivism encouraged the notion that the simple life in the midst of natural surroundings is more conducive to virtue than the over-refined atmosphere of the city, a view which appeared early in the works of Fénelon, Lamotte, and Prévost, and which was expressed with increasing frequency in the second half of the century. The call for a return to nature was not unconnected with sensationalism and the renewed interest in the concrete, material universe stimulated by the development of empirical science. 'On commence par la botanique et on finit par l'extase; on commence par étudier les cailloux, et on finit par grimper jusqu'aux cimes des Alpes pour y contempler, dans le ravissement, le lever du soleil.'[23]

Primitivism in one form or another was responsible for a number of important trends in eighteenth-century literature and esthetics besides the enthusiasm for natural scenery and the noble savage. There was a definite tendency, which was particularly marked after the mid-century, to contrast the undisciplined but 'sublime' production of genius, as exemplified particularly in the plays of Shakespeare, with the platitudes of authors who merely followed well-tried academic formulas. Imagination began to be valued more than the abstract conceptions of a noble style.

Nostalgia for an idealized past in which life was simpler and more 'natural', and at the same time more heroic and colourful, led to an interest in the age of chivalry and a veritable 'cult of antiquity', which reached its climax during the Revolution. The medieval period was sufficiently remote to be imaginatively reconstructed, yet close enough to supply subjects appealing to national pride. Antiquity was also a source of picturesqueness and patriotic feeling. What was chiefly admired was the austere, heroic spirit of

22. C. F. A. Lezay-Marnésia, *Essai sur la nature champêtre* (Paris, 1787), p. 17.
23. Paul Hazard, 'L'Homme du sentiment', *RR*, 28 (1937), 333.

the Roman Republic. The 'virtuous Roman' of eighteenth-century legend was a child of nature, who had much in common with the noble savage and could be used for the same purpose: to demonstrate by contrast the decadent frivolity of contemporary French manners.[24]

The preponderant role of the emotions was stressed by virtually all eighteenth-century thinkers. David Hume, a philosopher greatly admired by his French counterparts as one of the leading exponents of enlightenment thought, maintained that 'Reason is, and ought only to be the slave of the passions, and can never pretend to any other office than to serve and obey them.'[25] Helvétius adopted a similar thesis in *De l'esprit* (1758). Two of the chapter headings provide an eloquent summary of the author's attitude: 'De la supériorité d'esprit des gens passionnés sur les gens sensés'; 'Que l'on devient stupide, dès qu'on cesse d'être passionné.' D'Alembert, in the *Discours préliminaire* to the *Encyclopédie*, the work whose name has become synonymous with the Enlightenment, was highly critical of the tendency to introduce 'cold, didactic discussions' of philosophical matters into literature, which should be the domain of feeling.[26] The point of view of his colleague, Diderot, is well known: 'Tout ce que la passion inspire, je le pardonne. Il n'y a que les conséquences qui me choquent. Et puis, vous le savez, j'ai de tout temps été l'apologiste des passions fortes; elles seules m'émeuvent. Qu'elles m'inspirent de l'admiration ou de l'effroi, je sens fortement'.[27] La Mettrie

24. The comparison between North American Indians and Romans of the Republic was not uncommon in the Jesuit *Relations* of the seventeenth century. Both were contrasted with the fops of contemporary French society. See John H. Kennedy, *Jesuit and Savage in New France* (New Haven, 1950), p. 106.

25. David Hume, *A Treatise of Human Nature*, ed. L. A. Selby-Bigge (Oxford, 1896), p. 415.

26. Jean Le Rond d'Alembert, *Discours préliminaire de l'Encyclopédie*, ed. F. Pivacet (Paris, 1899), p. 118: 'On abuse des meilleures choses. Cet esprit philosophique, si à la mode aujourd'hui, qui veut tout voir et ne rien supposer, s'est répandu jusque dans les belles-lettres; on prétend même qu'il est nuisible à leurs progrès, et il est difficile de se le dissimuler. Notre siècle porté à la combinaison et à l'analyse, semble vouloir introduire les discussions froides et didactiques dans les choses de sentiment.'

27. *Œuvres complètes*, XIX, 87. See particularly the *Pensées philosophiques*, I, 127.

compared the delights of 'le désordre des passions' with 'la froide philosophie' and congratulated himself on having escaped corruption by 'le bel esprit'.[28] One of Chamfort's maxims was that 'Les passions font *vivre* l'homme; la sagesse le fait seulement *durer*.[29]'

Vauvenargues, Rousseau, and Condillac constantly returned to the same theme, best expressed by Grimm: 'Tout ce qu'il y a jamais eu de plus grand, de plus admirable, de plus sublime dans le monde, c'est l'ouvrage des passions.'[30] True happiness, according to Mme Du Châtelet, cannot be achieved without them: 'Les moralistes qui disent aux humains, *réprimez vos passions et maîtrisez vos désirs, si vous voulez être heureux*, ne connoissent pas le chemin du bonheur. . . . Ce seroit donc des passions qu'il faudroit demander à Dieu.'[31] The consequences of excessive indulgence of the passions were recognized, but it was generally felt that the danger lay in their perversion, especially through the misdirection of religious 'enthusiasm', rather than in their intensity.

Any number of quotations from minor writers could be added to show that one of the central dogmas of eighteenth-century thought was that feeling takes precedence over reason.[32] Moreover, it was not merely a question of theory. The *philosophes* were far from being cynical and frivolous voluptuaries; in general, they were earnest reformers, who were particularly sensitive to the charge of indifference and lack of sensibility. Their enemies were more inclined to regard them as dangerous fanatics.

28. *L'art de jouir* in *Œuvres philosophiques* (Amsterdam, 1753), II, 4–6.
29. *Maximes et anecdotes*, ed. Jean Mistler (Monaco, 1944), p. 34. See also p. 29: 'La nature, en faisant naître à la fois la raison et les passions, semble avoir voulu, par le second présent, aider l'homme à s'étourdir sur le mal qu'elle lui a fait par le premier, et, en ne le laissant vivre que peu d'années après la perte de ses passions, semble prendre pitié de lui, en le délivrant bientôt d'une vie qui le réduit à la raison pour toute ressource.'
30. Quoted by Roger Mercier, *La Réhabilitation de la nature humaine (1700–1750)* (Villemonble, 1960), p. 370.
31. *Réflexions sur le bonheur*, pp. 338–339.
32. For a comprehensive treatment of the question, see Mauzi, *L'Idée du bonheur* and Mercier, *La Réhabilitation de la nature humaine.*

It is perhaps significant that eighteenth-century imagery generally associated the 'light' in enlightenment with fire as the source of light; 'feu' and 'lumière' appeared frequently together. For all its emphasis on the role of the critical intelligence, the Enlightenment did not create a mental climate unfavourable to the emotions. The age of enlightenment and the age of sensibility developed concurrently. The outstanding figures of the century belonged to both. The typical *philosophe* prided himself on his sensibility; the typical man of feeling valued freedom of thought. Reason and sentiment were not regarded as antithetical but as complementary; the problem was how to bring them into harmony. In the words of Roland Mortier, '"Sensibilité" et "lumières" appartiennent à des ordres différents, mais elles peuvent se fortifier mutuellement, elles vont dans le même sens et tendent vers la réalisation d'un type humain complet, dont le bonheur consistera, non à se mutiler d'une part de soi-même (comme la princesse de Clèves), mais à assumer pleinement *tous* les aspects de son "moi".' [33]

As recent criticism has shown, there is no clear-cut division between an 'age of reason' and an 'age of sensibility',[34] but rather a gradual shift in literary fashion which began well before the mid-century. The notion that a period which experienced such a profound change of ideas was incapable of creating its own literature and that its writers must therefore be divided into neoclassicists (to 1750) and preromantics (from 1750 on) has long since been demolished.[35] It would be equally logical to refer to the late seventeenth century as 'pre-enlightenment' or to the romantics as

33. Roland Mortier, 'Unité ou scission du siècle des lumières?' *SV*, XXVI, 1220.
34. See particularly Roland Mortier, 'Unité ou scission du siècle des lumières?' *SV*, XXVI, 1207–21; Peter Gay, *The Party of Humanity: Essays in the French Enlightenment* (New York, 1964); Robert Mauzi, *L'Idée du bonheur au XVIII⁰ siècle* (Paris, 1967); Jean Fabre, *Lumières et romantisme, énergie et nostalgie, de Rousseau à Mickiewicz* (Paris, 1963); Roger Mercier, *La Réhabilitation de la nature humaine (1700–1750)* (Villemonble, 1960); Norman Hampson, *The Enlightenment* (Harmondsworth, 1968).
35. See A. Cherel, 'XVIII⁰ siècle et romantisme', *Revue politique et littéraire*, 71 (1933), 533; Mauzi, *L'Idée du bonheur*, p. 235; Gay, *Party of Humanity*, pp. 115–116.

'neo-*philosophes*'. What Henri Peyre has called the first
and most important wave of romanticism,[36] which reached
its peak towards the end of the century, was the result of a
fusion of reason and feeling, of enlightenment and sensibility.

Voltaire, Diderot, and the other *philosophes* would no
doubt have been shocked to learn that they would one day
be considered 'arid souls'[37] and leaders of a faction opposed
to sensibility and artistic freedom. This myth seems to have
originated in the early nineteenth century. There are indications of it in Mme de Staël's critical works, in which writers
of the Enlightenment, with the exception of Rousseau, are
taken to task for their materialism and their 'frivolous'
attitude to the great questions of human destiny. It was
further reinforced by the early pseudo-romantic school,
made up of *bien pensants* and reactionaries, who saw the
Revolution as the work of the *philosophes*; consequently, in
spite of liberal protest,[38] feeling became associated with
piety and political conservatism, while the *philosophes*
were identified with the losing cause of anemic neoclassicism.
A clear exposition of the paradox appeared in 1824 in a
work by Cyprien Desmarais,[39] who concluded: 'Le dix-
huitième siècle m'a paru avoir étrangement abusé de ce

36. 'Romantic Poetry and Rhetoric', *Yale French Studies*, XIII, 39–40:
'The so-called Romantic movement of 1820–1840 was in fact only one
wave (and probably the most timid, the most classical or pseudo-classical
one) in the long history of French Romanticism. The first now convenient-
ly termed pre-Romanticism (1760–75) was far bolder and more authentic
in everything but poetry.'

37. Paul Hazard, *La Pensée européenne au XVIIIᵉ siècle de Montesquieu à Lessing* (Paris, 1946), I, iv: 'Ames sèches, et dont la sécheresse
fait surgir, par contraste, les passionnés et les mystiques. . . . Ames que
n'ont pas émues la forêt, la montagne ou la mer; intelligences sans
merci.'

38. See R. Fargher, 'The Retreat from Voltaireanism (1800–1815)'
in *The French Mind, Studies in Honour of Gustave Rudler* (Oxford,
1952), pp. 220–237.

39. *Essai sur les classiques et les romantiques* (Paris, 1824), p. 103:
'Qui ne voit d'ailleurs que le genre classique, tel qu'on le conçoit aujourd'
hui, n'a pu arriver jusqu'à nous qu'en passant par les idées et les systèmes du dix-huitième siècle, et en contractant, plus ou moins, quelque
chose de cette morgue irréligieuse, par laquelle Voltaire l'avait comme
profané! Aussi le *classique* est-il surtout aujourd'hui, opiniâtrément,
quoique faiblement défendu par quelques vieux champions de l'Encyclopédie, soldats fidèles d'une puissance que personne n'attaque plus,
depuis qu'elle s'est écroulée d'elle-même.'

qu'on peut appeler la civilisation de l'esprit, et avoir ainsi
préparé les causes qui devaient, sinon flétrir, au moins dis-
créditer sa littérature: il a offert à l'histoire l'exemple d'une
de ces époques où, par un abus des facultés intellectuelles,
on en vient à considérér comme des chimères, les émotions
du cœur et les jouissances de l'imagination.'[40]

The persistence of this simplistic view is understandable.
One tends to judge the eighteenth century, or any other
period for that matter, in terms of works which have stood
the test of time and to ignore or minimize features which
were important to contemporaries but which, being tied to
an ephemeral fashion, disappeared along with it. Hence
Marivaux is the author of half a dozen light and charming
comedies on the subject of nascent love. One thinks of
Diderot primarily as the editor of the *Encyclopédie* and the
creator of such undisputed masterpieces as *Le Neveu de
Rameau, Jacques le fataliste*, or *Le Rêve de d'Alembert*;
his tedious sentimental dramas are museum pieces. Figaro,
as he appears in Beaumarchais' *Le Barbier de Séville* and
*Le Mariage de Figaro*, is taken to be eminently typical of
his age. But who remembers the Figaro of *La Mère coupable*,
'drame moral'?[41]

Voltaire is a prime example of the strange effects of partial
survival. Everyone has heard of him, but who, as Lytton
Strachey asked, has read him?

It is by his name that ye shall know him, and not by his
works. With the exception of his letters, of *Candide*, of
*Akakia*, and of a few other of his shorter pieces, the vast

---

40. p. iii. According to Desmarais, 'Les écrivains, qui sont restés
fidèles aux doctrines de l'Encyclopédie, ont très-bien senti que les inspira-
tions religieuses de la littérature romantique, ne pouvaient être filles de
la philosophie du dix-huitième siècle, et qu'on ne pouvait receuillir
l'héritage de Voltaire et de Diderot, et prétendre en même temps avoir
des droits au domaine du romantisme' (p. 55).

41. The differences between Fielding's novel, *Tom Jones*, and the
film version, skilfully adapted to suit mid-twentieth-century taste, are
revealing in this respect. The earthy humour and the emphasis on
sexual adventure, gaiety, and *joie de vivre* have been admirably captured,
but almost all traces of eighteenth-century sensibility have disappeared.
Allworthy is a figure of fun and a foil for Squire Western. The episodes
showing Tom's *bienfaisance* have been omitted.

mass of his productions has been already consigned to oblivion. How many persons now living have travelled through *La Henriade* or *La Pucelle*? How many have so much as glanced at the imposing volumes of *L'Esprit des Mœurs*? *Zadig* and *Zaïre*, *Mérope* and *Charles XII* still linger, perhaps, in the schoolroom; but what has become of *Oreste*, and of *Mahomet*, and of *Alzire? Où sont les neiges d'antan?*[42]

It is instructive to compare that statement with a contemporary forecast of Voltaire's future reputation. In 1771, Louis Sébastien Mercier published a book in which the narrator found himself transported into the year 2440. While browsing in the national library, he learned of posterity's judgment on Voltaire and his works:

On ne peut lui refuser la premiere, la plus noble, la plus grande des vertus, l'amour de l'humanité. Il a combattu avec chaleur pour les intérêts de l'homme. Il a détesté, il a flétri la persécution, les tyrans de toute espece. Il a mis sur la scene la morale raisonnée & touchante. Il a peint l'héroïsme sous ses véritables traits. Il a été enfin le plus grand poëte des François. Nous avons conservé son poëme, quoique le plan en soit mesquin; mais le nom de Henri IV le rendra immortel. Nous sommes surtout idolâtres de ses belles tragédies, où règne un pinceau si facile, si varié, si vrai. Nous avons conservé tous les morceaux de prose où il n'est pas bouffon, dur ou mauvais plaisant: c'est-là qu'il est vraiment original.[43]

One suspects that the prose works in which Voltaire is 'bouffon, dur ou mauvais plaisant' are precisely those which have retained their appeal. The 'belles tragédies', on the other hand, with their touching morality, are no longer read or performed except as historical curiosities; *La Henriade* is considered 'unreadable'; long philosophical poems are no longer in fashion; and the histories have been rendered

42. *Books and Characters* (London, 1922), p. 140.
43. *L'An 2440*, pp. 217–218.

obsolete by two centuries of scholarship. What remains—
a few *contes*, the light verse, some vigorous polemical prose,
and the superb correspondence—is sufficient, certainly, for
anyone's reputation, but hardly adequate for a true picture
of the man who was the most influential writer of his age.

It is normal for authors of this stature to be the victims
of legend and Voltaire has suffered more than most. The
innumerable catch phrases which have been attached to his
name have proved remarkably tenacious. It is hardly possible
to mention Voltaire without talking about his 'hideux
sourire', but there are many others: 'le prince des moqueurs'
(Mme de Staël); 'ce singe de génie' (Victor Hugo); 'le
prince des persifleurs' (Stendhal); 'un chaos d'idées claires'
(Emile Faguet). Baudelaire supplied a whole collection in one
outburst: 'l'anti-poète, le roi des badauds, le prince des
superficiels, l'anti-artiste, le prédicateur des concierges'.

Voltaire's name, in fact, seems to have been destined to
attract simplified labels. In the nineteenth century, many of
his admirers and critics alike identified him with one element
in his work—anticlericalism. Hence Littré's definition of
Voltaireanism as 'esprit d'incrédulité railleuse à l'égard du
christianisme'. The views of the so-called 'Voltaireans', a
group distinguished mainly by their cynicism and lack of
real convictions, were attributed to the object of the cult,
who thus became a kind of eighteenth-century Monsieur
Homais.

Their opponents viewed him in essentially the same light.
Voltaire thought of himself as the enemy, not of religion,
but of its dangerous excrescences, superstition and fanaticism.
But the distinction is sometimes difficult to draw. He attacked
what for many, in his own time and later, were basic and
cherished beliefs, and he attacked them with every weapon
at his command, including a formidable arsenal of ridicule.
The reaction was inevitable. Whoever deliberately sets out
to destroy a hallowed tradition is necessarily shallow, unfeeling, irreverent, and flippant, a monster of insensibility.

Voltaire undoubtedly was, or appeared to be, some of
these things some of the time. What both the nineteenth-
century Voltaireans and anti-Voltaireans failed to see, but

Flaubert clearly saw, was that his campaign against fanaticism was itself a form of fanaticism, and that he was sincerely convinced that its object was the good of humanity:

> Voltaire, c'est pour moi un *saint!* Pourquoi s'obstiner à voir un farceur dans un homme qui était un fanatique? . . . Je m'étonne que vous n'admiriez pas cette grande palpitation qui a remué le monde. Est-ce qu'on obtient de tels résultats quand on n'est pas sincère? . . . Bref, cet homme-là me semble ardent, acharné, convaincu, superbe. Son 'Ecrasons l'infâme' me fait l'effet d'un cri de croisade. Toute son intelligence était une machine de guerre. Et ce qui me le fait chérir, c'est le dégoût que m'inspirent les voltairiens, des gens qui rient sur les grandes choses! Est-ce qu'il riait, lui? Il grinçait! [44]

The picture of Voltaire as a shallow cynic was not, however, an invention of the nineteenth century. There was no shortage in his own day of critics who were ready to give a derogatory twist to any statement or action which might be used to show that the idol had feet of clay. A simple expression of modesty such as the following, from a letter to Henri Pitot in 1737, was later offered as positive proof that Voltaire admitted his superficiality: 'Vous trouvez que je m'explique assez clairement; je suis comme les petits ruisseaux; ils sont transparents parce qu'ils sont peu profonds.' [45]

An anonymous character-sketch which appeared in 1735 is the most likely source of many of the subsequent 'portraits'. As R. A. Leigh remarks in his interesting study, the whole episode throws 'a strange and somewhat disturbing light on the way reputations are made and perpetuated'. [46] Voltaire is depicted as an unscrupulous, vain, avaricious, changeable man and a witty, superficial writer with few original ideas. He is further accused of lack of patriotism.

44. 'Voltaire jugé par Flaubert', ed. Theodore Besterman, *SV*, I, 143.
45. Best. D1341. See Lepan's comment in his *Vie de Voltaire* (Paris, 1817), pp. xiv–xv.
46. R. A. Leigh, 'An anonymous eighteenth-century character-sketch of Voltaire', *SV*, II, 241–272.

The physical description clearly foreshadows the 'hideous smile' immortalized by Musset: 'Il est maigre: D'un temperament sec: Il a la bile brûlée: Le Visage décharné: L'air spirituel & caustique: Les yeux étincelans & malins'.[47]

Voltaire's reaction is worth noting. He denied that it was a good likeness, not because it was uncomplimentary, but because his real faults were different. The one charge that he specifically rejected was that he was lacking in sensibility or generosity: 'J'ai vu le portrait qu'on a fait de moi. Il n'est pas, je crois, ressemblant. J'ai beaucoup plus de défauts qu'on ne m'en reproche dans cet ouvrage & je n'ai pas les talents qu'on m'y attribue; mais je suis bien certain que je ne mérite point les reproches d'insensibilité & d'avarice que l'on me fait.'[48]

Nevertheless, the 'portrait' enjoyed a great success. Its main features were reproduced by numerous critics and from it emerged the familiar stereotype. Voltaire is forever identified with his alter ego: a thin, dry, skeleton-like figure with a sardonic smile; a man of limitless energy directed to destructive ends; a witty, polished writer and master of devastating irony, but somewhat cynical and lacking in depth and originality; a clear, sharp, analytical intelligence which illuminates but does not penetrate, and whose end product is a 'chaos of clear ideas'.

This image, or something like it, has strongly influenced innumerable biographies, books, plays and critical articles. Voltaire's 'sensibility', when it is mentioned at all, is generally thought of in terms of impetuosity rather than sentiment, which is assumed to be nonexistent. Yet doubts must occur to anyone who is acquainted with Voltaire's theatre, which cannot be ignored or explained away as an unimportant pastime. He devoted a large part of his time and energy to it and achieved fame by writing tearful tragedies and comedies, in other words, thinly disguised sentimental melodrama. He was universally recognized in his own age as a master of the genre, which he may be said to have perfected, if not invented.

47. Leigh, pp. 242–243.
48. To Berger, 4 Aug. 1735 (Best. D896).

It is also curious that a writer who is admired, almost exclusively, as a wit, as a satirist, and as a 'philosopher of common sense' should have had so little good to say about wit,[49] satire,[50] and common sense.[51] No man who was guided by common sense would have set out to rehabilitate Calas or to destroy the power of the Church. Moreover, if Voltaire was the arch-enemy of sensibility, we must cast him in the unlikely role of leader of the opposition to the general trend of the age. His enormous influence and prestige, particularly during the latter part of the century, then become extremely difficult to explain.

Obviously the stereotype contains a considerable element of truth, but it is true of only one aspect of his character, philosophy, and literary career. The real reason for its persistence is perhaps that it stresses some of the qualities which characterize his best work. Intelligence of this order is rare and wit which defies the centuries is rarer still. The popular Voltaire is the perfect embodiment of an extreme attitude to experience to which one turns with relief after a surfeit of sentiment. It provides an antidote to pomposity, hysteria, bigotry, and cant, and since there is always an unlimited supply of these, every society and every age needs a Voltaire. His immortality is assured, even if all his works are ultimately forgotten.

The purpose of this study is to provide a glimpse of the other Voltaire, better known to his contemporaries than to twentieth-century readers, to show that the iconoclast was also a sentimentalist, 'une manière d'apôtre, vibrant d'idéal, chaleureux, utopique, enthousiaste',[52] and that his role in the development of eighteenth-century sensibility has been underestimated.

49. 'Ce n'est pas ce qu'on appelle *esprit*, c'est le sublime et le simple qui font la vraie beauté' (M. XIX, 5); 'Oh! qui est ce qui n'a pas d'esprit dans ce siècle? mais du talent, du génie, où les trouve-t-on? Quand on n'a que de l'esprit avec l'envie de paraître, on fait un mauvais livre' (Best. 7328); see also M. X, 76; XIX, 252 and especially the article 'Esprit' in the *Dictionnaire philosophique* (M. XIX, 3–9).

50. Voltaire describes satire as 'le poison de la littérature' (Best. 13128). See M. III, 376; X, 76; X, 400; XXIII, 53; Best. D415.

51. See the article 'Sens commun' of the *Dictionnaire philosophique*.

52. Jacques Van den Heuvel, 'Voltaire' in *Encyclopédie de la Pléiade, Histoire des littératures* (Paris, 1958), III, 714.

# CHAPTER 1

# *The Man of Feeling*

From the beginning of his career, Voltaire lived in a constant glare of publicity. Almost every important detail of his life is known. Yet few writers have been more reticent about their inner feelings. Voltaire was not given to self-analysis and it is impossible to imagine him writing *Confessions* in the manner of Rousseau. In the absence of any such document, we are forced to rely for an assessment of his character on the evidence of his actions, on the general tenor of his writings, and on the testimony of his contemporaries.

His occasional self-portraits and the references to himself in the correspondence at least establish beyond doubt that he considered himself to be *un homme sensible* in the sense in which this term was generally used in the eighteenth century. In the *Epitre dédicatoire* to his tragedy, *L'Orphelin de la Chine*, there is a striking phrase which has the ring of an epitaph: 'Je n'ai consulté que mon cœur; il me conduit seul; il a toujours inspiré mes actions et mes paroles' (M. V, 295). The word 'sensible' occurs frequently. He was born, he says, 'extrêmement sensible' and remained so for the whole of his long life.[1] He therefore rejected any suggested comparison with Fontenelle: 'Oh bien, je ne suis pas comme Fontenelle, car j'ay le cœur sensible' (Best. 8593). His idea of a *philosophe* was quite different: 'O que j'aime qu'un philosophe soit sensible! Pour moi je suis plus sensible que philosophe' (Best. 13923).

Nowhere in the published work or in the correspondence

1. 'Je suis né extrêmement sensible. Je le suis à soixante et seize ans comme à vingt cinq' (Best. 15089); 'ce squelette possède une vieille âme très sensible' (Best. 15585); 'je suis sensible comme un enfant' (Best. 13263).

does Voltaire exalt the mind above the heart. Nor did he think of himself as a wit or as a dispassionate intellectual. He found it difficult in fact to imagine how one could be coldly detached and still continue to exist: 'Je n'ai jamais conçu comment l'on peut être froid; cela me passe, quiconque n'est pas animé est indigne de vivre. Je le compte au rang des morts' (Best. 10921). He admitted that he had 'les passions vives', in spite of age and sickness,[2] and apologized to d'Argental for his combative enthusiasm; but this was the price one had to pay for excessive sensibility, there was no help for it: 'Il est d'un cœur né sensible, et qui ne sçait point haïr ne sçait point aimer' (Best. 8812).

In the unperformed comedy, *L'Envieux* (1738), a thinly disguised allegory concerning the Desfontaines affair, Voltaire portrays himself in the role of Ariston, 'un homme vertueux', victim of fanaticism and envy, who disdains place-seeking and prizes the tender consolations of friendship above all else.[3] He is obliging, 'un ami tendre et sûr', eminently *bienfaisant*, and willing to forgive his enemies— even Desfontaines. This somewhat idealized autobiographical sketch is similar to that in the *Discours sur l'homme*, composed about the same time,[4] and does not differ substantially from later self-portraits.[5]

2. Best. 15349; 8301; 15692.
3. M. III, 534:

> ces places désirées
> Ne seraient à mes yeux que des chaînes dorées.
> Mon esprit est trop libre, il craint trop ces liens:
> On ne vit plus alors pour soi ni pour les siens.
> L'homme (on le voit souvent) se perd dans l'homme en place.
> Je vis auprès de vous: tout le reste est disgrâce.
> La tranquille amitié, voilà ma passion:
> Je suis heureux sans faste et sans ambition.

4. M. IX, 420:

> Pour moi, loin des cités, sur les bords du Permesse
> Je suivais la nature, et cherchais la sagesse;
> Et des bords de la sphère où s'emporta Milton,
> Et de ceux de l'abîme où pénétra Newton,
> Je les voyais franchir leur carrière infinie;
> Amant de tous les arts et de tout grand génie,
> Implacable ennemi du calomniateur,
> Du fanatique absurde, et du vil delateur;
> Ami sans artifice, auteur sans jalousie;
> Adorateur d'un Dieu, mais sans hypocrisie;
> Dans un corps languissant, de cent maux attaqué,

One aspect of Voltaire's many-sided career which offers an unusually revealing glimpse of the man is his life-long passion for theatricals. A born dramatist and director, an avid spectator, enthusiastic to the point of eccentricity, he was also an actor of considerable renown. From his first brief but memorable appearance as train-bearer to the High Priest in his own *Œdipe* to the gala nights at Ferney, he took every opportunity to exercise his talents and was never happy unless there was a private theatre in the vicinity.

Contemporary opinions on Voltaire the actor vary almost as widely as those on Voltaire the man. Gibbon described him as 'a very ranting, unnatural performer' (Best. 10520). Lekain, on the other hand, considered him sublime[6] and there are numerous tributes to his extraordinary ability to evoke emotion. He certainly possessed what his contemporaries called 'le don des larmes'; even when reading excerpts from his historical works, he could move his listeners to tears.[7]

His qualities and faults as an actor spring from an impetuous, highly emotional temperament and coincide with those of the dramatist. Voltaire's tragedies, full of touching recognition scenes, coups de théâtre, sudden reversals of fortune, and noble gestures, depended for success on the intensity of the acting. Voltaire the dramatist, like Voltaire the actor, was constantly striving for dramatic effect, to which he willingly sacrificed probability. Hence his passionate concern

---

Gardant un esprit libre, à l'étude appliqué,
Et sachant qu'ici-bas la félicité pure
Ne fut jamais permise à l'humaine nature.

5. e.g. in *La Défense de mon oncle*, he is 'pétri de douceur et d'indulgence' (M. XXVI, 399) and his speech 'fit verser des larmes de tendresse' (M. XXVI, 409); in *La Tactique*, he is 'un vieillard philosophe, ami du monde entier', whose 'cœur attendri' will not permit him to say anything good about the military profession (M. X, 191); in the *Dictionnaire philosophique*, art. 'Persécution', he is the benevolent patriarch: 'Tu adores un Dieu, tu prêches la vertu, et tu la pratiques; tu as servi les hommes, et tu les a consolés; tu as établi l'orpheline, tu as secouru le pauvre, tu as changé les déserts où quelques esclaves traînaient une vie misérable en campagnes fertiles peuplées de familles heureuses.'

6. J.-J. Olivier, *Voltaire et les comédiens interprètes de son théâtre* (Paris, 1900), p. xiv.

7. Longchamp and Wagnière, *Mémoires sur Voltaire et sur ses ouvrages* (Paris, 1826), II, 224.

for the way his plays were performed, his attempt to set an example, and his joy at discovering in Lekain an actor who embodied his own ideals.

In one respect, however, Voltaire differed from his disciple: to the end he clung to the outmoded tradition of rhythmical declamation. He rejected the newer, more realistic style of acting developed to suit the *comédie larmoyante*, not because it was sentimental, but on the contrary because he considered 'cette façon misérable de réciter des vers comme on lit sa gazette'[8] as too dry and conversational, lacking the poetic force which serious drama demands.

Voltaire himself combined this elevated tone with his chief characteristic, a total absorption in the part he was playing. He is a perfect example of Diderot's paradox of the actor endowed with excessive sensibility who exhausts himself by adopting the passions of the character he is portraying and who is ultimately less successful than the calculating professional. Voltaire became so involved in his roles that he would not infrequently break down and skip half his lines. His phenomenal memory, which could retain whole acts of Racine without effort, failed him at crucial moments[9] and he found his own verses strangely difficult to memorize.[10] The same tendency to identify completely with characters of his own invention explains his unreasonably severe criticisms of the performances of other actors.[11] Even Lekain was censured for presuming to play Cicero.

Voltaire by no means restricted himself to one type. He sometimes took the romantic lead as the violently jealous Orosmane or the tyrannical Gengis-kan. As might be expected, he excelled in comedy. Yet contemporary evidence and his own remarks clearly indicate that he specialized in certain roles. Since what a man would like to be is an important part of what he is, it is unfortunate that they have been largely overlooked by critics and biographers.

8. L. Perey and G. Maugras, *La Vie intime de Voltaire aux Délices et à Ferney, 1754–1778* (Paris, 1885), p. 128.

9. Longchamp and Wagnière, I, 49.

10. Longchamp and Wagnière, I, 51.

11. Olivier, *Voltaire et les comédiens*, p. 304.

They provide a clue, not only to some of his deepest aspirations, but also to the nature of his image and influence in his own century.

None of the three characters he preferred to impersonate—the patriot, the sentimental patriarch, and the high priest—accords very well with the sterotype. The role of the patriot, depicted not as an irresponsible chauvinist but as an elder statesman who warns his fellow citizens against the dangers of indifference and frivolity by recalling the essential virtues of republicanism, notably love of freedom and devotion to the state, recurs frequently, especially in the Roman plays. Voltaire gave an inspired performance as Cicero in *Rome sauvée*; so much so that Longchamp recalled meeting, thirty years later, people who still talked about it as though they had seen it the day before.[12] As Condorcet tells it,

Jamais, dans aucun rôle, aucun auteur n'a porté si loin l'illusion: on croyait voir le consul. Ce n'étaient pas des vers récités de mémoire qu'on entendait, mais un discours sortant de l'âme de l'orateur. Ceux qui ont assisté à ce spectacle, il y a plus de trente ans, se souviennent encore du moment où l'auteur de *Rome sauvée* s'écriait:

Romains, j'aime la gloire et ne veux point m'en taire, avec une vérité si frappante qu'on ne savait si ce noble aveu venait d'échapper à l'âme de Cicéron ou à celle de Voltaire. (M. V, 203)

It seems clear from this and other descriptions that Voltaire was playing himself, or rather an idealized version of himself, with such force and conviction that for the spectators the illusion was complete. Lekain confirms this impression while stressing Voltaire's chief attributes as an actor—enthusiasm, sincerity, and a gift for pathos. 'Je ne crois pas,' he writes, 'qu'il soit possible de rien entendre de plus vrai, de plus pathétique et de plus enthousiaste que M. de Voltaire dans ce rôle. C'était en vérité Cicéron lui-même

12. Longchamp and Wagnière, II, 281.

tonnant à la tribune aux harangues contre le destructeur de la patrie, des lois, des mœurs et de la religion.'[13]

Voltaire's projection of himself in the person of Cicero is not surprising if we consider that he consistently eulogized the latter, not only as the champion of freedom and the rule of law against tyranny, but also as a kind of Roman *philosophe* (M. VI, 210) and the greatest poet of his age after Lucretius (Best. 11020). In other words, he saw Cicero as a perfect example of a man of letters who was also a man of action and a man of feeling (M. V, 208). Forced to play a rather less direct role in political affairs, Voltaire's aim was to be, as indeed to a considerable extent he was, the Cicero of the eighteenth century, using his prestige, influence, and example to direct public opinion.

Undoubtedly his greatest 'succès de sensibilité' was his incarnation of Lusignan, benevolent leader of the Christian knights in *Zaïre*, who finds his long-lost daughter only to be separated from her by death, and whose appearance was invariably the signal for a torrent of tears. 'Rien de moins voltairien que ce rôle préféré de Voltaire', remarks René Pomeau.[14] This is true enough if the term 'Voltairean' is used in its narrow modern sense. But contemporary audiences saw nothing incongruous in the performance. Voltaire was the acknowledged master of sensibility in the theatre. Given his definition of 'true Christianity' as the practice of benevolence, the forgiveness of enemies, and the worship of God, as exemplified in the character of Alvarez in *Alzire* and the noble and sentimental patriarchs of his later plays, it was not implausible that he should pose as the defender of religion.

Moreover, it was perfectly logical for him to go one step further and provide himself with the key role as the high priest of deism. *Sémiramis* contains an edifying portrait of a religious leader as seen by Voltaire. His particular favourite, however, was the Hiérophante in *Olympie*, first performed at Ferney in 1762. It must have been an impressive spectacle.

13. J.-J. Olivier, *Henri-Louis Le Kain de la Comédie-Française* (Paris, 1907), p. 21, n.
14. *Voltaire par lui-même* (Paris, 1955), p. 18.

'J'ai représenté ce personnage,' he writes, 'moi qui vous parle; j'avais une grande barbe blanche avec une mitre de deux pieds de haut, et un manteau beaucoup plus beau que celui d'Aaron. Mais quelle onction était dans mes paroles! Je faisais pleurer les petits garçons' (Best. 10921). That Voltaire spoke flippantly about his role in private correspondence is no indication that he played it with anything less than his usual seriousness. The Hiérophante, apostle of *bienfaisance* and enlightened minister of a God of clemency, is a figure he had no difficulty in impersonating. He more than once hinted that he thought of himself as the prophet of a new, universal religion,[15] a minimum creed acceptable to all reasonable men. And for all his ferocious attacks on clerical intolerance, bigotry, and fanaticism, he had no desire to see the priesthood abolished.

Another important item in the dossier of Voltaire as *homme sensible* is his friendship for Vauvenargues, which has been justly called 'one of the keenest, and certainly one of the most durable feelings in a life crowded with violent emotions of every type'.[16] If the stereotype of Voltaire were true, the strong attraction to each other felt by both men would be quite inexplicable. Each had a very high opinion of the other's taste and literary talent, but all the evidence shows that something deeper than mutual respect was involved. Voltaire was genuinely devoted to the marquis; Vauvenargues recognized in Voltaire not only a great writer but a great man. Marmontel, an intimate friend of both and an eye-witness of their meetings, sums up their relationship as follows: 'C'était, d'un côté, le respect de Vauvenargues pour le génie de Voltaire, et de l'autre, la tendre vénération de Voltaire pour la vertu de Vauvenargues.'[17] The choice of words here is significant: a 'tender' veneration for 'virtue'. Voltaire saw in his young friend an admirable living example of his own conception of sensibility and *grandeur d'âme*.

15. e.g. M. X, 404: 'J'ai fait plus en mon temps que Luther et Calvin.'
16. May Wallas, *Luc de Clapiers, Marquis de Vauvenargues* (Cambridge, 1928), p. 116. See also Fernand Vial, 'Vauvenargues et Voltaire', *RR*, 33 (1942), 41–57.
17. *Mémoires*, quoted in M. I, xxxviii.

Vauvenargues was not, as is sometimes made to appear, a premature exponent of sensibility in a totally unreceptive environment. His philosophy was in accord with the general trends noted in the preceding chapter. It was exceptional in the intensity with which it was expressed and in its emphasis on the need to rise above mediocrity by entertaining a vision of greatness. His view of man was optimistic in that he affirmed the existence of something magnanimous in man's nature which makes life worth living and which is not divorced from feelings of pleasure. Without denying the importance of reason or the dangers of uncontrolled passion, he admired strong feelings as the indispensable attribute of greatness. Like the *philosophes*, Vauvenargues attacked the misuse of reason in constructing dogmatic systems in defiance of experience. In particular, he deplored any attempt to impose a rigid, puritanical concept of morality, since the repression of natural instincts is a denial of life itself. At the same time, he was even more opposed to the other extreme of vulgar hedonism. Any definition of happiness, in his view, should go beyond the enjoyment of mediocre material comforts and take into account man's noble and heroic instincts. Hence his vigorous denunciation of those features of contemporary life which he felt to be petty and frivolous.

Given his stress on feelings, his dislike of cynicism and scepticism, and his ethical doctrine, it is surely significant that Vauvenargues should have seen evidence of the kind of greatness that he most admired in Voltaire, whom he described as 'philosophe et peintre sublime, qui a semé avec éclat dans ses écrits tout ce qu'il y a de grand dans l'esprit des hommes, qui a représenté les passions avec des traits de feu et de lumière'.[18]

Vauvenargues was not the only contemporary to refer to Voltaire's genius in terms of fire as well as light, but he recognized more clearly than most the vein of idealism which characterizes Voltaire's 'prestige' productions. What he found particularly admirable was their reflection of the author's 'humanity' and 'vast imagination', which caused him to feel acutely for the victims of intolerance and oppression.

18. Quoted in Longchamp and Wagnière, *Mémoires*, II, 503.

He had no hesitation in calling *La Henriade* 'le plus grand ouvrage de ce siècle'.[19] In the tragedies, he praised 'les grandes passions qui y règnent' and 'la manière forte dont les passions y sont ordinairement conduites'.[20]

Voltaire in turn recognized similar qualities in Vauvenargues. In Voltaire's correspondence there is a marked difference, as Condorcet has pointed out, between obvious flattery directed at the vanity of influential persons who might conceivably be useful to the cause, and the language of sincere admiration.[21] The accent of sincerity in the letters to Vauvenargues is unmistakeable. In spite of the difference in age and literary eminence, Voltaire saw him as an equal, as a kindred spirit, and as a mirror of all that was best in his own character: 'Aimable créature, beau génie, j'ay lu votre premier manuscrit, et j'y ay admiré cette hauteur d'une grande âme qui s'élève si fort au dessus des petits brillants des Isocrates. Si vous étiez né quelques années plutôt mes ouvrages en vaudroient mieux. Mais au moins sur la fin de ma carrière, vous m'affermissez dans la route que vous suivez. Le grand, le pathétique, le sentiment, voylà mes premiers maîtres. Vous êtes le dernier.'[22]

Above all else, Voltaire was captivated by Vauvenargues' sensibility, 'cet esprit de profondeur et de sentiment' which he correctly perceived to be the marquis' dominating quality (Best. 3085), and which inclined him to give the advantage to Vauvenargues over Horace in a comparison between the two writers: 'Il me semble que son cœur n'était pas si sensible que le vôtre. C'est cette extrême sensibilité que j'aime' (Best. 2869).

Whether the depiction of passion in Voltairean tragedy is as successful as Vauvenargues believed is a matter of opinion; but there is considerable evidence that his assessment of Voltaire's character is nearer the truth than the standard portrait would suggest. No-one who has consulted the correspondence or read Desnoiresterres' biography can be in any

19. Vauvenargues, *Œuvres*, ed. Pierre Varillon (Paris, 1929), I, 276.
20. *Œuvres*, I, 276.
21. *Vie de Voltaire*, M. I, 274.
22. 5 April [1744], Best. 2751.

doubt that Voltaire was a passionate, impulsive man, notwithstanding his tact, politeness, and sense of propriety and the impression left by some of his most celebrated works, in which irony and an apparently casual attitude predominate. Formey's judgment that 'jamais homme ne fut moins libre que lui, cédant à tous les mouvemens qui le dominoient, sans délibération ni réflexion' [23] is an exaggeration, but less so than the myth of the cold rationalist.

'All fire and fickleness' is the way Byron described him. This is an inept caricature according to Peter Gay, who protests with reason against the accusation of dilettantism: 'He was, rather, a methodical, systematic, hard-working, and thoughtful scholar.' [24] The truth is that he was both ardent and studious, combining a vivacious and sensitive temperament with an astonishing capacity for patient research and hard work. But the passionate outbursts cannot be dismissed as mere eccentricity; they are the key to his character and also to some of his qualities and defects as a writer. In Voltaire's case there is a particularly close connection, as many critics have pointed out, between temperament and ideas.[25]

Few writers have lived more in the present or have been more affected by events. It is no accident that Voltaire excelled in improvisation and in a superior form of journalism. He needed the stimulus of strong emotion and was often at his best when responding to an immediate situation: the Lisbon earthquake, the judicial murders of Calas and La Barre, the attacks of his literary, philosophical, and personal enemies. Even historical events were rendered actual by his extraordinary capacity for suffering with the victims. The periods of calm are deceptive, like the polished surface of his best writing.

23. Formey, *Souvenirs d'un citoyen*, I, 234.
24. *Party of Humanity*, p. 59.
25. 'Ce sont ses problèmes, ses conflits sur le plan émotif qui expliqueront peut-être le mieux cette œuvre dans sa multiplicité et sa variété. La sensibilité de Voltaire expliquant ses idées: une preuve n'en est-elle pas sa réaction au tremblement de terre de Lisbonne? Sous le coup, il rejette soudain les réponses dont il se contentait naguère.' (André Delattre, *Voltaire l'impétueux; essai présenté par R. Pomeau* [Paris, 1957], p. 14). See also R. Pomeau, *La Religion de Voltaire* (Paris, 1956), p. 123; Naves, *Voltaire*, p. 88; Theodore Besterman, 'Voltaire et le désastre de Lisbonne: ou, la mort de l'optimisme', *SV*, II, 17.

The words which occur most frequently in contemporary descriptions of Voltaire and his work are 'feu',[26] 'ardent', and 'sensible'. Mme Suard spoke of 'le feu de ses yeux' and his 'physionomie pleine de feu';[27] Linguet of his 'tempérament plein de feu', his 'sensibilité excessive', his 'imagination impétueuse' and his 'désir ardent du bonheur des hommes'.[28] La Harpe deplored the fact that his 'tête vive' and his 'âme ardente' were too often deaf to the voice of calm reason.[29] Bret ('Je ne voyais en lui qu'une sensibilité trop grande, que trop peu de défiance pour ses premiers mouvements')[30] and Grétry ('la nature, en créant l'homme de génie, commença par le rendre vif, sensible, passionné, et rarement assez pacifique pour résister au plaisir d'une juste vengeance')[31] expressed the same view. Servières found in *Sémiramis* 'cette force, ce feu, cette supériorité de pathétique, qui n'est propre aujourd'hui qu'à M. de *Voltaire*'.[32] Pierre Clément criticized *La Henriade* as being merely the product of 'une imagination vive et hardie, et une grande sensibilité d'âme'.[33] According to Trublet, no poet had 'plus d'imagination, plus de feu, et plus de graces que *Voltaire*'.[34]

Hostile and sympathetic critics were agreed on this one

26. 'Feu' was often used in the eighteenth century as a synonym for poetic inspiration and imaginative power. In the art. 'Verve' of the *Encyclopédie*, Jaucourt speaks of 'un cœur plein d'un feu noble et qui s'allume aisément à la vue des objets' and of the poet's soul at the moment of inspiration as 'enflammée comme d'un feu divin'.

27. Quoted by Marcel Hervier, *Les Ecrivains français jugés par leurs contemporains*, vol. II, *Le Dix-huitième siècle* (Paris, 1936), p. 98. It is worth noting that Mme Suard describes Voltaire's smile, not as 'hideux', but on the contrary as 'enchanteur'.

28. S. N. H. Linguet, *Examen des ouvrages de M. de Voltaire, considéré comme Poëte, comme Prosateur, comme Philosophe* (Brussels, 1788), pp. 1–5.

29. J. F. de la Harpe, *Lycée ou Cours de littérature ancienne et moderne* (Paris, 1798), X, 72.

30. *Correspondance littéraire, philosophique et critique par Grimm, Diderot, Raynal, Meister*, etc., ed. Maurice Tourneux (Paris, 1877–82), I, 306.

31. in *Lettres de Mme de Graffigny*, ed. Eugène Asse (Paris, 1879), p. 370.

32. *Mémoires*, II, 206.

33. *Les Cinq Années littéraires* (Berlin, 1755), II, 92.

34. Nicolas Trublet, *Essais sur divers sujets de littérature et de morale*, 4ᵉ éd. (Paris, 1749), IV, 218–219.

point: that Voltaire's highly emotional nature was chiefly responsible for his qualities and faults. The famous 'portrait' included the following comment: 'Tout le feu que vous trouvez dans ses Ouvrages, il l'a dans son action: Vif jusqu'à l'étourderie: C'est un ardent qui va & vient, qui vous éblouit & qui pétille.' [35] And Pellegrin, in his analysis of Œdipe, concluded that Voltaire relied too much on inspiration to be a great poet: 'S'il ne falloit avoir que du feu, de l'imagination et de l'esprit pour faire un bon Poëte, Mr de Voltaire s'éleveroit au premier rang; mais dans le dramatique et dans l'épique il faut sur tout de l'ordre, et cet ordre est souvent incompatible avec ce grand feu, qui l'emporte au-delà de lui-même, et qui ne lui permet de connoître d'autre raison que l'enthousiasme.' [36]

On the other hand, Goldsmith, who met Voltaire at his house in Lausanne, was more impressed by his 'elegant sensibility' and by the warmth of his personality: 'In company which he either disliked or despised, few could be more reserved than he; but when he was warmed in discourse, and had got over a hesitating manner which sometimes he was subject to, it was rapture to hear him. His meagre visage seemed insensibly to gather beauty; every muscle in it had meaning, and his eyes beamed with unusual brightness.' [37]

Voltaire's impulsiveness was one of his most endearing characteristics, as Jean-Jacques Rousseau was the first to admit.[38] The acts of kindness to which it gave rise were legion. A typical example among many was his adoption of Mlle Corneille, a descendant of the great dramatist, in 1760. When Le Brun wrote to Voltaire asking him to take the impoverished young lady under his protection, he made the request in the form of a hymn to *bienfaisance*:

35. Leigh, 'An anonymous eighteenth-century character-sketch of Voltaire', *SV*, II, 242–243.

36. S. J. Pellegrin, 'Dissertation sur l'Œdipe de Corneille, et sur celui de M. de Voltaire', *Mercure* (June 1729), pp. 1316–17.

37. 'Voltaire's British Visitors', ed. Sir Gavin de Beer, *SV*, IV, 8–9.

38. 'Je ne sache point d'homme sur la terre dont les premiers mouvements aient été plus beaux que les siens' (*Œuvres complètes*, ed. G. Petitain [Paris, 1839], I, 666).

BIENFAISANCE sublime, ô Déesse adorée!
Toujours à tes regards l'infortune est sacrée.
Qu'il est beau d'accueillir la vertu malheureuse!
        Une âme généreuse
Enchaîne tous les cœurs par le nœud des bienfaits.[39]

Le Brun knew his man. Voltaire could never resist this kind
of appeal and promptly replied in the affirmative.

His impulses were not always generous; they frequently
involved him in endless petty squabbles. Voltaire was a
living confirmation of the current theory that the source
of magnanimity and greatness could also be the cause of a
great deal of suffering and conflict. He himself admitted as
much. He needed, he said, to exercise constant self-control,
'sentir et réprimer ma vive impatience'.[40] His lack of restraint
in responding to provocation was deplored by his friends as
well as his enemies. Both Gui de Chabanon and Mme
Suard felt unable to grant him the full title of 'homme
vertueux', in spite of his formidable qualifications, because,
as the former explained, 'Il fut toute sa vie un enfant indis-
cipliné, esclave de ses passions, et n'ayant jamais eu le projet
de les réprimer. . . . Voltaire avait le correctif de son implacable vengeance dans une sensibilité naturelle, que la moindre
prévenance suffisait pour intéresser; mais rarement ceux
qui l'avaient offensé ont eu recours à sa clémence.'[41]

Voltaire's impulsiveness may help to explain a curious

39. Quoted by C. Palissot, *Eloge de M. de Voltaire* (London, 1778), p.
92. For Voltaire's reply, see Best. 8619.
40. *Epître au roi de Prusse*, M. X, 333. In 1737, he wrote to Thieriot:
'Il est vray mon cher amy que j'ay été très malade, mais la vivacité de
mon tempérament me tient lieu de force. Ce sont des ressorts délicats
qui me mettent au tombeau et qui m'en retirent bien vite' (Best.
D1262).
41. *Lettres de Mme de Graffigny*, p. 364. Mme Suard's comment:
'En adorant le génie et l'âme passionnée de Voltaire pour les intérêts de
ses semblables, je ne prétends pas approuver les excès où l'a souvent
entraîné la violence de ses passions. Je ne le considère point comme un
modèle de vertu dans sa vie, quoique remplie d'actions nobles et généreuses, je l'envisage encore moins comme un exemple de sagesse dans
tous ses ouvrages. Je réserve le culte que nous devons à la parfaite vertu,
pour les Antonins, les Marc-Aurèles et les Fénelons' (*Lettres de Mme de
Graffigny*, pp. 375–376). It is clear that 'vertu' is being used in the
Stoic sense, in accordance with the trend of the late eighteenth century.

streak of naïveté in his character and an occasional tendency to indulge in romanesque behaviour, so completely out of keeping with the common-sense image. One thinks, for example, of his obsessive determination to fight a duel with the chevalier de Rohan, of his illusions about Frederick, of the innumerable complicated intrigues in which he seems to have been perpetually involved.[42] Collini relates an amusing and revealing episode which occurred when Voltaire was anxious to leave Prussia after his quarrel with the King:

> Ecoutez, me dit-il, j'ai imaginé un moyen de sortir de ce pays. Vous pourriez acheter deux chevaux. Il ne sera pas difficile de faire ensuite emplette d'un chariot. Lorsqu'on aura des chevaux, il ne paraîtra pas étrange que l'on fasse provision de foin.—Eh bien, monsieur lui dis-je, que ferons-nous du chariot, des chevaux et du foin?—Le voici: nous emplirons le chariot de foin. Au milieu du foin nous mettrons tout notre bagage. Je me placerai, déguisé, sur le foin, et me donnerai pour un curé réformé qui va voir une de ses filles mariées dans le bourg voisin.[43]

Fortunately, Collini persuaded Voltaire to abandon this scheme, worthy of the hero of a Prévost novel.

Equally reminiscent of Prévost, more particularly of his *Manon Lescaut*, is the story of the young Arouet's love affair with Olympe Dunoyer—too familiar to bear repetition here—[44] which has all the romantic ingredients one could wish for, including secret meetings, disguises, plans for elopement, hostile parents, and protestations of eternal love. In spite of the latter, the affair only lasted a few months and had little influence on Voltaire's life, although with characteristic generosity he tried to send Olympe money and over twenty

42. Commenting on a particularly clumsy intervention in the Palissot affair, R. Naves remarks: 'Nous l'avons déjà laissé entendre: avec son air roublard et ses manœuvres compliquées, Voltaire est très souvent un grand naïf' (*Voltaire et l'Encyclopédie* [Paris, 1938], p. 78).

43. C. A. Collini, *Mon Séjour auprès de Voltaire, et lettres inédites que m'écrivit cet homme célèbre jusqu'à la dernière année de sa vie* (Paris, 1807), p. 54.

44. There are detailed accounts in F. Allizé, 'Voltaire à La Haye en 1713', *Revue de Paris*, 22 (15 November 1922), pp. 321–324 and Arnelle, *Les Filles de Mme Du Noyer* (1663–1720) (Paris, 1920).

years later gave her a handsome present. What is particularly interesting is the accent of passionate sincerity in Voltaire's earliest love letters. Even the young lady's formidable mother agreed that they merited comparison with the *Lettres portugaises* and the letters of Héloïse and Abélard, especially, she noted, in 'cette manière d'exagérer les malheurs et les besoins qu'on a de se consoler mutuellement l'un l'autre, par une tendresse et une confiance mutuelle'.[45]

The escapade at The Hague was the first of a considerable number of love affairs, which have too often been dismissed as inconsequential or as arrangements of convenience, devoid of that true passion which Voltaire is supposed to have reserved for the battle of ideas. His rapid recovery of equilibrium and good humour when thwarted in love is cited as proof that he did not take them seriously. Sainte-Beuve stated flatly, 'Au fond, Voltaire n'était pas et ne pouvait être un véritable amant. Il n'avait que des admirations d'esprit, et était surtout capable d'amitié.'[46]

This view of the author of *Zaïre* is too glib to be accepted without comment. It is true that Voltaire was well aware of the ephemeral nature of love between the sexes and for that reason placed a higher value on friendship.[47] He was wise enough to accept the inevitable and too sensitive to the feelings of others to play the romantic hero oblivious to everything but his own passion. But he was very far from being either a frivolous libertine or a sexless philosopher.

Michelet has pointed out that the reputation of the eighteenth century generally in this regard is undeserved: 'L'amour est grand au dix-huitième siècle. A travers le caprice désordonné et la mobilité, il subsiste adoré, et surtout admiré. Il n'a pas la fadeur des Astrées, des Cyrus. Il est fort et réel, et il semble une religion, accrue des ruines de l'ancienne.'[48] Voltaire's fame as a poet of this

45. Allizé, p. 324.
46. *Causeries du lundi*, 2ᵉ éd. (Paris, 1869), II, 276.
47. e.g. M. X, 501:
Il vaut mieux être amis tout le temps de sa vie
Que d'être amants pour quelques jours.
48. Jules Michelet, *Histoire de France* (Paris, 1893–1897), XIV, 306. Mauzi (*Bonheur*, pp. 472–483) has shown that love was equated with virtue and *grandeur d'âme* throughout the century.

conception of love exceeded that of Racine. Like Puccini a century or so later, he was renowned for the portrayal of unhappy heroines—Zaïre, Alzire, Adélaïde, Aménaïde—and of ardent, tender love. So much so that he became the prisoner of his own success and was forced to bow to public demand. 'Comment', asked one critic, upset by Voltaire's new style in tragedy, 'M. de *Voltaire* qui manie l'amour avec tant de délicatesse, et qui en connait toute la véhemence et toute l'étenduë, s'est-il oublié dans celui de *Sémiramis*?'[49]

As Voltaire himself insisted, one cannot depict passion successfully without having personally experienced its effects.[50] His two most important liaisons, with Mme Du Châtelet and with Mme Denis, show that he was both tender and passionate. In spite of stormy crises and the fact that each had become involved with someone else before the end, the relationship between Voltaire and his beloved Emilie was one of extraordinary mutual devotion, which can hardly be accounted for by intellectual affinity alone. Few men would have been as forgiving, sympathetic, and willing to offer practical assistance as was Voltaire after what must have seemed a blatant betrayal, and fewer still would have been capable of the poignant grief so simply and movingly expressed in the letters to d'Argental after Mme Du Châtelet's death.[51] Anyone who still thinks of Voltaire as a 'frigid intellectual' has not read the *Lettres d'amour de Voltaire à sa nièce*.[52] These completely confidential letters, filled with expressions of affection, passion, jealousy, and frank sexual desire, provide a revealing glimpse of one aspect of Voltaire's real nature. As their editor states, 'It is impossible

49. [Dupuy-Demportes], *Parallèle de Sémiramis de M. de Voltaire et de celle de M. de Crébillon* (Paris, 1748), p. 19.

50. To Gui de Chabanon, 3 October 1766 (Best. 12757): 'Vous prétendez donc que j'ai été amoureux dans mon temps tout comme un autre? Vous pouriez ne vous pas tromper. Quiconque peint les passions les a ressenties.'

51. Best. 3472, 3474, E. Champion justly comments: 'Comparez ces lettres à celles où Racine parle de la mort de la Champmeslé avec tant d'indifférence, de dureté. Et c'est Racine qui a le cœur tendre, tandis que Voltaire a le cœur sec!' (*Voltaire. Etudes critiques*, 3⁰ éd. [Paris, 1921], p. 15, n.).

52. ed. Theodore Besterman (Paris, 1957).

to doubt that Voltaire loved his niece sincerely, tenderly, passionately, and often blindly.'[53]

Terms such as 'passionate', 'impulsive', and 'impetuous' are not therefore inappropriate to descriptions of Voltaire's character, as many commentators would now readily agree. It is difficult to see why 'sentimental'—one of the more important meanings of *sensible* as used in the eighteenth century—should be excluded. We learn from several sources that he was in the habit of weeping frequently, copiously, openly, and at the slightest provocation: 'On sait qu'à la Comédie-Française, le jour de son couronnement, il répandit des pleurs. Il en avait l'usage familier et quelquefois immodéré.'[54] According to Duvernet, 'On le surprit souvent seul, versant des larmes de pitié & de douleur, sur les malheurs de l'espece humaine.'[55] Mme de Graffigny who, as the author of the *Lettres d'une Péruvienne*, must be considered something of an expert on the subject, had no doubts about Voltaire's tender and compassionate sensibility; she recognized a kindred spirit who was not ashamed of showing feelings.[56] 'Je l'ai fait pleurer hier, mais pleurer à chaudes larmes,' she exclaimed in a letter written to Devaux during her stay at Cirey, 'en lui contant ce que Léopold avait fait pour la *M*. . . . Il n'entend jamais parler d'une belle action sans attendrissement' (Best. D1700).

This last observation is confirmed by a number of other contemporaries who knew him well. Gui de Chabanon, for example, relates the following typical incident: 'Un jour, il vint à table tenant à la main un plaidoyer de M. Servan, en faveur d'une protestante mariée avec un catholique. Il voulut nous en lire la péroraison: les larmes le suffoquaient; il sentait que son émotion était plus forte que le discours ne le comportait, quoique noble et touchant. "Je pleure plus que je ne devrais, nous dit-il; mais je ne puis

---

53. Theodore Besterman, *Voltaire* (London, 1969), p. 262.
54. Gui de Chabanon in *Lettres de Mme de Graffigny*, p. 359.
55. *La Vie de Voltaire* (Geneva, 1786), pp. 247–248.
56. '[Mme Du Châtelet] riait pour s'empêcher de pleurer; Voltaire, l'humain Voltaire, fondait en larmes, car il n'a pas honte de paraître sensible' (*Lettres*, p. 106).

me retenir." Telles étaient les émotions dont il était susceptible.'[57]

Thierot said that he preferred Voltaire's heart to his mind; Baculard d'Arnaud that Voltaire could never be accused of sacrificing the former to the latter.[58] Mme de Duras described him as 'sensible, aimable'; Mme Du Deffand as 'une âme sensible'; Mlle Clairon as 'cette âme compatissante et sensible'. Mme Du Châtelet said of him, 'Il avait le cœur bon et tendre: il aimait à aimer.'[59]

In 1778, Voltaire's secretary left him in Paris to return to Ferney. The scene, as described by Wagnière, might have provided an ideal subject for the brush of Greuze:

> J'entrai dans cet instant, et me jetai dans ses bras. Il me tint long-temps serré, sans que nous pussions proférer une parole, et fondant tous deux en larmes; je lui dis enfin: 'Puissé-je, mon cher maître, vous revoir bientôt en bonne santé!' *Hélas! mon ami*, répondit-il, *je souhaite de vivre pour te revoir et de mourir dans tes bras*. Je m'arrachai alors des siens, et me retirai sans pouvoir lui rien dire de plus, tant j'étais plein de trouble et d'agitation.
>
> Telles sont les dernières paroles que j'ai entendu prononcer à ce grand homme, à cet être extraordinaire, vertueux et bon, à mon cher maître, mon père, mon ami, qu'un destin fatal n'a pas permis que je revisse, et que je pleure chaque jour.[60]

If, as the cliché has it, Voltaire's life resembles a novel, it is a typically eighteenth-century novel, full of improbable incidents, philosophical digressions, noble sentiments, and torrents of tears.

One of Voltaire's virtues which certainly cannot be denied and which is indicative of the nature of his sensibility is his capacity for friendship. Friendship meant much more to him than simply being on good terms with a few close

57. *Lettres de Mme de Graffigny*, pp. 359–360.
58. *Les Amusements du cœur et de l'esprit* (La Haye, 1742), IV, 290.
59. All quoted by Charles Oulmont, *Voltaire en robe de chambre* (Paris, 1936), pp. 139–140.
60. Longchamp and Wagnière, *Mémoires*, I, 152.

acquaintances; it was a sacred and inviolable pact, almost an article of faith. He expressed surprise that it was not a part of religious instruction (M. XVIII, 74). When he touches on the subject in the *Discours sur l'homme*, a philosophical discourse in verse is suddenly transformed into a fervent hymn of praise:

> O divine amitié! félicité parfaite,
> Seul mouvement de l'âme où l'excès soit permis,
> Change en bien tous les maux où le ciel m'a soumis;
> Compagne de mes pas dans toutes mes demeures,
> Dans toutes les saisons et dans toutes les heures:
> Sans toi tout homme est seul; il peut par ton appui
> Multiplier son être, et vivre dans autrui.
> Idole d'un cœur juste, et passion du sage,
> Amitié, que ton nom couronne cet ouvrage![61]

According to Voltaire's definition, friendship is inseparable from sensibility, virtue, and 'douceur'.[62] Only men and women of feeling are granted this most precious of all God's gifts and the strength or weakness of the ties depends on the degree of sensibility on both sides (M. XVII, 171). One of the most moving of Voltaire's poems, *Aux mânes de M. de Genonville*, emphasizes the point:

> Loin de nous à jamais ces mortels endurcis,
> Indignes du beau nom, du nom sacré d'amis,
> Ou toujours remplis d'eux, ou toujours hors d'eux-mêmes:
> Au monde, à l'inconstance ardents à se livrer,
> Malheureux, dont le cœur ne sait pas comme on aime,
> Et qui n'ont point connu la douceur de pleurer!
>
> (M. X, 266)

61. M. IX, 405. See also M. IX, 423–424.
62. *Dictionnaire philosophique*, art. 'Amitié': 'C'est un contrat tacite entre deux personnes sensibles et vertueuses'; 'ce contrat entre deux âmes tendres et honnêtes'; 'les hommes vertueux ont seuls des amis.' *L'Envieux*, M. III, 535:

> Un ami vertueux, éclairé, doux, et sage,
> Est un présent du ciel, et son plus digne ouvrage.

It is of particular significance therefore that Voltaire prided himself, justifiably, on possessing this talent to the highest degree. The emphasis placed on his resounding quarrels has left a false impression of general irritability and vindictiveness. The correspondence tells a different story. Dr. Besterman has pointed out that very few people can claim to have maintained such a close relationship with such a variety of acquaintances over such a long period of time.[63] Tending to judge other people's ardour by his own, Voltaire expected a great deal of his friends and counted on their loyalty and support; in return, he was always at their disposal—with money, with his pen, with advice and consolation, even with that most precious of all commodities, time. Yet he was unusually kind, forgiving and tolerant of faults and idiosyncracies, as is clear from his relations with Saint-Lambert, the impossible Thieriot and a host of ungrateful protégés. His instinct was to overlook occasional lapses of disloyalty and to see the best rather than the worst in others. Whatever their respective theories, in practice it was Voltaire and not the misanthropic Rousseau who was optimistic about human nature.[64]

This optimism is all the more remarkable when one considers that his kindness was not infrequently repaid by betrayal, especially in his repeated attempts to assist struggling, unknown writers. To readers of the correspondence or of Desnoiresterres' biography, the pattern becomes depressingly familiar: Voltaire receives an appeal for help from a young author, responds promptly and discreetly with financial and other assistance, and is subsequently exploited or abused. One can only endorse Desnoiresterres' conclusion: 'Ces infiniment petits que Voltaire traîne à sa

63. 'Le Vrai Voltaire par ses lettres', *SV*, X, 16–17. Voltaire maintained regular correspondence with thirty-five people for twenty years or more and with some twenty for over thirty years. And as Condorcet noted (M. I, 282), 'On voit dans ses ouvrages que peu d'hommes sensibles ont conservé aussi longtemps que lui le souvenir des amis qu'ils ont perdus dans la jeunesse.'

64. According to Wagnière (*Mémoires*, I, 301), Voltaire hated people to think he was in good health and exaggerated his illnesses for the same reason that he exaggerated his age: he persisted in believing that no-one would persecute a sick old man.

suite, Thiériot, Linant, d'Arnaud, Lamarre, Mouhy et les autres, aident à le connaître, à l'apprécier, et révèlent les côtés généreux, voire ingénus, de ce terrible enfant, comme Diderot l'appellera un jour, qui aima véritablement ses amis, leur pardonna avec une mansuétude peu ordinaire, et s'obstina en dépit de tout à n'écouter que le penchant qui l'attirait vers eux.'[65]

Unprejudiced readers of the correspondence will find it difficult to disagree with its editor's claim that Voltaire emerges from its pages as 'a very human, a kindly and a lovable man'.[66] In view of the wide gap between reputation and reality in the case of Voltaire, it is hardly surprising that one of the most generous of all famous men has been repeatedly accused of meanness. If any refutation were needed outside the correspondence itself, there is ample evidence in the testimony of contemporaries. His kindness is stressed by, among others, Condorcet, La Harpe, Mme de Graffigny, Marmontel, Lekain, and Palissot, who said that 'le fond de son caractère' was 'naturellement bon et sensible' and spoke of 'cette effusion du cœur qui a été en lui le principe de tant d'actions généreuses'.[67] Métra, who was not particularly well-disposed towards Voltaire, agreed that he was 'sans contredit l'homme opulent qui a donné le plus d'or, et fait le plus d'ingrats'.[68]

A particularly striking corroboration of these traits in Voltaire's character is provided by three men who knew him more intimately than most, his personal secretaries. Voltaire proves to be an exception to the rule that no man is a hero to his servants. Longchamp, recounting an unfortunate first day spent in his service, notes his quick temper but adds: 'Je vis de plus en plus dans la suite qu'autant ses vivacités étaient passagères, et, pour ainsi dire, superficielles, autant son indulgence et sa bonté étaient des qualités solides et durables.'[69] Voltaire was, in fact, more than

65. G. Desnoiresterres, *Voltaire et la société au dix-huitième siècle* (Paris, 1871–6), 2ᵉ éd., II, 150.

66. Besterman, *Voltaire*, p. 485.

67 Palissot, *Eloge*, pp. 31–32.

68. *Correspondance littéraire secrète*, 15 (23 November 1783), p. 235. This is confirmed by Collini and Wagnière. See also Best. D1134.

69. *Mémoires*, II, 136.

kind to this rather unscrupulous man, who kept unauthorized copies of his manuscripts. When Longchamp saw him again in 1778 after a long interval, he was moved to tears.[70]

Collini writes that his greatest happiness was to be in Voltaire's company,[71] and that he left *les Délices* 'les larmes aux yeux'.[72] He remembers his former employer as a generous, humane, and tolerant man: 'Le grand homme dont j'étais commensal, portait un cœur sensible, un esprit égal et tolérant, jamais l'ennui ne venait altérer son humeur; avec de telles qualités, il établissait sans peine dans sa maison l'accord domestique, partie essentielle du bonheur de la vie privée.'[73]

Wagnière is even more emphatic, praising particularly Voltaire's interest in the welfare of young people and his paternal concern for the inhabitants of Ferney. This is his description of the departure for Paris in 1778: 'La douleur et la consternation étaient dans Ferney lorsque M. *de Voltaire* en sortit. Tous les colons fondaient en larmes et semblaient prévoir leur malheur. Lui-même pleurait d'attendrissement. Il leur promettait que dans un mois et demi, sans faute, il serait de retour, et au milieu de ses enfants.'[74] Again, one has the impression of reading an extract from a contemporary *roman sensible*.

The same might be said of Mme Suard's account of her visit to Ferney in 1775. Her portrait of the 'Dieu bienfaisant de Ferney' is imbued with the sentimental enthusiasm characteristic of the literature of the period:

Comme le soir de mon arrivée, M. Audibert lui apprit qu'on venait de mettre à la Bastille l'abbé du B*** et se saisir de ses papiers, il versa des larmes sur son malheur, et parla avec la plus vive indignation de cet acte de despotisme. C'est cette sensibilité si vraie qui me le fait adorer; c'est ce feu sacré qui éclaire et échauffe tout ce qu'il touche; c'est cette imagination si vive, si facile à

70. *Mémoires*, II, 360.
71. *Séjour*, p. 177.
72. *Séjour*, p. 176.
73. *Séjour*, p. 118.
74. *Mémoires*, I, 120.

émouvoir, qui le transforme à l'instant dans la personne opprimée pour lui prêter l'appui de tout son génie, et crée peut-être son génie; car je crois, avec Vauvenargues, que le génie vient de l'accord et de l'harmonie entre l'âme et l'esprit. Qui jamais a pris en main la cause des opprimés avec plus de chaleur et l'a poursuivie, à travers les obstacles, avec plus de constance? Eh! qu'on ne dise point que c'était la gloire qu'il poursuivait en cherchait à les sauver: non; c'en était le bonheur! L'amour de la gloire se laisse rebuter par toutes les choses où le génie ne peut se montrer; ce n'est que l'amour de l'humanité qui se soumet à cette multitude de détails nécessaires au succès des affaires, et qui peut seul y trouver sa plus douce récompense.[75]

Several points in this passage are worth underlining: Voltaire possessed to a really extraordinary degree the rare gift of true compassion; his sensibility was perfectly attuned to that of the late eighteenth century; and his humanity was genuine, not a mere pose, as Mme Suard astutely proves.

*Bienfaisance*, in fact, meant far more to Voltaire than an abstract concept or a useful gambit in the philosophical campaign against *l'Infâme*; it was a deeply rooted conviction that kindness and magnanimity in one's relations with others is the greatest source of happiness and the key to both personal fulfilment and to the progress of humanity in general. As he put it, 'Le vrai salut est la bienfaisance' (Best. 13016); or, to quote a line from the *Epitre à Horace* which became proverbial: 'J'ai fait un peu de bien; c'est mon meilleur ouvrage' (M. X, 443).

Too much importance has been accorded to Voltaire's doctrine of the 'Dieu gendarme' and his supposed fear of being robbed,[76] and too little to his positive approach to ethics, his desire to set an example and to encourage altruistic behaviour. Voltaire was acutely conscious of his failings, but he always maintained that his aim was the pursuit of virtue. He saw himself in much the same light as readers

75. *Lettres de Mme de Graffigny*, pp. 398–399.
76. cf. Collini's remark: 'Je n'ai jamais connu d'homme que ses domestiques pussent voler plus facilement' (*Séjour*, p. 184).

viewed the typical eighteenth-century hero—Gil Blas, Tom Jones, Candide, Des Grieux—as a man whose actions were sometimes doubtful, but whose intentions were excellent: 'J'ai bien fait des fautes dans le cours de ma vie. Les amertumes et les souffrances qui en ont marqué presque tous les jours ont été souvent mon ouvrage. Je sens le peu que je vaux, mes faiblesses me font pitié et mes fautes me font horreur; mais dieu m'est témoin que j'aime la vertu.' [77] The majority of his contemporaries were inclined to agree; in the long run, they were willing to overlook his faults because in spite of them Voltaire remained the most outstanding example of *bienfaisance* as understood by the eighteenth century: a combination of reason and sentiment in the service of humanity.

Condorcet has established a distinction, which is not absolute but which has some validity, between its private and public manifestations, the former being characteristic of Voltaire's earlier career and the latter of his years at Ferney (M. I, 237). Voltaire's interest in the broader concept of 'humanity' did not, of course, date from 1760. He was a *philosophe* and an active campaigner from the outset. By 1759, he was already being hailed by Villaret as a model of humane behaviour.[78] But it was undoubtedly his reputation as the genial patriarch, benefactor, and protector of the inhabitants of Ferney,[79] and above all his unprecedented one-man crusade on behalf of the victims of injustice—Byng, La Barre, d'Etallonde, Calas, Sirven, Monbailly, Lally-Tolendal, the comte de Morangiés—which linked his name inseparably with public *bienfaisance*[80] and provoked a great wave of humanitarian sensibility during the last decades of the century.

77. To Mlle Bessières, 15 October [1726], Best. D302.
78. C. Villaret, *L'Esprit de M. de Voltaire* (Paris, 1759), p. 4.
79. For details, see F. Caussy, *Voltaire seigneur de village* (Paris, 1912). Voltaire said that his purpose in buying Ferney was to 'do a little good' (Best. 7234). In a book bathed in sensibility and recommending a return to nature, Lezay-Marnésia praises Voltaire's 'bienfaisance champêtre' and cites him as a perfect example of the *seigneur* who spreads prosperity and happiness in the country (*Le Bonheur dans les campagnes* [Neufchâtel, 1785], p. 58).
80. The marquis de Langallerie thought that the abbé de Saint-Pierre might well have invented the term for Voltaire's benefit (Best. 13931).

Why, at the very moment when he was most painfully aware of the inevitability of human suffering, when he appeared to be counselling resignation and a 'mind-your-own-business' attitude in *Candide*, did Voltaire become involved, against the advice of his friends, in a series of apparently hopeless compaigns to right judicial wrongs? Already the most famous writer in Europe, he had no need of further publicity. He can hardly have been motivated by the hope of increasing his political influence; such risky manœuvres were likely to get him into still more trouble at Versailles, where he was definitely a *persona non grata*. Nor was it simply a question of pressing the attack against the *Infâme*; religion had nothing to do with the Byng, Lally-Tolendal, and other cases. The answer can only be that Voltaire was naturally *bienfaisant*. Cideville, like Vauvenargues and many other contemporaries, was right in relating the *grandeur d'âme* of Voltaire's tragic heroes to the example of the Calas case: 'C'est donc de cette sensibilité précieuse que découle dans vostre belle âme ces grands sentimens, ces pensées fortes, ces situations déchirantes et ce charme inexprimable qui anime tous vos drames et les moindres actions de vostre vie, c'est parceque vous estes humain, c'est parceque vous savés aimer que vous estes l'autheur le plus touchant, l'ami le plus désirable et le plus aimé.'[81]

The 'Don Quixote of the Alps', as he nicknamed himself, was never happier than when marshalling his forces against the odds to fight for a principle exemplified in a concrete case.[82] His sensitivity to human suffering actually increased with age, along with his determination to eliminate some of the causes. The more outwardly pessimistic he became, the more urgently he felt the need for exemplary action. His faith in *bienfaisance*, which implies a fundamental optimism concerning human nature, was the one indestructible factor in the midst of increasing uncertainty and disillusionment.

81. 29 December 1762, Best. 10050.
82. 'J'aime passionnément à dire des vérités que d'autres n'osent pas dire, et à remplir des devoirs que d'autres n'osent pas remplir' (Best. 16186).

In spite of his habit of turning anything, however sacred or tragic, into a joke when he felt the need to relieve tension, there is no mistaking Voltaire's passionate concern. During Mme Suard's visit to Ferney, she noticed an engraving of the Calas family placed beside his bed as a constant reminder. When she reproached him, he replied, 'Ah! Madame, pendant onze ans j'ai été sans cesse occupé de cette malheureuse famille et de celle des Sirvens; et pendant tout ce temps, Madame, je me suis reproché comme un crime le moindre sourire qui m'est échappé.'[83]

As Flaubert insisted, Voltaire had in his nature something akin to fanatical idealism. How else can one explain the results he achieved? For a period of some twenty years he constituted himself the 'conscience of Europe', and the European conscience has never been the same since. He convincingly demonstrated the power of what has come to be known as 'public opinion'. For many despairing unfortunates Ferney represented a last hope and became, among other things, 'a sort of clearinghouse for Protestant affairs'.[84]

During the last two decades of his life, Voltaire was viewed more and more as the model of a man of feeling and public benefactor. The *Mercure* publicized this image of him, faithfully reporting his good actions over a period of more than thirty years.[85] Even the *Correspondance secrète* paid homage to his influence on French sensibility.[86] He was

83. *Lettres de Mme de Graffigny*, p. 395.

84. Ira O. Wade, *The Search for a New Voltaire; Studies Based upon Material Deposited at the American Philosophical Society* (Philadelphia, 1958), p. 21: 'When one of them is sent to the galleys for preaching or listening to a sermon in a Protestant gathering, Voltaire busies himself in securing the victim's release. When the legitimacy of a Protestant marriage is questioned, Voltaire occupies himself in having the marriage validated. In all cases, where an injustice has been committed through some act of intolerance, Voltaire stands ready to seek a rectification of the injustice.'

85. Madeleine Fields, 'Voltaire et le *Mercure de France*', *SV*, XX, 189.

86. Vol. XVI (3 March 1784), 26–27:

Tout homme au cœur dur, inflexible,
Devant Dieu, voilà le païen.
Mais quiconque a l'ame sensible
Fut-il né Turc, est bon Chrétien.
Jadis, en prêchant chez Valere
Je tenois à des préjugés,
Depuis nous avons lu Voltaire,
Voltaire nous a bien changés. . . .

constantly referred to as 'protecteur de l'humanité',[87] 'réparateur des torts de l'humanité',[88] 'le grand ami du genre humain',[89] 'le philosophe sensible'.[90] 'Jamais', wrote Damilaville after the successful conclusion of the Calas case, 'la philosophie ne m'a paru si belle qu'en la voyant baignée de larmes, arracher par vos mains les innocentes victimes, aux fureurs de l'exécrable fanatisme. Je l'ai cru voir elle même tracer les traits sublimes et touchants dont vous la peignez. Oui, tel est le philosophe, et vous en êtes le modèle' (Best. 11599). Diderot's reaction was equally enthusiastic. 'Oh! mon amie,' he exclaimed to Sophie Volland, 'le bel emploi du génie! Il faut que cet homme ait de l'âme, de la sensibilité, que l'injustice le révolte, et qu'il sente l'attrait de la vertu. . . . Quand il y auroit un Christ, je vous assure que De Voltaire seroit sauvé.'[91]

Readers of *La Bienfaisance française* were informed that 'Toute l'Europe a retenti de cette affaire; les larmes ont coulé de toutes parts, tous les cœurs se sont émus, et j'ai vu les François vaincre par leur sensibilité toutes les autres Nations de l'Europe.'[92] A Protestant minister confessed to Voltaire that he was the true inspiration of his own love for mankind and virtue: 'Je sais que la Philosophie bienfaisante, cette amie de l'humanité, doit ses progrès autant à vos touchans exemples qu'à vos élégantes leçons; je vous avouêrai même que je n'aime les hommes, que le goût du bien ne s'est profondément enraciné dans mon cœur que depuis la lecture de vos immortels ouvrages.'[93]

This wave of humanitarian sensibility reached its peak during Voltaire's triumphant return to Paris in 1778, when the man who had been a virtual exile for most of his life, who was accused in some quarters of unpatriotic behaviour, whose very presence was an affront to all 'right-thinking'

---

87. J. A. Comparet, *La Vérité, ode à M. de Voltaire* (London, 1765), p. 16.

88. Hennin, Best. 14277.

89. Pomaret, Best. 13665.

90. D'Alembert, on the occasion of the reception of Ducis at the Académie Française, 4 March 1779.

91. 8 August 1762, *Correspondance*, ed. G. Roth (Paris, 1955–), IV, 97.

92. Dagues de Clairfontaine, *La Bienfaisance française*, II, 364–365.

93. Pierre Lombard, 7 February 1774, Best. 17701.

people, was hailed as a public hero and a living legend, in defiance of the wishes of the court. Everywhere he went, to the Comédie Française for a memorable performance of *Irène*,[94] to the Académie, where he gave his blessing to Franklin's grandson,[95] tears were shed in abundance. Crowds followed him shouting 'Vive l'auteur de *Zaïre* et *Alzire!*' and 'Gloire au défenseur des Calas, gloire au sauveur des Sirven et des Montbailli!' It was obviously no mocking sceptic who was being venerated. We may take Condorcet's word for it: 'Jamais homme n'a reçu des marques plus touchantes de l'admiration, de la tendresse publique; jamais le génie n'a été honoré par un hommage plus flatteur. Ce n'était point à sa puissance, c'était au bien qu'il avait fait, que s'adressait cet hommage. Un grand poëte n'aurait eu que des applaudissements; les larmes coulaient sur le philosophe qui avait brisé les fers de la raison et vengé la cause de l'humanité' (M. I, 275).

Another outburst of sensibility followed Voltaire's death. Paris was inundated with poems, plays and *éloges* celebrating his goodness of heart, his concern for public welfare, and the emotive power of his poetry. Their tone can best be illustrated by a few extracts:

Jouissez, il jouit; sa vieillesse attendrie
Renaît pour respirer l'encens de la Patrie.
Vos cris ont retenti dans son cœur consolé;
Vous avez vu ses pleurs, et vos pleurs ont coulé.[96]

O Fernex! ô retraite aux malheureux si chere!
De ce peuple orphelin qui plaindra la misere?[97]

94. 'Dans l'excès de la joie dont tous les cœurs étaient pleins, des hommes raisonnables versaient des larmes d'attendrissement, tandis que des Dames debout dans leurs loges, & dans les transports de l'ivresse commune, levaient les mains vers lui, comme vers un être qu'on vénere & qu'on invoque' (Duvernet, *Vie*, pp. 332–333). Voltaire himself was in tears and was unable to reply.

95. Voltaire says that 'Tous les assistans versèrent des larmes d'attendrissement' (Best. 19912). According to Bernard Fäy, 'nul ne se méprit sur le sens de la cérémonie. La philosophie, trop longtemps esclave du raisonnement abstrait, pénétrait les cœurs et apportait enfin des spectacles et des enseignements sensibles' (*L'Esprit révolutionnaire en France et aux Etats-Unis à la fin du XVIIIᵉ siècle* [Paris, 1925], pp. 72–73).

96. La Harpe, *Aux mânes de Voltaire* (Paris, 1779), p. 4.

97. Gui de Chabanon, *Vers sur Voltaire* (s.l., 1778), p. 6.

O sainte humanité, trop long-temps ignorée,
Première des vertus, qu'étouffaient nos erreurs,
C'est VOLTAIRE surtout, dans l'Europe éclairée,
Qui t'ouvrit tous les cœurs.[98]

Que vois-je! une contrée entiere
Donne ses pleurs à sa poussiere
Et redemande un bienfaiteur.[99]

La haine s'amollit au cri du sentiment,
L'esprit est désarmé lorsque le cœur soupire,
Le cœur préfère à tout les malheurs de Zaïre.[100]

De la cendre des Grecs cet Art ressuscité
Ce grand art d'émouvoir, tu l'aurois inventé![101]

L'amour du bien public sous la plume respire;
De son vaste génie on voit la profondeur,
Et nous applaudissons la bonté de son cœur.
De deux moteurs puissants la force irrésistible
Animait tour-à-tour cette âme si sensible;
L'impérieux désir de l'immortalité,
Et pour les malheureux l'ardente activité.[102]

Horace avoit-il vu, sur ses pas élancés,
Des Habitants nombreux autour de lui pressés,
Des talents, des vertus admirer l'assemblage,
Et par des cris touchans exprimer leur hommage?
'C'est VOLTAIRE lui-même: oui, nos regards charmés
'Contemplent le vengeur des Calas opprimés.
'Ah! que la bienfaisance honore le Génie!'[103]

The Revolution saw yet another sentimental apotheosis.
By decree of the National Assembly, Voltaire's remains were
transferred to the Panthéon with lavish pomp and ceremony
on 11 July 1791. The sarcophagus, surrounded by students

98. Ode by the editor of Longchamp et Wagnière, *Mémoires*, II, 402.
99. P.L.A. Veau de Launay, *Voltaire, Ode et autres poésies* (London, 1780), p. 8.
100. A. P. Shuvalov, *Lettre à Voltaire* (Amsterdam, 1779), p. 9.
101. R. F. C. Doigny Du Ponceau, *Aux mânes de Voltaire, par un citoyen de l'univers* (Amsterdam, 1779), p. 7.
102. P. J. B. Nougaret, *Eloge de Voltaire* (Paris, 1779), p. 11.
103. C. E. C. de Pastoret, *Eloges de Voltaire* (Amsterdam, 1779), p. 11.

from the Beaux-Arts dressed in costumes of antiquity, was adorned with the inscription, 'Il vengea Calas, La Barre, Sirven et Montbailly.—Poète, philosophe, historien, il a fait prendre un grand essor à l'esprit humain, et nous a préparés à devenir libres.'[104] Members of the Calas family were there, as was Mme de Villette who, 'les yeux baignés des pleurs délicieuses du sentiment, le visage animé par les douces émotions de la piété filiale', placed a wreath on Voltaire's statue to delirious applause from the crowd.[105]

It was fitting that Voltaire should have been honoured in this way. His influence on the Revolution, especially during the early years when it was still possible to express genuine enthusiasm, was considerable: the National Assembly was Voltairean in outlook; his Roman tragedies and his sentimental melodramas enjoyed great popularity; and orators of the period often sounded like characters from *Brutus* or *La Mort de César*. The general atmosphere of deistic sensibility and of veneration for *humanité*, *vertu*, and *bienfaisance* must surely be attributable at least as much to Voltaire as to Rousseau.[106]

The titles of plays about Voltaire performed in the years 1790 and 1791—two tragedies entitled *Jean Calas*,[107] *Calas ou le fanatisme*,[108] *La Veuve Calas à Paris*,[109] *La Bienfaisance de Voltaire*[110]—indicate clearly enough the image projected

104. For a description of the ceremony, see Julien Tiersot, *Les Fêtes et les chants de la Révolution française* (Paris, 1908), pp. 54–60.

105. From the account in the *Chronique de Paris*, 12 July 1791, quoted by Jean Stern, *Belle et Bonne, une fervente amie de Voltaire (1757–1822)* (Paris, 1938), p. 147.

106. Almost every speech and pamphlet of the early revolutionary period contained expressions such as 'âmes sensibles et vertueuses', 'âmes sensibles et généreuses', 'âmes courageuses et sensibles'. When the first death sentence was passed, the judges, jury, and most of the spectators burst into tears. See C. A. Fusil, *La Contagion sacrée ou Jean-Jacques Rousseau de 1778 à 1820* (Paris, 1932).

107. J. L. Laya, *Jean Calas* (Paris, 1791), performed at the Théâtre de la Nation, 18 December 1790; M. J. B. Chénier, *Jean Calas* (Paris, 1793), performed at the Théâtre de la République, 6 July 1791.

108. A. J. Lemierre d'Argy, *Calas, ou le Fanatisme* (Paris, 1791), performed at the Palais-Royal, 17 December 1790.

109. M. J. B. Pujoulx, *La Veuve Calas à Paris ou le Triomphe de Voltaire* (Paris, 1791), performed at the Théâtre Italien, 31 July 1791.

110. Willemain d'Abancourt, *La Bienfaisance de Voltaire* (Paris, 1791), performed at the Théâtre de la Nation, 30 May 1791.

during the Revolution. In all of them, Voltaire is a god-like benefactor, 'une âme sensible et vertueuse', a friend of youth and an implacable enemy of injustice.

Willemain d'Abancourt's play, *La Bienfaisance de Voltaire*, performed in 1791 with great success, according to the author, has Voltaire ('Ame noble et sensible!') speaking such lines as the following:

> J'ai de la gloire aussi connu la jouissance;
> Mais la gloire n'est rien près de la bienfaisance.
> Ah! s'il le connaissait ce besoin d'un bon cœur,
> Que le riche aisément trouverait le bonheur!
> Il lui coûterait moins que ces plaisirs futiles,
> Qu'il paye au poids de l'or dans le sein de nos villes.[111]

> Le Ciel fit la vertu, l'homme en fit l'apparence;
> Il peut la revêtir d'imposture et d'erreur;
> Mais ne peut la changer: son juge est dans son cœur.[112]

In the course of an incredibly naïve dénouement, Voltaire accurately foresees the Revolution and the triumphal transfer of his remains to Paris. His last words are:

> J'ai fait un peu de bien, c'est mon meilleur ouvrage,
> Ouvrage fortuné, qui vivra d'âge en âge,
> Le seul qui maintenant puisse flatter mon cœur!—
> L'être bienfaisant seul a des droits au bonheur.[113]

This play was imitated two months later by Pujoulx in *La Veuve Calas à Paris*, the intention of which was to 'exciter dans les cœurs sensibles le désir de défendre les opprimés'. The first scene takes place in a room with a bust of Voltaire bearing the inscription, 'Au plus grand Génie, au cœur le plus sensible.'[114] In the final scene, Voltaire ponders it: 'Lisons: "au plus grand génie"(*avec indifférence*); oh! . . . "Au cœur le plus sensible". (*Avec sensibilité*); oh! oui!'—and surreptitiously makes off with the inscription.[115]

111. *Bienfaisance*, p. 27.
112. *Bienfaisance*, p. 31.
113. *Bienfaisance*, p. 46.
114. *Veuve Calas*, p. 3.
115. *Veuve Calas*, p. 11.

Voltaire cannot, of course, be held responsible for this kind of absurd exaggeration. The caricature is as gross as in the opposing stereotype; both omit an essential part of his character. The contradictions have often been pointed out by his biographers.[116] Even his appearance expressed ambivalence: Mme de Genlis was struck by the contrast between the tenderness of his eyes and the malicious smile.[117] It is difficult to reconcile the two extremes: on the one hand, the patient, generous, kindly patriarch, apostle of tolerance and model of *bienfaisance*, and on the other the irreverent wit, constantly embroiled in scandal and pursuing interminable vendettas. The man most responsible for establishing the principle of freedom of conscience and speech spent a great deal of his energy trying to persuade the authorities to punish insignificant adversaries and to suppress their writings. While it is possible to find excuses— Voltaire was always unwilling to start a quarrel[118] and usually ready to go more than half way if there was any chance of a reconciliation—there is no doubt that these undignified public brawls disfigure the image of the benevolent *philosophe*.

Observers have also noted his susceptibility to sudden, disconcerting changes of mood—from tears to laughter, from rage to sentimental concern. Palissot considered that all these 'weaknesses' were due to extreme sensibility.[119] Is not this in fact the most likely explanation? Voltaire was

116. e.g. R. Naves, *Voltaire, l'homme et l'œuvre* (Paris, 1942), pp. 79–81.

117. *Mémoires* (Paris, 1928), I, 153–154. See also John Moore's description in *Lettres de Mme de Graffigny*, p. 442.

118. Desnoiresterres' assertion (*Voltaire*, III, 62) is confirmed by the evidence of the correspondence: 'Est-il écrivain qui ait été plus attaqué que Voltaire, qui ait été le but des calomnies, des noirceurs de toute espèce? Son tort incontestable, c'est de n'avoir pas assez méprisé ces méprisables machinations. . . . Encore est-il (et il est bon de le redire) qu'il ne fait que se défendre, et que c'est de l'ennemi que partent les premiers coups: Desfontaines, Saint-Hyacinthe, Fréron, La Beaumelle, Clément, auront pris l'initiative, et par conséquent, assumé les responsabilités de l'agression.'

119. 'Naturellement bon, humain, généreux, comme il est aisé de le prouver par une suite non interrompue de belles actions dont sa vie est semée, les contrariétés, les injustices, les persécutions, aigrirent quelquefois son caractere, au point de lui inspirer, du moins en apparence, des haines très-violentes' (*Eloge*, p. 29).

*sensible* in the full eighteenth-century sense of the term: passionate, impulsive, and changeable, as well as sentimental. His gaiety was his way of coping with misfortune and remaining sane in a mad world. He combined deep feelings and an almost pathological sympathy with suffering with an unparalleled verve, wit, and sense of the absurd. The great romantic historian, Michelet, understood this; he called Voltaire 'le rieur plein de larmes'.[120]

120. *Histoire de France*, XV, 388. 'La tendresse, l'esprit satirique, l'amour, la guerre ne sont point opposés. La bonté, la pitié, chez quelques-uns sont violentes, et pleines d'un esprit de combat. Elles rendent impitoyables pour toute chose cruelle, pour toute idée barbare, pour tout dogme inhumain. Ces deux dispositions nullement contraires se rencontrent chez tous les grands hommes de ce siècle, spécialement chez Montesquieu' (*Histoire de France*, XIV, 385).

# CHAPTER 2

# *Le Philosophe Sensible*

For all his caution in sifting evidence and his reliance on reason as an antidote to superstition and prejudice, Voltaire was neither a sceptic nor a rationalist. A man who believes in the existence of a benevolent deity, natural law, and divine justice can hardly be called a sceptic,[1] and Voltaire was highly critical of abstract, all-inclusive systems of thought, whether derived from theology or from the a priori reasoning of philosophers. The well-known comparison in the *Lettres philosophiques* between 'notre Descartes, né pour découvrir les erreurs de l'antiquité, mais pour y substituer les siennes, et entraîné par cet esprit systématique qui aveugle les plus grands hommes' and Locke, who, 'ayant bien établi que toutes nos idées nous viennent par les sens . . . considère enfin l'étendue, ou plutôt le néant des connaissances humaines',[2] set a pattern followed by most enlightenment thinkers.

Locke's influence on the direction of Voltaire's philosophy and hence on that of eighteenth-century France is well established. While Voltaire's views diverged in several important respects from those of the English philosopher, he remained a convinced sensationalist. He never ceased proclaiming 'cette vérité que toutes les idées nous viennent par les sens' (Best. 10618). The clearest statement is in the chapter of the *Traité de métaphysique* entitled 'Que toutes les idées viennent par les sens'. As in the *Lettres philosophiques*, he concludes that the superiority of the empirical method is fully demonstrated. A priori reasoning, he says,

1. 'Le scepticisme détruit tout et se détruit lui-même, comme Samson accablé sous les ruines du temple' (*Sottisier*, p. 59).
2. *Lettres philosophiques*, M. XXII, 122–123.

55

is even more dangerous than scholasticism, because a clear thinker can easily recognize scholastic jargon as nonsense, whereas an ingenious hypothesis, logically developed, appeals strongly to our pride in the power of the human intellect.[3] Sensationalist principles are developed in several articles of the *Dictionnaire philosophique*, particularly that on 'Sensation', in which Locke's French disciple, Condillac, is referred to as 'un grand philosophe'.

If sensationalism, as some commentators believe, is the key to the intellectual and cultural revolution of the eighteenth century since it insists on critical examination of the facts of experience as opposed to speculation, metaphysics, or appeal to authority and at the same time implies a rehabilitation of the passions, instincts, and feelings, then the importance of Voltaire's role as the most effective early popularizer of Locke's ideas in France can scarcely be overrated. He was delighted to find in Locke a 'modest' philosopher honest enough to admit ignorance where there is an insufficiency of factual evidence. He saw the empirical method as a way of separating truth from hypothesis and as a convenient weapon with which to belabour the pretensions of those who claim certainty where there is in fact doubt.[4]

But he was also conscious of the other implications of sensationalism. Like Diderot, Rousseau, and the vast majority of eighteenth-century thinkers, he considered feeling, not thought, to be primary. In the article 'Vie' of the *Dictionnaire philosophique*, he argues that sensation is absolutely necessary to existence, whereas thought is not. Feeling is just as miraculous a demonstration of God's power as thought[5] and invariably precedes it.[6] Moreover, 'la matière a pensé à proportion de la finesse de ses sens, . . .

3. *Traité de métaphysique*, M. XXII, 202–203.
4. 'Il est clair qu'il ne faut jamais faire d'hypothèse; il ne faut point dire: Commençons par inventer des principes avec lesquels nous tâcherons de tout expliquer. Mais il faut dire: Faisons exactement l'analyse des choses, et ensuite nous tâcherons de voir avec beaucoup de défiance si elles se rapportent avec quelques principes' (M. XXII, 203).
5. 'Nous sommes étonnées de la pensée; mais le sentiment est tout aussi merveilleux. Un pouvoir divin éclate dans la sensation du dernier des insectes comme dans le cerveau de Newton' (M. XX, 419).
6. *Dictionnaire philosophique*, M. XX, 420. See also M. XXII, 203.

ce sont eux qui sont les portes et la mesure de nos idées.'[7] It follows that sensibility is as important for the thinker and for the ordinary man as for the artist and should be cultivated if one is to savour the fullness and variety of life: 'Il faut donner à son âme toutes les formes possibles. C'est un feu que dieu nous a confié, nous devons le nourir de ce que nous trouvons de plus précieux. Il faut faire entrer dans notre être, tous les modes imaginables, ouvrir toutes les portes de son âme à toutes les sciences et à tous les sentiments. Pourvu que tout cela n'entre pas pêle mêle, il y a place pour tout le monde' (Best. D1285).

Reason, for Voltaire, was an admirable and essential instrument, but one which was not without its dangers. When perverted, it can turn men into ferocious animals (M. VI, 503); yet when properly used it is the only effective means of turning such animals back into men. History shows that the multitude can be induced to accept the most preposterous absurdities as truth and be led into acts of violence by misguided prophets or clever scoundrels. 'Enthusiasm' which hardens into a system normally gives rise to fanaticism. Voltaire saw this as the most pernicious of all human failings and the source of many of the evils which have beset society. Hence the recurring Voltairean myth of the origin and development of fanatical sects. An unscrupulous individual takes advantage of the superstitious gullibility of the masses in order to seize power: 'Le fanatisme commence; la fourberie achève. Un homme puissant vient; il voit une foule qui s'est mis une selle sur le dos et un mors à la bouche; il monte sur elle et la conduit.'[8] He stays in power by repressing criticism and freedom of thought. This is the real message of Voltaire's most powerful pièce à thèse, Mahomet; it is reiterated with a number of variations throughout his works.[9]

Reason, rightly understood, is therefore of capital import-

7. *Mélanges*, Pléiade, p. 46.
8. *Catéchisme de l'honnête homme*, M. XXIV, 537.
9. However absurd as an explanation of the origin of great religions, Voltaire's theory is not as naïve as it may appear. If fanaticism is taken to include the uncritical promotion of ideologies—and Voltaire was concerned with political as well as religious intolerance (M. XXIV, 432)—it is more appropriate to the twentieth than to the eighteenth century.

ance in Voltaire's philosophy. Its all-important task is to destroy fanaticism at its roots: 'En un mot, moins de superstitions, moins de fanatisme; et moins de fanatisme, moins de malheurs' (M. XX, 456); and the only possible remedy for superstition is the prudent analysis of the facts in the light of critical reason. Yet he was as suspicious of reason and as aware of its shortcomings as any other *philosophe*. Excessive confidence in its powers is as hazardous as the other extreme. Since we are much more certain of the truth of our own thoughts and feelings than of the existence of external objects (Best. D637), it is just as easy to arrive at rigid, life-destroying systems by logical processes as through ignorance and imposture. Voltaire's best-known satire is not directed against the religious establishment but against the claims to omniscience of certain rationalist philosophers. He was opposed to philosophical optimism as an all-embracing system justifying God's purposes for the same reason that he was opposed to religious dogma: because it claimed to explain the inexplicable and reduced the mystery of existence to a few tenets which an appeal to experience immediately destroys. Moreover, philosophers, like theologians, have a distressing tendency to become so involved with ideas that the human dimension is omitted entirely. It is one thing to reason calmly about the nature of evil, quite another to *feel* the anguish of human beings: 'Leibnits et Shaftsburi, et Bollingbroke et Pope n'ont songé qu'à avoir de l'esprit. Pour moy, je soufre et je le dis' (Best. 6066).

In Voltaire's view, atheists and materialists were equally guilty of intellectual arrogance. The status of Lucretius as one of the saints of the Enlightenment and the chief enemy of superstition among the ancients did not exempt him from criticism on this score.[10] Nor was Voltaire particularly partial to the cruder form of reason known as 'common sense'. As he pointed out in his article on the subject in the *Dictionnaire philosophique*, it is almost as insulting to be called a man of common sense as to be said to be lacking in

10. In the *Dialogues entre Lucrèce et Posidonius* (M. XXIV, 69), Lucretius is advised to give up the 'dogmas' of Epicurus. Voltaire concludes: 'Tout ce que nous pouvons faire, c'est de sentir notre impuissance, de reconnaître un être tout-puissant, et de nous garder de ces systèmes.'

it, since the description implies that one is neither intelligent nor completely stupid. He preferred the original Latin term which includes both sense and sensibility: '*Sensus communis* signifiait chez les Romains, non-seulement sens commun, mais humanité, sensibilité. Comme nous ne valons pas les Romains, ce mot ne dit chez nous que la moitié de ce qu'il disait chez eux' (M. XX, 417).

Thus, while Voltaire considered reason, as the only effective weapon against fanaticism and its resultant evils, to be vital to human happiness and progress, he was fully aware of its severe limitations. True philosophy, he maintained, consists of recognizing these and knowing when to stop (M. XXII, 205). The most important questions will always remain unanswered, and compared with this vast unknown reason explains very little. Its inappropriate application to metaphysics is as potentially dangerous to society as its excessive intrusion into esthetic matters is detrimental to the development of great art.

Whatever the importance which should be accorded to reason, Voltaire was in no doubt that the real force governing human action and achievement has its source in the passions. These he defines as 'des désirs vifs et continus de quelque bien que ce puisse être', and goes on to argue, in accordance with Locke's theory of 'uneasiness', that they are always accompanied by a form of suffering. We suffer from the absence of whatever it is that is desired, and this impels us to act. Passions in themselves, he concludes, are neither good nor evil; they may lead to virtuous or vicious behaviour, depending on their object (M. IX, 410–411).

The best-known expression of Voltaire's theory of the passions occurs in *Zadig*. Using a well-worn image,[11] the hermit endowed with divine wisdom contradicts the traditional view that the passions should be condemned as the source of vice. On the contrary, he says, they are the driving force which makes life possible: 'Ce sont les vents qui enflent les voiles du vaisseau . . . elles le submergent quelquefois; mais sans elles il ne pourrait voguer. La bile rend colère

11. See Ira O. Wade, 'A Favourite Metaphor of Voltaire', *RR*, 26 (1935), 330–334.

et malade; mais sans la bile l'homme ne saurait vivre' (M. XXI, 88).

Voltaire had discussed the question at some length in the *Traité de métaphysique*. Taking up the ideas of Mandeville and Shaftesbury, but inclining towards the latter's optimism[12] he sees the passions as the essential foundation of society. Besides the nobler motive of altruism—always, for Voltaire, a feeling as well as a product of reason—pride, ambition, avarice, and envy provide the stimulus needed to develop the arts and techniques without which civilized society would be impossible. 'Ces passions', he concludes, 'dont l'abus fait à la vérité tant de mal, sont en effet la principale cause de l'ordre que nous voyons aujourd'hui sur la terre' (M. XXII, 222).

In the *Discours sur l'homme*, he attacks Stoicism and its modern equivalents—Jansenism, puritanism, and Christian asceticism—for engaging in an unnatural and futile attempt to suppress them.[13] As he had already said in his reply to Pascal, 'Qui veut détruire les passions au lieu de les régler veut faire l'ange', and 'qui veut faire l'ange fait la bête.'[14] The sensible course is to exploit their possibilities for good. The passions are gifts from God which, dangerous though they are, make possible 'great actions'.[15] Without them, men would be lazy and cowardly (Best. 11239) and, worse still, indifferent. 'Tout ce que je crains,' he wrote to Chauvelin, a minister of the government, 'c'est d'acquérir de l'indiférence avec l'âge—l'indiférence glace les talents. Qui voit les choses de sang froid, n'est bon que pour votre illustre métier.'[16] The pleasure afforded by the most sublime of all

12. Voltaire was probably influenced also by the views of Mme Du Châtelet who, like Shaftesbury, preferred to emphasize the role of natural benevolence. See Ira O. Wade, *Voltaire and Madame Du Châtelet, An Essay on the Intellectual Activity at Cirey* (Princeton, 1941), pp. 30–31.

13. M. IX, 412:
> Voilà votre portrait, stoïques abusés,
> Vous voulez changer l'homme, et vous le détruisez.

14. M. XXII, 53. (The second quotation is from Pascal, the first is Voltaire's comment). *Memnon* is the satirical portrait of man who fears the passions so much that he falls into the opposite excess.

15. *Discours en vers sur l'homme*, M. IX, 410. 'Les grandes passions donnent les forces' (Best. 13494).

16. 5 January [1763], Best. 10070. In the same letter, he writes, 'Je ne peins que des passions: / Il faut les sentir pour les peindre.'

the passions, love, is a proof of their divine origin and sufficient in itself to establish the existence of God (M. XXVIII, 314).

Voltaire never, of course, recommended that conduct should be exclusively governed by 'enthusiasm'; he was only too familiar with the consequences. Guidance is necessary if we are to avoid private and public disaster and reason urges moderation. But guidance and moderation do not imply repression. The man who lives according to reason alone—supposing such a person could exist—is far from being Voltaire's ideal. He advocated self-control provided that discipline does not result in coldness and indifference through the atrophy of feelings and normal instinctive responses. In a letter to Mme Du Deffand written when he had reached the venerable age of eighty, he asserted that he preferred the solitude of Ferney to the distractions of Paris because 'la retraitte rend les passions plus vives et plus profondes' (Best. 18153).

Voltaire was thus in theory as well as by temperament a 'man of feeling'. In common with many other writers of his age, he was seeking the perfect integration of the heart and the mind. Without going so far as to say with Hume that reason is and ought to be the slave of the passions, he recognized the primacy of feeling and sensation over thought and made a major contribution, before Diderot or Rousseau, to the rehabilitation of the passions as the mainspring of human achievement and the sine qua non of a viable society.[17]

In spite of these views and of the optimism evident in the early philosophical works—the Lettres philosophiques, the Traité de métaphysique, the Discours sur l'homme—Voltaire could hardly be accused of blind faith in man's natural goodness. It would not be difficult to assemble an impressive number of quotations with a marked Pascalian flavour. Thanks to the popularity of Candide, Voltaireanism is commonly associated with a somewhat jaundiced view of human nature and the human condition. His pessimistic

17. See R. Mercier's assessment of the importance of Voltaire's contribution in La Réhabilitation de la nature humaine, p. 254.

statement that history is a long record of crimes and follies is often cited, as are his repeated affirmations that a belief in the deity, whether justified or not, is necessary in order to restrain man's baser impulses. 'Tout le monde n'est pas philosophe. Nous avons affaire à force fripons qui ont peu réfléchi; à une foule de petites gens, brutaux, ivrognes, voleurs. Prêchez-leur, si vous voulez, qu'il n'y a point d'enfer, et que l'âme est mortelle. Pour moi, je leur crierai dans les oreilles qu'ils seront damnés s'ils me volent' (M. XVIII, 547).

It is, moreover, a well-known axiom of romantic philosophy that the exceptional individual who has been granted that 'fatal présent du ciel', an excess of sensibility, is inclined to melancholy and periods of black despair. Voltaire was aware of this[18] and was himself, to some extent, a case in point. He was physically affected by the thought of the Saint Bartholomew's Day massacre and by similar crimes and catastrophes, such as the execution of La Barre or the Lisbon earthquake. War, in particular, always brought out his pessimism, as in the article on the subject in the *Dictionnaire philosophique*, which is a cry of rage and despair rather than a reasoned analysis. Even during the period of *Le Mondain*, passages such as the following occur in the correspondence: 'On ne croit point la paix faite; je n'en sais rien: tout ce que je sais c'est que nous sommes des moutons, à qui jamais le boucher ne dit quand il les tuera.'[19]

This is not, however, Voltaire's last word. As usual when there was a strong element of uncertainty, his views varied, or seemed to vary, depending on his mood or the particular question at issue at a given moment. He considered the concept of an avenging deity useful to society and 'in any case harmless'. To make the point effectively, he found it convenient to blacken human nature. But in the same work, the *Dictionnaire philosophique*, he presents a very different picture: 'L'homme n'est point né méchant; il le devient, comme il devient malade. . . . Vous avez donc tout au plus sur la terre, dans les temps les plus orageux, un homme sur

18. 'Le plus modéré, le moins inquiet, et en même temps le plus sensible, est le plus heureux; mais malheureusement le plus sensible est presque toujours le moins modéré' (M. XIX, 345).
19. Best. D1187. See also Best. D1558.

mille qu'on peut appeler méchant; encore ne l'est-il pas toujours. Il y a donc infiniment moins de mal sur la terre qu'on ne croit. Il y en a encore trop, sans doute: on voit des malheurs et des crimes horribles; mais le plaisir de se plaindre et d'exagérer est si grand qu'à la moindre égratignure vous criez que la terre regorge de sang' (M. XX, 54–56).

The catastrophes which befall the characters of *Candide*, as has frequently been pointed out, do not imply that Voltaire shared Martin's pessimism. The exaggeration of misfortune to the point where constantly repeated accumulations of misery become comic rather than tragic is a literary device ideally suited to the achievement of Voltaire's polemical and artistic aims. Besides man's natural propensity to knavery and foolishness, the novel also demonstrates some of his more admirable qualities and ends, not in despair, but in the attainment of a middling kind of happiness. In any case, *Candide* is far from being the sum of Voltairean wisdom. The doctrine of resignation preached by its hero is the opposite of that practised by his creator, the 'Don Quichotte des malheureux'. The literary productions which Voltaire took more seriously, notably the plays and his epic poem, are ample evidence that he leaned more frequently to idealizing optimism: 'Epopée, chevalerie, sensibilité, vertu, autant de manifestations optimistes et d'actes de foi dans l'homme.'[20]

When all allowances have been made for variations of mood and circumstances, Voltaire's conception of human nature is reasonably clear and consistent. Like Rousseau, he rejects the Christian attitude based on original sin.[21] This is, indeed, the major point at issue in the *Remarques*

20. Naves, *Voltaire l'homme et l'œuvre*, p. 117.
21. Voltaire's marginal comments on Rousseau's *Lettre à M. de Beaumont* show how close they were on the question of man's natural goodness, as Professor Havens has noted: 'Certainly there are important divergences between the two men, but it is striking how near together they are on the theory which is most closely associated with Rousseau and in connection with which he is too often made to stand in a unique position' (*Voltaire's Marginalia on the Pages of Rousseau* [New York, 1966], p. 147). Rousseau, for his part, is quoted as saying of the *Dictionnaire philosophique*, 'Plût à Dieu que la morale de ce livre fût dans tous les cœurs et dans celui de l'auteur' (J. M. Quérard, *Bibliographie voltairienne* [Paris, 1842], p. xxvii).

*sur Pascal.* Whereas Pascal 's'acharne à nous peindre tous méchants et malheureux', Voltaire 'ose prendre le parti de l'humanité contre ce misanthrope sublime.'[22] Neither angel nor brute, man occupies his rightful place in the universe and is endowed with faculties which enable him to attain a measure of happiness.

The point of view expressed much later in the *Dictionnaire philosophique* is not dissimilar. Without stating definitely that man is by nature good, Voltaire protests vigorously against the notion that he is basically evil. 'Ne paraît-il pas démontré que l'homme n'est point né pervers et enfant du diable?' Why then does he behave so badly? 'N'est-ce pas que, n'étant né ni bon ni méchant, l'éducation, l'exemple, le gouvernement dans lequel il se trouve jeté, l'occasion enfin, le déterminent à la vertu ou au crime?'[23] Human nature is fixed and immutable; circumstances and education determine whether we incline to good or evil. Voltaire's optimism lies in the belief that at least a partial and precarious progress can be achieved by changing the social environment and above all by releasing the natural forces for good. Man will be happy insofar as he is free to satisfy his aspirations without interfering with those of others. On this point, he can learn something from the animals: 'Il est certain que si les animaux raisonnaient avec les hommes ils auraient toujours raison, car ils suivent la nature, et nous l'avons corrompue' (Best. 13114).

Man possesses, however, one great advantage over all other animals: 'Non-seulement il a cet amour-propre nécessaire pour sa conservation, mais il a aussi, pour son espèce, une bienveillance naturelle qui ne se remarque point dans les bêtes' (M. XXII, 222). The same idea is expressed in the *Eléments de la philosophie de Newton* and elsewhere. This compassionate feeling for others is as common as any of the other instincts (M. XXII, 421); it is variously

22. M. XXII, 28. See also Best. D877.
23. Art. 'Homme', M. XIX, 381. This is exactly Diderot's view: 'Non, chère amie, la nature ne nous a pas faits méchants; c'est la mauvaise éducation, le mauvais exemple, la mauvaise législation qui nous corrompent' (*Correspondance*, III, 226).

referred to as *humanité, vertu, bienveillance,* or *bienfaisance*; and it includes all the chief Voltairean virtues: love, tolerance, magnanimity, humanitarian concern. It inspires courage to express unpopular truths and defend oppressed innocence. Voltaire spoke of it as the guiding principle of all his thoughts.[24] Although he could not go so far as to agree with the more naïve followers of Shaftesbury that *bienfaisance* necessarily brings happiness,[25] he saw it as the ultimate criterion for judging a man's value to the society in which he lives. What he admired most in his heroes was their *moral* greatness.[26] The seventh *Discours sur l'homme* is a veritable hymn to *bienfaisance* which includes a warm tribute to the idealism of the inventor of the word, the abbé de Saint-Pierre.[27]

In his earliest writings, Voltaire tended to emphasize the role of pleasure. This is understandable in the context of his opposition to asceticism and puritanism. He was also briefly attracted by Mandeville's paradox that society is founded on passions which are normally considered to be vices, such as pride, ambition, and vanity.[28] The general direction of his ethics is, however, quite different. Despite occasional nostalgic references to pleasure as the supreme law, hedonism is rarely advocated in his mature work. He defines virtue as 'what is useful to society', because morality is meaningless except in terms of one's relationship with others: 'La vertu et le vice, le bien et le mal moral, est donc en tout pays ce qui est utile ou nuisible à la société.' But he immediately adds, 'et dans tous les lieux et dans tous les temps, celui qui sacrifie le plus au public est celui qu'on appellera le plus vertueux' (M. XXII, 225). When he lists

24. To Frederick, [15 October 1737], Best. D1376.
25. In the art. 'Bien (Souverain Bien)' of the *Dictionnaire philosophique,* he maintains that virtue and happiness belong to different categories: 'Un homme vertueux avec la pierre et la goutte, sans appui, sans amis, privé du nécessaire, persécuté, enchaîné par un tyran voluptueux qui se porte bien, est très-malheureux.' (M. XVII, 576). A similar theme runs through *Zadig.*
26. See R. Pomeau, 'Voltaire et le Héros', *Revue des Sciences Humaines,* 64 (October–December 1951), pp. 345–351.
27. See especially M. IX, 424.
28. This is particularly evident in the *Traité de métaphysique.* Even here, however, Voltaire places greater emphasis on altruism.

the virtues most useful to society, they turn out to be 'la fidélité, la magnanimité, la bienfaisance, la tolérance, etc.' (M. XVIII, 75). Not only is concern for others and, for the exceptional individual, self-sacrifice, essential for the common welfare, but in any case

Le premier des plaisirs et la plus belle gloire,
C'est de prodiguer les bienfaits. (M. VIII, 545)

Voltaire's considered opinion seems to have been that man is provided by nature with two instincts without which society cannot exist: self-preservation and benevolence. The former is necessarily much the stronger of the two; altruism needs to be reinforced by reason and example. Nevertheless, both are 'gifts from God' and common to all men, from the most primitive to the most civilized. 'Cette morale est si pure, si sainte, si universelle, si claire, si ancienne, qu'elle semble venir de Dieu même.... N'a-t-il pas donné aux hommes l'amour-propre, pour veiller à leur conservation; la bienveillance, la bienfaisance, la vertu, pour veiller sur l'amour-propre; les besoins mutuels, pour former la société; le plaisir, pour en jouir; la douleur, qui avertit de jouir avec modération; les passions, qui nous portent aux grandes choses, et la sagesse, qui met un frein à ces passions?'[29] Unfortunately, the ideal equilibrium is difficult to preserve and man's imperfect laws are therefore necessary to ensure social order.

There is no doubt, however, that Voltaire considered 'natural law'—the consciousness of right and wrong—to be primary, universal, and engraved on men's hearts by God. It is one of the basic principles of his philosophy and is frequently given literary expression in his poetry and plays.[30] He never tired of repeating that 'La morale est une, elle vient de Dieu; les dogmes sont différents, ils viennent de nous' (M. XIX, 549); that all great philosophers have taught essentially the same precepts; that customs differ but the concept of virtue is the same everywhere. Even

29. *Les Questions de Zapata* (M. XXVI, 188–189).
30. e.g. M. VIII, 172, 438; IX, 440, 444, 445; XI, 22, 156; XV, 430; XXII, 421; XXIV, 223. See also below, chaps. 6 and 7.

the most backward people will, in the long run, recognize which laws are best because of their innate sense of what is right and just.[31]

The clearest affirmation occurs in the *Poème sur la loi naturelle*. God is within us,[32] operating through conscience and remorse to ensure that egoism is to some extent offset by love for our neighbour:

Ainsi l'Etre éternel qui nous daigne animer
Jeta dans tous les cœurs une même semence.
Le ciel fit la vertu; l'homme en fit l'apparence.

(M. IX, 445)

To avoid directly contradicting Locke on the question of innate ideas, Voltaire argues that man is not born with a fully developed moral sense; it evolves gradually in much the same way as his ability to walk or to reason; but the seed is implanted by God (M. IX, 450). In practice, it is very difficult to make any very clear distinction between this idea of natural law or 'universal reason' and the faculty designated by other terms in popular use in the eighteenth century, such as 'right reason', 'moral sense', 'the voice of the conscience', 'the voice of the heart', or 'the voice of nature'. In all cases, a benevolent deity is guiding man along the path of virtue through an inner feeling and without resort to revelation.

Voltaire's moral philosophy is thus not as far removed as has generally been supposed from the 'nature doctrine'[33] which is one of the foundations of eighteenth-century sensibility. Man is, if not born good, at least not 'né pervers'; if he will only heed it, the voice of the heart will incline him to generosity and compassion. The greater one's capacity for feeling, the more virtuous one is likely to be: 'Malheur aux cœurs durs! Dieu bénira les âmes tendres. Il y a je ne sais quoi de réprouvé à être insensible; aussi s^te Thérèse

31. *La Philosophie de l'histoire*, ed. J. H. Brumfitt. *The Complete Works of Voltaire*, vol. 59, p. 114.

32. 'Si Dieu n'est pas dans nous, il n'exista jamais' (M. IX, 442).

33. See George R. Havens, 'The Nature Doctrine of Voltaire', *PMLA*, 40 (1925), p. 862: 'Nothing could be more Rousseauistic than this unexpected Voltairean opinion [on man's natural instinct for good].'

définissait elle le diable, le malheureux qui ne sait point aimer.'[34] Hence the true Voltairean hero—Henri IV, Cicero, Confucius, Socrates—is the man who combines sensibility with the ability to see things as they are.[35] This is also Voltaire's definition of a *philosophe*: not simply a clear-sighted and courageous critic of the status quo, but a man of feeling and a champion of humanity.[36]

In one respect, however, Voltaire differed from many of the eighteenth-century theorists of sensibility. He was too much of an activist to be satisfied with feelings of sympathy and compassion. It is not difficult to decide what is right since we are informed by both instinct and reason and all philosophies, all religions teach the same lesson. The difficult and essential thing is to act,[37] above all to set an example. While he did not go so far as to propose worship of the benefactors of mankind, Voltaire considered it a 'pardonable superstition' (M. XX, 454) and would have liked to see a system of public awards for virtuous actions instituted such as that which existed in China (M. XVIII, 158).

Voltaire's doctrine of *bienfaisance* is inseparable from his religion. 'La loi naturelle' and 'la religion naturelle' are, in fact, synonymous;[38] both assume the existence of a beneficent deity. Reduced to its essentials, natural religion consists of two items: the worship of God and the practice of virtue, in the Voltairean sense.[39] He admits that the first

34. To Frederick, 12 August [1739], Best. D2062.
35. cf. his disillusionment with Frederick: 'Vous avez été mon idole pendant vingt années de suitte. Je l'ay dit à la terre, au ciel, à Gusman même. Mais votre métier de héros et votre place de roy ne rendent pas le cœur bien sensible' (To Frederick, 19 May [1759], Best. 7586).
36. In the *Dictionnaire philosophique*, he defines a *philosophe* as a man who loves truth, by which he means primarily moral truth, since scientific truth is fallible and relative (art. 'Philosophe'). Truth, therefore, coincides with virtue and the *philosophe* should set an example: 'Il est bon que vous soyez philosophe, mais il est nécessaire que vous soyez juste' (art. 'Catéchisme chinois').
37. 'Rien n'est plus commun que gens qui conseillent, rien de plus rare que ceux qui secourent' (M. XIX, 505).
38. 'J'entends par religion naturelle les principes de morale communs au genre humain' (M. XXII, 419).
39. '. . . le vrai culte, la vraie piété, la vraie sagesse est d'adorer dieu comme le père commun de tous les hommes sans distinction, et d'être bienfaisant' (To Frederick, October 1769, Best. 14992).

is not in itself sufficient to constitute a religion, but 'celui qui pense que Dieu a daigné mettre un rapport entre lui et les hommes, qu'il les a faits libres, capables du bien et du mal, et qu'il leur a donné à tous ce bon sens qui est l'instinct de l'homme, et sur lequel est fondée la loi naturelle, celui-là sans doute a une religion' (M. XX, 506).

In spite of the consistency with which Voltaire repeated these fundamental principles throughout his life, his religion remains a matter of controversy. Even such a basic question as whether he really believed in the existence of God is still debated. That Voltaire was not a 'believer' in the traditional Christian sense is obvious. Yet it is inconceivable that a man who proclaimed over and over again, often with passionate conviction, his faith in a supreme being, who was obsessed with the problem of evil, who considered atheism personally repugnant and socially disastrous,[40] should have been himself an atheist. 'Les athées qui veulent me mettre de leur parti', he protested, 'me semblent aussi ridicules que ceux qui ont voulu faire passer s$^t$ Augustin pour un moliniste.'[41] Professor Pomeau's conclusion in his authoritative study is surely indisputable: 'Ce qui compte, c'est ce que Voltaire a répété toute sa vie; ce qui compte, ce sont ses entêtements, et ce sont ses obsessions. Or, d'un bout à l'autre de cette longue vie, Voltaire fut déiste ardemment, agressivement. Pendant quelque soixante années, il a cherché des justifications historiques et philosophiques. Un Fontenelle, un Anatole France furent peut-être des frivoles rationalistes en surface, et comme par distraction. Il n'a cessé, lui, de combattre *pour et contre*, pour la religion dite naturelle, et contre la chrétienne.'[42]

As the last sentence of this quotation indicates, there are two sides to Voltaire's religion, corresponding to what Leslie Stephen called 'constructive deism' and 'critical

40. Voltaire had a genuine horror of the consequences of the spread of atheism. See, for example, his description of fifteenth-century Italy in the *Essai sur les mœurs*, ed. R. Pomeau (Paris, 1963), II, 71–72.

41. To d'Argental, 4 August 1775, Best. 18467. See also *Lettre au docteur Pansophe* (M. XXVI, 19): 'Je ne suis athée ni dans mon cœur, ni dans mes livres.'

42. *Religion de Voltaire*, p. 455.

deism'.[43] Constructive deism is a positive belief in the existence of God and natural law. Critical deism arises from the realization that institutional Christianity as it then existed, particularly in the Roman Catholic Church, was a major obstacle to natural morality and intellectual progress and must therefore be weakened or destroyed. For obvious reasons, Voltaire's attacks on traditional beliefs and practices have received far more attention than his attempt to promote a universal religion. He was quickly 'outflanked on the left' by militant atheists and materialists and deism has had very little appeal since the eighteenth century. His criticisms of some of the foundations of Christianity, on the other hand, were highly effective; so much so that Voltaire still scandalizes the faithful and 'Voltairean' has become synonymous with anticlerical, or even antireligious.

It is not altogether surprising therefore that his real views have been somewhat obscured and that a man who thought of himself as a kind of religious leader—the Luther of the Enlightenment—[44] should be commonly regarded as a sceptic. Voltaire recognized that before his idea of a reasonable, humane, and universal religion had any chance of being established, someone would have to take on the Herculean task of clearing away the myths and hallowed traditions of centuries, firmly anchored by enormous vested interests. Having ascertained that the alliance between a liberal form of Christianity and Voltairean deism, of which he dreamed in earlier moments of optimism, was unlikely to become a reality, he calmly set out to crush the 'infamous' obstacle by a massive and unprecedented frontal attack on public opinion.

But even at the height of his campaign he was careful

43. Leslie Stephen, *History of English Thought in the Eighteenth Century* (London, 1881), I.

44. M. X, 404:
> J'ai fait plus en mon temps que Luther et Calvin.
> On les vit opposer, par une erreur fatale,
> Les abus aux abus, le scandale au scandale.
> Parmi les factions ardents à se jeter,
> Ils condamnaient le pape, et voulaient l'imiter.
> L'Europe par eux tous fut longtemps désolée;
> Ils ont troublé la terre, et je l'ai consolée.

to preserve a balance between his assault on the religious establishment and a more constructive approach. He never supposed that religion could be dispensed with altogether or that a society of atheists was desirable.[45] His utopias are far from being godless states. He argued that all religions are good insofar as they all contain a core of essential truth, and that in any case a bad religion is better than none at all.[46]

Since religion was Voltaire's favourite topic, it is not difficult to ascertain his views. They were established early and remained remarkably consistent, in spite of tactical changes of emphasis. The doctrine expounded in the *Traité de métaphysique* of 1734 is very close to that which emerges from the *Histoire de Jenni*, published in 1775. What matters, as Professor Pomeau rightly insists, is not the occasional discrepancy, but the frequency with which Voltaire returns to certain fundamental principles. Even before his exile in England, he was already a deist. His serious works of the period from 1711 to 1726—the *Odes*, *Œdipe*, *La Henriade*— show him to be a firm believer in God, ardently in favour of tolerance and highly critical of dogmatic Christianity. Reacting against the Jansenism of his immediate family and against Christian pessimism generally, he tended to emphasize divine benevolence and the legitimate pleasure to be derived from the satisfaction of the instincts. This early deism, reinforced by his acquaintance with English writers, especially Pope and Shaftesbury, was definitely, although cautiously, optimistic. In the *Traité de métaphysique*, he recognized the existence of evil as a 'difficulty' but did not see it as an insuperable objection.

By the time *Zadig* appeared, the problem had begun to assume the proportions of an obsession. Voltaire was too much of a realist and too suspicious of abstract 'explanations' of the universe to be convinced by metaphysical optimism as a thoroughgoing system. Moreover, he came to realize that

45. See, e.g., the *Traité sur la tolérance* (M. XXV, 100): 'Partout où il y a une société établie, une religion est nécessaire.' In the *Dictionnaire philosophique*, art. 'Religion', he describes in detail what the ideal state religion should be.

46. 'Il est indubitable que, dans une ville policée, il est infiniment plus utile d'avoir une religion, même mauvaise, que n'en avoir point du tout' (M. XVII, 474).

it was, in fact, not optimistic at all, but a philosophy of despair and resignation. The crisis which came to a head with the news of the Lisbon earthquake did not destroy his belief in Providence or the rightness of the natural instincts, but it forced him to shift his ground. Since nature is inscrutable and apparently 'cares little about the individual', even though we know that her ultimate purpose is benign, humanity and *bienfaisance* become all the more important. In *Candide*, God is still the 'master of the vessel', but Voltaire's devotion is to the mice swarming over it. The thread which runs through most of his pronouncements of this period is best expressed in the line from the *Poème sur le désastre de Lisbonne*: 'Je respecte mon dieu, mais j'aime l'univers'. This cannot be said to represent a profound change of view. Voltaire had never envisaged the deity as a personal God in the Christian sense. If anything, belief in a particular rather than a general Providence seems to have tempted him more in his later years.[47]

It was during this period also that he placed increasing stress on the social value of religion. According to Voltaire, even if all the indisputable evidence of God's existence were false, belief in divine justice would still be necessary. Without a super-policeman to detect and punish secret crimes, especially those of the great and powerful, 'everything is permitted' and the foundations of morality disintegrate, with consequences too terrible to contemplate. However much one may regret Voltaire's insistence on this rather crude theology, there is no denying that it was one of his major preoccupations.[48] It should be added, however, that he was clearly motivated by a genuine concern for social order, in spite of the personal terms in which he sometimes expressed the idea. Given the force of human passions and the precarious nature of civilization, he saw no harm in

47. e.g. M. XXI, 547.
48. A typical statement is the following from *L'Histoire de Jenni* (M. XXI, 573): 'Qui retiendra les grands et les rois dans leurs vengeances, dans leur ambition, à laquelle ils veulent tout immoler? Un roi athée est plus dangereux qu'un Ravaillac fanatique.' See also M. X, 199, 403; XI, 180; XVII, 462; XXV, 100; XXVI, 525; XXVII, 399–400; XXVIII, 133; XXIX, 282.

utilizing a metaphysical hypothesis for praiseworthy ends. If he was guilty of the false logic which he condemned in Pascal,[49] his attitude can be described as cynical only if he was indeed an unavowed atheist. But commenting on the famous dictum 'Si Dieu n'existait pas, il faudrait l'inventer', he was careful to point out that God is a necessary concept intellectually as well as morally: 'Ainsi Dieu est nécessaire au monde en tout sens' (M. XXIX, 10).

Voltaire's intellectual caution kept him from tying up the loose ends too neatly and ensured that there would be large areas of doubt, hesitation, and contradiction. His aim was not to replace one set of dogmas by another, but to present what he considered to be extremely probable inferences from the known facts and, by a process of discarding superstitious accretions, to arrive at the essential element of truth common to all religions and philosophies. When he ventures beyond the simple affirmations into the realm of metaphysics, he wavers. How does God punish the wicked and reward the virtuous? He hesitates between two possible answers, both unacceptable to reason: that justice is done here on earth—but in that case how does one explain 'qu'il est et qu'il sera toujours dans cette vie des vertus malheureuses et des crimes impunis'? (M. XVIII, 67); or that justice is meted out in an afterworld—but this involves a leap of faith which Voltaire's prudence was reluctant to accept and a belief in damnation which offended his sensibility. Can evil be explained as the contribution of the part to the whole? He accepts this solution in the *Traité de métaphysique* but rejects it in the *Poème sur le désastre de Lisbonne* and makes fun of it in *Candide*. Yet some version of this doctrine is unavoidable for the deist. If God is benevolent and omnipotent, evil must in some unknown way be part of the divine plan. We laugh with Voltaire at the philosophical optimists, but logic is on their side rather than his. He was no more successful than they in finding a way out of the dilemma. Yet, to judge by the renewed expression of his faith in the last period of his life, his deism does

49. 'L'intérêt que j'ai à croire une chose n'est pas une preuve de l'existence de cette chose' (M. XXII, 32).

73

not seem to have been shaken—surely proof that his religion was founded on a feeling so deep-rooted that it could withstand the cold blasts of reason.

The fact is that despite his lifelong fascination with it, Voltaire disliked and feared metaphysics. For intellectual, moral, and sentimental reasons, he needed a religion, but one which would contain the minimum of doubtful speculation. He was happiest therefore when he could reduce it to a simple formula, as in his definition of a 'théiste': 'Faire le bien, voilà son culte; être soumis à Dieu, voilà sa doctrine' (M. XX, 508). If God exists, he must be just and *bienfaisant*.[50] But to Voltaire, the existence of God was obvious; the evidence from design is overwhelming. The universe obeys mathematical laws; there must therefore be a mathematician. His justice is a different matter. This is a question of *feeling*, not of reason or revelation: 'Toute la nature vous a démontré l'existence du Dieu suprême: c'est à votre cœur à sentir l'existence du Dieu juste' (M. XXVI, 440). The only true religion is that which is common to all men, the religion of the heart: 'Je mourrai consolé en voyant la véritable religion, c'est à dire celle du cœur, établie sur la ruine des simagrées. Je n'ai jamais prêché que l'adoration d'un dieu, la bienfaisance et l'indulgence. Avec ces sentiments je brave le diable qui n'existe point, et les vrais diables fanatiques qui n'existent que trop.'[51] Hence Voltaire's approval of Rousseau's fervent and sentimental brand of deism, as expressed in the *Lettre à M. de Beaumont* and elsewhere.[52]

This simplified definition of 'true religion', with its direct appeal to sensibility, provides the key to Voltaire's

50. 'Il ne paraît pas qu'il y ait un milieu: ou il n'y a point de Dieu, ou Dieu est juste' (M. XXVI, 321).

51. To Jean Dufour, 20 December 1768, Best. 14412.

52. e.g. in the *Lettre à M. de Beaumont*: 'Enfin plus je m'efforce de contempler son essence infinie, moins je la conçois; mais elle est, cela me suffit; moins je la conçois, plus je l'adore. Je m'humilie & lui dis: "Etre des êtres, je suis parce que tu es; c'est m'élever à ma source que de te méditer sans cesse. Le plus digne usage de ma raison, est de s'anéantir devant toi: c'est mon ravissement d'esprit, c'est le charme de ma foiblesse de me sentir accablé de ta grandeur".' Voltaire's comment in the margin: 'très beau' (Havens, *Voltaire's Marginalia*, pp. 159–160). For Voltaire's favourable comments on the *Profession de foi d'un vicaire savoyard*, see, e.g., Best. 10491, 11149, 12278, 12476; M. XXVII, 118.

apparently contradictory attitude to Christianity. How does one reconcile his claim to be a Christian and his admiration for some aspects of Christianity with his avowed aim of destroying it? How could he be taken seriously by his contemporaries, and later by Chateaubriand, as the author of 'Christian tragedies'? The answer is clear: Voltaire distinguished between 'true Christianity', which he took to be the real message of Christ, and the 'infernal doctrine'[53] masquerading in its name. 'Je crois avec Jésus-Christ', proclaims the saintly hero of *L'Histoire de Jenni*, 'qu'il faut aimer Dieu et son prochain, pardonner les injures et réparer ses torts. Croyez-moi: adorez Dieu, soyez juste et bienfaisant; voilà tout l'homme. Ce sont là les maximes de Jésus.'[54]

Such a definition would hardly, of course, satisfy the majority of Christians, even in the late twentieth century. Voltaire undoubtedly felt that this rapprochement between Christianity and his own deistic principles was a good tactical move insofar as it would tend to establish his own respectability, divide the faithful, and enlist the support of some liberal Christians. There is no reason, however, to suppose that he was insincere. Alvarez and Lusignan were highly successful portraits of Christian patriarchs who were intended to be admired. As indeed they were: on the whole, eighteenth century spectators and critics agreed with Duvernet and La Harpe that the final act of *Alzire* was the 'triumph of Christian morality'.[55]

Voltaire's views on the related topics of primitivism, luxury, and civilization have also been subject to considerable

53. 'Je suis chrétien comme l'était Jésus, dont on a changé la doctrine céleste en doctrine infernale' (M. XXV, 131–132). See also M. XIX. 549; XXVI, 352; XXVII, 229.

54. *Histoire de Jenni*, M. XXI, 532.

55. Duvernet, *Vie de Voltaire*, p. 113; La Harpe, *Lycée*, IX, 361. Du Chasteau uses similar terms to describe the dénouement of *Alzire* in his *Epistre à monsieur de Voltaire sur la nouvelle tragédie d'Alzire* (Paris, 1736), pp. 6–7:

> Ce trait, Voltaire, attendrit tous les cœurs;
> Tu sçais changer en vrais adorateurs
> Les esprits forts d'un Parterre idolâtre,
> Accoutumés à des Dieux de Théâtre.
> Ah! quel plaisir d'entendre célébrer
> Le Maître seul que l'on doit adorer!

distortion; so much so, that he is commonly regarded as an outright antiprimitivist and the chief defender of worldly values against the proponents of the simple life and the virtues of the noble savage. Most of the major figures of the eighteenth century, including Voltaire, did not see these questions in such black-and-white terms. Voltaire certainly believed civilization to be preferable to barbarism and knowledge to ignorance. He was completely opposed to the thesis that the arts and sciences have been a source of corruption, and even more adamant in rejecting another contention of Rousseau, that man in his original 'state of nature' was a solitary individualist. According to Voltaire, man is by nature, and always has been, a social animal; even the most primitive of savages live in some kind of society. Such an unequivocal stand on certain issues has led most commentators to discount the considerable body of evidence showing that he was, on the whole, inclined to favour what might be called moderate primitivism.

The notion that Voltaire was a champion of luxury is certainly an exaggeration. He considered luxury to be essential to the welfare of a large state, since economic prosperity depends upon it and the development of the arts and crafts and therefore of taste, refinement, and culture generally, requires the support of an affluent minority. *Le Mondain*, an amusing rebuttal of the simplistic theory that life was better in some past golden age, is his best-known tribute to 'le superflu, chose très nécessaire'. But *Le Mondain* was not Voltaire's last word on the subject and was certainly not intended to endorse the values of the eighteenth-century equivalent of the playboy. It should be taken for what it was—an excellent example of the poet's skill in handling light verse and a not-too-serious attack on asceticism and pious hypocrisy. Voltaire himself called it a 'badinage' (Best. D1222, 3631), a 'plaisanterie' (Best. 3635) which did not reflect his own tastes.[56] The following comment by the

---

56. 'Au reste monseigneur,' he wrote to Frederick, 'c'est par pure humanité que je conseille les plaisirs. Le mien n'est guères que L'étude et la solitude. Mais il y a mille façons d'être heureux' (January 1737, Best. D1251).

Kehl editors expresses accurately enough the contemporary
view and places the poem in its true perspective:

> Nous avouerons ... que la vie d'un honnête homme,
> peinte dans *le Mondain*, est celle d'un sybarite, et que
> tout homme qui mène cette vie ne peut être, même
> sans avoir aucun vice, qu'un homme aussi méprisable
> qu'ennuyé; mais il est aisé de voir que c'est une pure
> plaisanterie. Un homme qui, pendant soixante et dix ans,
> n'a point peut-être passé un seul jour sans écrire ou sans
> agir en faveur de l'humanité, aurait-il approuvé une vie
> consumée dans de vains plaisirs? Il a voulu dire seulement
> qu'une vie inutile, perdue dans les voluptés, est moins
> criminelle et moins méprisable qu'une vie austère
> employée dans l'intrigue, souillée par les ruses de l'hypo-
> crisie, ou les manœuvres de l'avidité. (M. X, 82)

Voltaire attacked excessive luxury as vigorously as he
defended the values of civilized society. He admitted that
small republics could be corrupted by it (M. X, 91), and
even went so far as to approve sumptuary laws in certain
circumstances.[57] The *Discours sur l'homme*, published shortly
after *Le Mondain*, has a quite different message:

> O vous, qui ramenez dans les murs de Paris
> Tous les excès honteux des mœurs de Sybaris;
> Qui, plongés dans le luxe, énervés de mollesse,
> Nourrissez dans votre âme une éternelle ivresse;
> Apprenez, insensés qui cherchez le plaisir,
> Et l'art de connaître, et celui de jouir. (M. IX, 404)

On the whole, Voltaire advocated moderation, recognizing
that in certain conditions unrestrained luxury may lead to
decadence, but refusing to admit that the harmless pursuit
of legitimate pleasure can be seriously condemned.[58]

Voltaire had a good deal to say about the 'noble savage'.
He returned to the theme, in fact, much more insistently

57. M. XX, 17; XXIV, 417.
58. M. X, 94; XX, 17; Best. 17163.

than Rousseau[59] and displayed a considerable familiarity with the extensive literature on the subject. In view of his theory of instinctive behaviour and the universality of moral law, it would be surprising if his attitude were as completely negative as has often been suggested. According to Gilbert Chinard, for example, 'Pour les vrais sauvages, Voltaire n'aura jamais ni sympathie ni admiration'.[60] But this is true only if a 'true savage' is taken to mean the solitary animal described in Rousseau's *Discours sur l'iné-galité*. Voltaire simply refused to believe that such a creature could have existed (M. XXVII, 354). Even for Rousseau, 'man in a state of nature' was a hypothetical being, not a portrait of the noble savage: our remote ancestor is depicted in the *Discours* as little more than a brute, neither happy nor unhappy and neither good nor bad, since morality has no meaning except in society.

Several of the tragedies are concerned with a comparison between civilized and semicivilized or primitive peoples. *Alzire* is by no means a simple endorsement of the primitivist thesis. Voltaire finds much to admire and condemn in both Americans and Europeans. If he reserves his harshest criticisms for the latter, described as brutal and unscrupulous colonizers, it is nevertheless the Spaniard, Alvarez, who is presented as a model of virtue, compassion, and *bienfaisance*, and another Spaniard, Gusman, whose sudden conversion to 'humanity' in the last act provides the moral. But Alvarez is a shining exception among the Spaniards and Gusman's is an exceptional act; in the direct comparison,

59. In spite of fundamental differences, notably on whether man has always been a social animal, the two philosophers were by no means in total opposition. In the heat of controversy, Voltaire sarcastically referred to Rousseau as the 'judicieux admirateur de la bêtise et de la brutalité des sauvages' (M. XXVI, 19). This is, of course, an absurd caricature. Recent critics have even denied that Rousseau was a primitivist (e.g. Arthur O. Lovejoy, 'The Supposed Primitivism of Rousseau's Discourse of Inequality', *MP*, 21 [1923], 165–186; Lester G. Crocker, *Nature and Culture. Ethical Thought in the French Enlightenment* [Baltimore, 1963], pp. 134–152). Both Voltaire and Rousseau painted sympathetic, if not idyllic, pictures of the semi-civilized North American Indians, and neither considered that a return to the primitive state was either possible or desirable.

60. Gilbert Chinard, *L'Amérique et le rêve exotique dans la littérature française au XVIIe et au XVIIIe siècles* (Paris, 1913), p. 242.

Voltaire leaves no doubt as to where his sympathies lie:

> Les Espagnols sont craints, mais ils sont en horreur:
> Fléaux du nouveau monde, injustes, vains, avares,
> Nous seuls en ces climats nous sommes les barbares.
> L'Américain, farouche en sa simplicité,
> Nous égale en courage, et nous passe en bonté.
>
> (M. III, 388)

Contemporary audiences and critics certainly took this to be the message of the play. Prévost, for example, in his review, admired 'la vertueuse barbarie des Amériquains' and complimented the actress playing the role of Alzire on expressing perfectly 'la tendresse, la constance et l'honneur, dans toute la simplicité de la nature, c'est-à-dire tels qu'ils devoient être avant la naissance du crime et dans l'âge d'or de son innocence',[61] while Cideville summarized Voltaire's achievement thus:

> A nostre ambition, à nostre Politique,
> A nos vices brillans il oppose les mœurs
> De la vertueuse Amerique,
> Et dans une Leçon publique
> Nous corrige en touchant nos cœurs.[62]

Primitives are also eulogized in the later tragedies. *Les Scythes* betrays a strong influence of Fénelon in the description of the Scythians as a dynamic people, proud of their equality and republican spirit[63] as opposed to the 'esclaves brillants' of Persia. They are by nature kind, generous, and hospitable, although they have retained barbarous customs. The Cydonians of *Les Lois de Minos*, portrayed as nomads ignorant of the arts and the use of money, are even closer to nature than the Scythians. Yet they compare very favourably with the civilized Greeks. Leading simple, healthy

61. *Le Pour et contre* (Paris, 1736), VIII, 105.
62. Best. D1002. See also d'Argens' comments in *Lettres juives* (La Haye, 1761), IV, 11–12 and those of Condorcet (M. I, 215).
63. M. VI, 278, 282, 296. For a discussion of primitivism in this play, see my *La Propagande philosophique dans les tragédies de Voltaire, SV*, XV (Geneva, 1961), pp. 205–211.

lives, they follow their instincts, and above all 'ce doux présent des dieux, l'instinct de la vertu' (M. VII, 205). Their religion, unlike that of the Greeks, is admirably free of dogma and superstition; they are content to worship a God whose temple is the woods, the fields, and the whole universe.[64]

As might be expected, expressions of primitivism are generally more restrained in the nondramatic works. Voltaire fluctuates between scorn for 'cet horrible état qui approche de la pure nature' (M. XIX, 384) and an occasional outburst of sentimental enthusiasm in the style of the late eighteenth century.[65] He was too committed to the values of refined civilization to be a whole-hearted supporter of the back-to-simple-nature movement. He was even prepared to argue that the development of the arts and sciences is 'natural', since it is in the nature of man to reach his full stature by gradually perfecting society (M. XXVII, 352–354). In any case, there is no turning back.

Nevertheless, his descriptions of primitive societies are, on the whole, sympathetic. Canadian Indians are depicted in the *Philosophie de l'histoire* as 'infinitely superior' to the serfs and peasants of Europe. They have a strong sense of dignity, honour, and patriotism and often display heroic energy. 'Ces Canadiens étaient des Spartiates, en comparison de nos rustres qui végètent dans nos villages, et des sybarites qui s'énervent dans nos villes' (M. XI, 19). In the *Essai sur les mœurs*, he describes the idyllic, semicivilized life of those natives of New Zealand who have progressed beyond cannibalism (M. XII, 423, n.). Even the Hottentots, according to the *Dictionnaire philosophique*, are 'libres, égaux entre eux, sans maîtres, sans sujets, sans argent, et presque sans besoins. La chair de leurs moutons les nourrit, leur peau les habille, des huttes de bois et de terre sont leurs retraites: ils sont les plus puants de tous les hommes, mais ils ne le

64. M. VII, 222–223. Voltaire's primitives are invariably deists, in accordance with his theory that religion evolved from primitive monotheism to complex polytheism and finally to the enlightened deism of the eighteenth century (M. XX, 349–351). Thus enlightenment and primitivism converge.

65. *L'Histoire de Jenni* (M. XXI, 546).

sentent pas; ils vivent et ils meurent plus doucement que nous' (M. XX, 184). Apart from the typically realistic detail, this is not a disapproving judgment. There is no suggestion that civilized man should attempt to imitate the Hottentots, but he might well envy them in some respects.

Savages, in Voltaire's view, are not morally inferior beings. They have the same instinct for justice as Europeans and make war for the same reasons. Cannibals are no worse than soldiers; their crime lies in killing, not eating, men, and they too experience feelings of remorse (Best. D1376). The great advantage enjoyed by the savage—and here Voltaire joins Rousseau—is his 'negative virtue'. His ignorance of metaphysical concepts and his native common sense preserve him from those 'errors associated with religion' which Voltaire considered to be one of the principal causes of misfortune in advanced societies.[66]

The 'return to nature' took several forms in the eighteenth century besides the popularity of the noble savage. One of the most important factors in the development of sensibility was the renewal of interest in natural surroundings, beginning with the fashion for English gardens, whose wild disorder, compared with the mathematical regularity of French parks, was felt to be closer to nature, and ending with the luxuriant exoticism of Bernardin de Saint-Pierre. Montesquieu transformed his park at La Brède in accordance with the new English style and dedicated a monument to James Thomson, author of *The Seasons*. This work enjoyed a considerable vogue in France and gave rise to innumerable imitations and translations,[67] notably Saint-Lambert's *Les Saisons*, which Voltaire hailed as a 'masterpiece'. By the third quarter of the century, comparisons between life in town and life in the country, to the advantage of the latter, were commonplace. A growing number of 'âmes sensibles' waxed sentimental over the simple pastoral life, the delights of solitude, the sense of freedom, and the solid virtues said to result from living in close communion with nature. In

66. See the *Entretiens d'un sauvage et d'un bachelier*, M. XXIV, 265–271. A similar argument is advanced in *L'Ingénu* (M. XXI, 256).

67. Margaret M. Cameron, *L'Influence des Saisons de Thomson sur la poésie descriptive en France (1759–1810)*, pp. 191–193.

contrast, city life seemed artificial and restricted, its pleasures shallow and unhealthy.

Largely because of his early reputation as a 'mondain', his obvious social talents and his brief career as a courtier, it is often assumed that Voltaire was a townsman *par excellence*, that he disliked solitude and was indifferent to natural beauty. Yet he confessed as early as 1723 that he was not born to live in the city: 'J'étois né pour être faune ou silvain, je ne suis point fait pour habiter dans une ville' (Best. D155). This was no idle statement, for he spent the greater part of his life away from Paris, much of it in country retreats. Nor was his 'exile' entirely involuntary; there is no doubt that the happiest periods of his life were those spent at Cirey and Ferney. The interlude at Versailles, on the other hand, he found frustrating and unsatisfactory. His dislike of courts and courtiers became a constantly recurring theme in his correspondence and literary works.[68]

His youthful admiration for things English seems to have included gardens. In the *Epître au prince royal de Prusse* (1738), he protests against the formality of French gardens and finds the wild freedom of nature more in accord with his temperament:

Trop d'art me révolte et m'ennuie.
J'aime mieux ces vastes forêts:
La nature, libre et hardie,
Irrégulière dans ses traits,
S'accorde avec ma fantaisie. (M. X, 308)

Voltaire even claimed to have introduced the vogue for English gardens into France.[69] Much to the amusement of visitors from across the Channel, he was fond of exhibiting his estate at Ferney as an example of a 'natural' park, free from 'French gewgaws' and 'quite in the English taste'.[70]

68. It appears in many of the plays and in some of the poems in praise of nature, e.g. in the *Epitre à Monsieur de Saint-Lambert* (M. X, 406) and the *Epitre XCII* (M. X, 378): 'C'est la cour qu'on doit fuir; c'est aux champs qu'il faut vivre.'

69. 'Ce fut moi qui introduisis cette mode en France, et tout le monde la saisit avec fureur' (M. I, 390).

70. Best. 11251; 'Voltaire's British Visitors', ed. de Beer, *SV*, IV, 44, 74, 122.

It is therefore not entirely surprising that when faced with the prospect of spending the rest of his life in the 'déserts' between the Alps and the Jura, Voltaire expressed, not the despair of an uprooted Parisian, but the joy of a man who has at last found a haven combining freedom and natural beauty.[71] After the move to Ferney, which enabled him to indulge his taste for country living and at the same time satisfy long-felt patriarchal ambitions, his letters are full of enthusiastic comments, interspersed with occasional cries of 'Vive la campagne!' or 'Vive la vie pastorale!' He can only be happy, he writes, in the country (Best. 12004, 12155) and he pities those who do not enjoy nature and who spend their entire lives without seeing it (Best. 10011). Crimes and follies are to be found only in the cities (Best. 11649), whose pleasures do not lead to true happiness but merely prevent one from being content to live anywhere else (Best. 14502).

It is true that Voltaire had good reasons, unconnected with the appeal of pastoral bliss, for disliking Paris. It is true also that Ferney, with its dinners, fêtes, and theatrical performances, was not exactly the solitary refuge he sometimes depicted. There is little trace in the correspondence or elsewhere of Rousseau's identification with nature or of a sentimental appreciation of mountain scenery. One may suspect that Voltaire had no time for 'rêveries' and that the chief attraction of country life lay in the challenge of healthy and constructive work (Best. 8174, 14722). But when all allowances have been made, it must surely be conceded that his enthusiasm was genuine. If it was a pretence, then it was a pretence which he maintained with every appearance of sincerity for over twenty years.

That he should have been particularly interested in practical matters is natural enough for a man of his energetic

---

71. Lamartine considered the poem entitled *L'Auteur arrivant dans sa terre, près du lac de Genève* an inspired hymn to nature as well as to liberty: 'Frappé de cette vue, il éprouva plus qu'il ne l'avait éprouvé jusque-là la poésie de la nature inanimée. Il chanta son lac dans des vers inspirés où le génie du paysage et le génie de la liberté se confondaient pour exalter son âme au-dessus d'elle-même' (*Cours familier de littérature* [Paris, 1856–69], XXVIII, 239).

and pragmatic temperament. As everyone knows, Candide's recipe for snatching a modest scrap of happiness from a harsh world is to cultivate one's garden. Whatever figurative meanings may be attached to this phrase, 'le vieux jardinier de Ferney' followed the advice quite literally. The gardeners he portrays tend to be rather like the mythical noble savage, simple, wise, and virtuous men of feeling, such as Arzéman in *Les Guèbres*, whose exaggerated qualities moved Flaubert to protest: 'Pour être jardinier, quelle admiration pour l'agriculture! à quelle époque donc n'y en a-t-il pas eu? pourquoi cet enthousiasme en entendant dire qu'elle arrosait des choux? La campagne est une chose dont on a cruellement abusé sous le point de vue vertueux; comment est-il plus louable de ratisser des allées ou de repiquer des oignons que de faire de la tapisserie ou de cirer des bottes?'[72]

Flaubert's is the voice of another age. For disciples of Rousseau, such as Lezay-Marnésia, the connection between country life and *bienfaisance* was obvious and Voltaire himself was an outstanding example:

> Ce n'est point parmi les distractions des villes que la pitié fait des impressions profondes et durables. Si l'on pleure au théâtre sur des infortunes imaginaires, dans le tourbillon de la société l'on reste froid sur des maux trop véritables. A Paris, Voltaire se serait encore plus occupé du soin de plaire, se serait livré davantage au désir de multiplier ses succès, et se serait moins souvent attendri. Plus à lui-même à Ferney, et par conséquent plus sensible et meilleur, l'humanité lui parlait avec empire; il en soutenait, il en rétablissait les droits, et du pied des Alpes sa voix entraînait la France entière.[73]

72. G. Flaubert, *Le Théâtre de Voltaire*, ed. Theodore Besterman, *SV*, L and LI (Geneva, 1967), LI, 405.
73. *Essai sur la nature champêtre*, pp. 28–29.

# CHAPTER 3

# *The Idealist*

Voltaire's reputation as a pessimist, political realist, and anti-romantic would seem to preclude any form of Utopianism. The most celebrated of his ideal societies is Eldorado and Eldorado, as numerous critics have pointed out, is a rejected Utopia. One wonders, however, whether this episode can plausibly be interpreted as an attack on idealism. Eldorado, where natural law is observed in its purest form and civilization is combined with simplicity, is the perfect realization of Voltairean values. It is described with no trace of irony. The likeable but mediocre hero of *Candide*, unable to imagine any other ideal than proximity to his mistress, is only too glad to load up his pebbles and leave. Given a choice between life in a tolerant, peace-loving community where inequality has no meaning in the midst of abundance, and the possibility of enjoying immense wealth in the normal, irrational world, he does not hesitate: 'Si nous restons ici, nous n'y serons que comme les autres; au lieu que si nous retournons dans notre monde seulement avec douze moutons chargés de cailloux d'Eldorado, nous serons plus riches que tous les rois ensemble, nous n'aurons plus d'inquisiteurs à craindre, et nous pourrons aisément reprendre Mlle Cunégonde.'[1]

Voltaire's satirical target is surely unmistakeable. In any case, Eldorado is by no means the only Voltairean Utopia. The complete works cover a wide range of eighteenth-century mythology, including several idealized societies, from ancient China to contemporary England, and a large selection of exemplary figures: the Good Quaker, the Patriotic Roman, the Chinese Sage, the Philosopher Prince, the Wise Old

1. *Candide*, M. XXI, 178.

Gardener, the Gallant Knight, and the occasional Noble Savage. Voltaire was perfectly capable of naïve enthusiasm, in life as in literature—witness his recurrent dream of establishing a haven for an élite group of philosophers who would live together in idyllic harmony—and the desire to be moved by outstanding examples of *grandeur d'âme* seems to have been a permanent feature of his sensibility.

His descriptions of China and India may properly be termed Utopian, since they conform to a preconceived ideal and were clearly intended to point up certain inadequacies in European civilization. As Frederick slyly remarked, they follow the pattern set by Tacitus, who praised the frugality and candour of the Germans, 'qui certainement ne méritaient pas alors d'être imités de personne', in order to stimulate the pursuit of virtue among his fellow-Romans (Best. 18916).

Voltaire's interest in India, dating from the 1740s, developed into a veritable fascination during the Ferney period. The fact that little was known about the sub-continent in the eighteenth century and that Voltaire's main sources of information are virtually worthless is of little consequence. He found precisely what he wanted to find: an ancient civilization, even older than that of China, exemplifying the principles of natural philosophy. The accounts of the Jesuits, supplemented by the *Shasta*, which he supposed to be the oldest book in the world, the false Hindu manuscript of the *Ezour Veidam* and a book by an Englishman, J. Z. Holwell,[2] gave him all the necessary details from which to construct the 'earthly paradise' depicted in the *Essai sur les mœurs*, the *Lettres chinoises*, and *La Princesse de Babylone*.

As in most of Voltaire's idealized societies, perfection is not quite achieved. The simple cult of benevolent deism has been overlaid in the course of time by various superstitions and sullied by the horrible practice of suttee. But the ancient religion of the Brahmins is described as the only one, apart

2. *Interesting Historical Events Relating to the Provinces of Bengal and the Empire* (London, 1766–1771). Voltaire received the first two volumes in 1767 (Best. 13663). See A. Debidour, "L'Indianisme de Voltaire", *RLC*, 4 (January–March 1924), pp. 26–40.

from that of the Chinese, which is not to some degree barbarous.[3] Even the doctrine of the transmigration of souls serves a useful social purpose by ensuring that citizens will obey the law, if only from fear of becoming vile insects or animals in another life.

An idyllic picture of life on the banks of the Ganges emerges from the pages of the *Lettres chinoises* and *La Princesse de Babylone*. It is a pastoral paradise, a fertile land favoured by a perfect climate. The inhabitants are worthy of it: they are pure, just, and pious, and this beauty of soul is equalled only by the beauty of their appearance. They are not 'savages', since the arts are cultivated, but they are clearly products of the primitivist tradition. In *La Princesse de Babylone*, there is a contrast between their frugal manners and the empty magnificence of the Babylonian court.[4] Unlike the less fortunate peoples of the West, 'les seuls Gangarides avaient conservé la nature et la dignité primitive de l'homme.'[5] They cherish freedom, equality, simplicity, and tolerance and are thoroughly republican in spirit. Their leader, Amazan, would consider it a loss of dignity to accept the title of king: 'Il aime trop ses compatriotes: il est berger comme eux.'[6]

The same process may be observed in the creation of a legendary image of China, which became a part of the faith of the Enlightenment and which Voltaire did more than anyone to establish and perpetuate. Again, available accounts are used to form a composite picture containing salutary lessons for corrupt Westerners who have strayed far from the path of natural law.

Since China is a huge country with flourishing cities and a civilization dating back several millennia, a republican form of government in the narrow political sense would be quite impossible. Voltaire insists, however, that it is not a despotism but a paternalistic system with rigid safeguards to ensure that absolutism does not infringe upon the laws.

3. *Essai sur les mœurs*, ed. R. Pomeau, I, 61.
4. M. XXI, 384, 395.
5. *Princesse de Babylone*, M. XXI, 427.
6. *Princesse de Babylone*, M. XXI, 384.

Like the English constitution, but in a different way, it combines the best features of royalism and republicanism. The laws are 'établies sur le pouvoir paternel, c'est-à-dire sur la loi la plus sacrée de la nature' (M. XXIX, 469), but it is impossible for the Emperor to act without first consulting elected legal experts (M. XIII, 162). Arbitrary punishment is eliminated by the need to have recourse to several tribunals. Not content with merely punishing crime, the enlightened Chinese actively encourage virtue by rewarding it (M. XI, 175; XVIII, 158). In short, their constitution is the best in the world (M. XVIII, 158).

They are, of course, deists. Voltaire protested as vehemently against the charge that the Chinese were atheists as against the notion that their Emperor was a tyrant. Their religion, or rather the religion of the élite, is 'simple, sage, auguste, libre de toute superstition et de toute barbarie' (M. XI, 57) and notable for the rigid control of the priesthood and the absence of fanatical factions. The prophet of this pure faith, and one of the most important figures in Voltaire's gallery of greatness, is Confucius. His message, as revealed in his writings on ethics, consists of two basic principles: first, that 'Dieu a gravé lui-même la vertu dans le cœur de l'homme', and second that 'l'homme n'est point né méchant et qu'il le devient par sa faute' (M. XI, 57). Confucius is obviously intended to be regarded as one of the earliest philosophers of *bienfaisance*. The period when men obeyed his maxims was, according to Voltaire, the happiest in human history (M. XI, 176).

Voltaire's glorification of these remote civilizations, whose antiquity, in the words of Geoffroy, 'donne un soufflet à la Bible',[7] was undoubtedly inspired in part by his hostility to Christianity. But his aim was much wider than this negative explanation would suggest. If, as he believed, the development of society and the arts is 'natural', China may be said to represent the true 'state of nature'. The very fact that the Chinese have retained their laws, religion, and institutions intact over thousands of years is a guarantee

7. *Cours de littérature dramatique* (Paris, 1825), III, 54.

that they are close to nature and nature's law.[8] In this respect they resemble the noble savage, but with the great advantage of having succeeded in combining the natural virtues with cultural progress. They have built cities and cultivated the arts without being corrupted; they are virtuous deists of simple manners but without the ignorance and aggressive tendencies of true primitives.

Like the legend of the wise and virtuous Chinese, the image of the good Quaker owed its enormous popularity in the eighteenth century to Voltaire's publicizing talents. They have much in common: both are remarkable for the purity of their religion and for their fidelity to an ethical code based on natural law; both love peace and practise tolerance; and both have made considerable progress towards the attainment of the perfect state through submission to wise laws. Moreover, Voltaire's Quakers, like his Chinese, represent an ideal blend of nature and civilization. They are constantly referred to as 'primitives' because of the extreme simplicity of their way of life; yet they are also men of the eighteenth century engaged in commerce.

There is, however, one important difference. The China of Confucius is a remote and somewhat abstract conception. Voltaire had direct personal experience of the Quakers; they are closer and more human. By stressing above all else their spirit of benevolence, he used them to express his own sentimental idealism, to such a degree and with such success that by the end of the century the mere mention of the word 'Quaker' was invariably the signal for the shedding of virtuous tears.

Voltaire was probably first attracted to the Quakers by their peculiarities, some of which, notably their habit of trembling, their mystical enthusiasm, and their scorn for conventional politeness, were not entirely to his taste. These are satirized, although without malice, in the *Lettres philosophiques*. In the same work, however, he devotes a disproportionate amount of space to enlarging on their more

8. 'Mais ce qui met les Chinois au-dessus de tous les peuples de la terre, c'est que ni leurs lois, ni leurs mœurs, ni la langue que parlent chez eux les lettrés, n'ont changé depuis environ quatre mille ans' (M. XIX, 349).

admirable traits and describing the enviable lot of the citizens of Pennsylvania, who live in a state where there are no priests, no wars, no oppressive laws, where all creeds are tolerated and all men, including savages, are regarded as brothers.

Voltaire was obviously profoundly impressed by these quiet revolutionaries, whose simple faith in the goodness of man had apparently been triumphantly vindicated. He returned to them again and again, in the *Essai sur les mœurs*, in the *Traité sur la tolérance*, in the *Dictionnaire philosophique*, with an increasing respect which became at times uncritical enthusiasm. The article entitled 'Quakers' in the *Dictionnaire philosophique* is thoroughly Utopian. After expressing his love for the Quakers and his desire to visit Pennsylvania, he depicts a never-never-land of perfect peace, tolerance, liberty, equality, and *bienfaisance*, an American haven where natural law is free to operate without the strain imposed by excessive civilization: 'On peut, pour douze guinées, acquérir cent arpents de très-bonne terre; et dans ces cent arpents on est véritablement roi, car on est libre, on est citoyen; vous ne pouvez faire de mal à personne, et personne ne peut vous en faire; vous pensez ce qu'il vous plaît, et vous le dites sans que personne vous persécute; vous ne connaissez point le fardeau des impôts, continuellement redoublé; vous n'avez point de cour à faire; vous ne redoutez point l'insolence d'un subalterne important' (M. XX, 312).

Those who cling to the view that Voltaire was an irreligious cynic will be hard put to explain this fascination. He was well aware that the Quakers were profoundly religious men and also that they were not deists. He repeatedly stressed their resemblance to early Christians, with whom he had considerable sympathy.[9] Like the saintly Alvarez in *Alzire*, they symbolize 'true Christianity', the simple doctrine of Christ, which has been obscured and disfigured by generations of theologians and which is sufficiently close to Voltairean deism to make any difference acceptable. Their

9. e.g. M. XX, 523: 'S'il est une secte qui rappelle les temps des premiers chrétiens, c'est sans contredit celle des premiers quakers'.

piety has not led to superstition or fanaticism; on the contrary, they condemn such rites as baptism and communion and they are the most tolerant of men. The important thing in Voltaire's view is that their religion is deeply felt but uncomplicated and places the emphasis where it should be, on the love of God and man rather than on ritual and dogma.

There is no mistaking Voltaire's genuine, not to say naïve, enthusiasm. As is often the case when the theme of *bienfaisance* is involved, realism and irony are noticeably absent. 'While we sit for our Picture to that able Painter,' noted Franklin, ''tis no small Advantage to us that he views us at a favourable Distance.'[10] But it was not simply a matter of remoteness fostering exaggeration. Pennsylvania fulfils the same role as any other Utopia: to provide the ideal by which to judge and therefore change the actual. In this respect Voltaire was remarkably successful. His message was taken up by the abbé Raynal and others who developed it into a mystique of Anglo-America as powerful as, and ultimately much more important than, that of the noble savage. Voltaire's idealized Quaker was a central figure in the eighteenth-century version of the 'American dream', as outlined by Raynal:

La violence a des bornes dans ses excès; elle se consume & s'éteint, comme le feu dans la cendre de ses aliments. Mais la vertu, quand elle est dirigée par l'enthousiasme de l'humanité, par l'esprit de fraternité, se ranime, comme l'arbre, sous le tranchant du fer. Les méchans ont besoin de la multitude, pour exécuter leurs projets sanguinaires. L'homme juste, le Quaker, ne demande qu'un frere pour en recevoir de l'assistance, ou lui donner du secours. Allez, peuples guerriers, peuples esclaves & tyrans, allez en Pensilvanie; vous y trouverez toutes les portes ouvertes, tous les biens à votre discrétion; pas un soldat, & beaucoup de marchands ou de laboureurs.[11]

10. Quoted by A. O. Aldridge, 'Benjamin Franklin and the *philosophes*', *SV*, XXIV, 44.
11. *Histoire philosophique et politique des Etablissements et du Commerce des Européens dans les deux Indes* (Geneva, 1780), IX, 35.

The search for *grandeur d'âme*, combined with a longing to escape into a more spontaneous, less corrupt and complicated existence undoubtedly had a great deal to do with the revival of interest in the age of chivalry, usually credited to the romantics. A lively curiosity about the Middle Ages began to manifest itself quite early in the eighteenth century, was given a powerful stimulus by the performance of Voltaire's *Zaïre* and *Adélaïde du Guesclin* and by the publication of Lacurne de Sainte-Pelaye's *Mémoires sur l'ancienne chevalerie*, and developed into a veritable cult, rivalling that of antiquity, after the enormously successful production of *Tancrède* in 1760. Innumerable plays, operas, comic operas, 'romances', novels, adaptations, and collections exploited the public taste for chivalrous deeds and tales of love and adventure in a medieval setting, while poets sang of honour, gallantry, and selfless devotion.

Voltaire's views on 'les temps grossiers qu'on nomme du moyen âge' were, of course, anything but Utopian. He saw the Crusades as a 'disease' and the Crusaders as monsters of violence and debauchery. The description of chivalry in the *Discours historique et critique sur la tragédie de Don Pèdre* is equally unromantic: 'On élève aussi quelquefois au ciel d'anciens chevaliers défenseurs ou oppresseurs des femmes et des églises, superstitieux et débauchés, tantôt voleurs, tantôt prodigues, combattant à outrance les uns contre les autres pour l'honneur de quelques princesses qui avaient très-peu d'honneur' (M. VII, 254).

The *Essai sur les mœurs* presents a more serious, balanced, sympathetic, and on the whole accurate account, in which the chivalric code is contrasted with the general brutality of the age: 'Ces temps de grossièreté, de séditions, de rapines et de meurtres, furent cependant le plus brillant de la chevalerie: elle servait de contre-poids à la férocité générale des mœurs . . . l'honneur, la générosité, joints à la galanterie, étaient ses principes.'[12]

The historian's indignation at the spectacle of anarchy and suffering inclined him to pessimism; he was less con-

12. M. XII, 28. See especially M. XII, 130–134.

cerned with idealism than with assessing the social value of a
system founded to establish order, suppress brigands, and
protect women. Voltaire's optimism and admiration for
heroic qualities are much more in evidence in the tragedies,
where pathos and epic grandeur combine naturally to reveal
both sides of his sensibility. Since he was also keenly aware
of the importance of spectacle and was the first French
dramatist to take a serious interest in local colour, it was
perhaps inevitable that he should be attracted sooner or
later to chivalry as a possible subject.

Voltaire has an undeserved reputation as a conservative,
or even reactionary, where literature is concerned. In fact,
he had an uncanny knack of anticipating public taste, sometimes by several decades. *Zaïre*, first performed in 1732, is a
case in point. To the modern reader, this tableau of the
Crusades seems timid and superficial; to contemporaries
it was a play full of daring and impressive innovations. Here
was a classical tragedy in which Frenchmen were among the
leading characters, in which the Seine was mentioned, which
made a strong appeal to patriotic and religious feelings, and
whose setting was a particularly colourful period of national
history. Looking back half a century later, the anonymous
author of a critical review in the *Journal des Savants* saw
it as marking a new epoch in the theatre: '*Enfin Voltaire
vint*, Voltaire nourri du théâtre anglais et de Shakespeare,
qu'il a fait connaître le premier en France; il fit entendre sur
la scène française des noms français, comme Shakespeare
avait mis sur la scène anglaise des personnages anglais.
On a donné plus d'étendue dans la suite à cette nouveauté
heureuse.' [13]

The Crusaders are, on the whole, sympathetically presented as worthy champions of the chivalric ideals of honour,
fidelity, and self-sacrifice. The excessive zeal of their leader,
Nérestan, precipitates the catastrophe and compares un-
favourably with the sultan Orosmane's magnanimity, but
his motives are noble and disinterested. Commenting on

13. Quoted by C. D. Brenner, *L'Histoire nationale dans la tragédie
française du XVIIIᵉ siècle* (Berkeley, 1929), p. 197.

his conduct, one of the Crusaders, Chatillon, sums up the code of the Christian knight:

> ... tout chrétien, tout digne chevalier,
> Pour sa religion se doit sacrifier;
> Et la félicité des cœurs tels que les nôtres
> Consiste à tout quitter pour le bonheur des autres.
>
> (M. II, 568)

Lusignan, the venerable patriarch of the Crusaders, a pathetic but dignified figure, whose speech beginning 'Mon Dieu! j'ai combattu soixante ans pour ta gloire' contributed greatly to the play's popularity as an early 'tragédie larmoyante', is a perfect instrument for the display of Voltaire's talents both as actor and playwright.

*Adélaïde du Guesclin* was less well received during its opening run in 1734, but made a considerable impression when it was revived some thirty years later. Encouraged by the success of *Zaïre*, Voltaire had the audacity not only to take as his subject an episode from medieval history, but to situate the action in France. Here the historical background, as Voltaire himself pointed out (Best. D675), is much less important than the theme of distorted passion. The impetuous Vendôme is hardly an exemplary knight, since his love for Adélaïde develops into an obsession which obliterates all other feelings, including compassion and honour, but he does express the chivalric ideal:

> Il n'est point de Français que l'amour avilisse:
> Amants aimés, heureux, ils cherchent les combats,
> Ils courent à la gloire. . . . (M. III, 91)

And Adélaïde herself is the tender and faithful lady of medieval romance.

Voltaire's most successful evocation of the spirit of chivalry was undoubtedly *Tancrède*. Immediately and ecstatically acclaimed by public and critics alike and constantly revived, it exerted an indisputable influence on the direction of

eighteenth-century, and even nineteenth-century, romanticism. It was the first acknowledged literary 'masterpiece'
to emerge from the cult of the Middle Ages and the prototype
of romantic melodrama. Gazon Dourxigné was merely echo-
ing the unanimous opinion of contemporary critics, including
Voltaire's arch-enemy, Fréron, when he referred to the play
as 'un magnifique et fidèle tableau des mœurs et des coutumes
de l'ancienne chevalerie'.[14] Later, the prophet of early
romanticism, Mme de Staël, sang its praises in no uncertain
fashion:

> Quel rôle est plus touchant au théâtre que celui de Tan-
> crède? Phèdre vous inspire de l'étonnement, de l'en-
> thousiasme; mais sa nature n'est point celle d'une femme
> sensible et délicate. Tancrède, on se le rappelle comme un
> héros qu'on aurait connu, comme un ami qu'on aurait
> regretté. La valeur, la mélancolie, l'amour, tout ce qui
> fait aimer et sacrifier la vie, tous les genres de volupté
> de l'âme sont réunis dans cet admirable sujet. Défendre
> la patrie qui nous a proscrits, sauver la femme qu'on
> aime alors qu'on la croit coupable, l'accabler de générosité,
> et ne se venger d'elle qu'en se dévouant à la mort,
> quelle nature sublime, et cependant en harmonie avec
> toutes les âmes tendres![15]

The long-overdue removal of benches from the stage of
the Comédie Française gave Voltaire the opportunity to
realize an old ambition: 'frapper l'âme et les yeux à la fois'
(M. V, 496). He took full advantage of it. Knights and
squires in full period costume with armour and banners
paraded across the stage and formed impressive tableaux.
Nothing like it had been seen before; in the words of the
author, the setting became 'a part of the plot' (M. V, 497).
But the play's originality is by no means confined to these
external trappings. Voltaire seems to have been inspired by
his subject to the point where *Tancrède* becomes a glorification of chivalry. There are several quotable tributes to

14. *L'Ami de la vérité* (Amsterdam, 1767), p. 105.
15. *Œuvres complètes* (Paris, 1836), I, 285.

gallant knights whose exploits, surprisingly, are related to the freedom of the 'people':

> Les soupçons n'entraient point dans leurs esprits altiers.
> L'honneur avait uni tous les grands chevaliers:
> Chez les seuls ennemis ils portaient les alarmes;
> Et le peuple, amoureux de leur autorité,
> Combattait pour leur gloire et pour sa liberté.
>
> (M. V, 518)

Tancrède and Aménaïde are typical characters of medieval romance literature. Both prefer death to dishonour and remain scrupulously faithful to their vows when faced with betrayal. Aménaïde dedicates herself exclusively to love, the source of her courage. Tancrède is true to the 'sacred words' of his banner, Love and Honour: ideals which take precedence even over his patriotism. Their pride, fidelity, and lofty conception of duty lead to the ultimate tragedy, which permits Voltaire to indulge to the full his gift for pathos.

It is perhaps significant that *Zaïre* and *Tancrède* were among Voltaire's most successful tragedies and also, with the exception of *Mahomet* and *Brutus*, the only ones which appear to have genuinely fired his imagination. However outmoded their creaking machinery, rudimentary psychology, and imitative style, they cannot be called 'cold'. Voltaire obviously found an outlet for his own emotions in the dramatic presentation of an attitude to life which transcends self-interest and seeks other goods than pleasure, material comfort, or peace of mind.

The awakening of interest in the Middle Ages and the vogue for themes drawn from national history, with overtones of pride in a colourful and glorious past and dedication to an ideal of service, are related to another, even more powerful manifestation of eighteenth-century sensibility in which Voltaire again played a key role as pioneer and popularizer: the cult of antiquity and the 'republicanism' from which it can hardly be separated. Since it was a comparatively short-lived phenomenon and is of only minor interest in the investigation of 'preromanticism', it has received less attention than it deserves. It was not only a vogue which lasted for several decades and which had a profound effect on almost every aspect of living from style in clothes and furniture to political oratory, but also an important literary and artistic movement, culminating in the works of Gluck, David, and André Chénier.

Enthusiasm for an idealized antiquity and for a concept of morality derived from the writings of Stoics and ancient historians is generally considered to date from the publication of Rousseau's first *Discours* in 1750. In fact, the origins go back to the 1730s, to Voltaire's *Brutus* and Montesquieu's analysis of the moral foundations of Rome's greatness and beyond these to Fénelon's descriptions of 'l'aimable simplicité du monde naissant'. Writing in a style often reminiscent of Latin writers, Montesquieu succeeded in imprinting on the minds of his contemporaries an image of Roman republicanism based on devotion to the state, pride in citizenship, love of freedom, and a toughness which was later softened and corrupted by the acquisition of wealth. Rousseau, an avid reader of Plutarch in his youth, according to the *Confessions*, took up the same theme in the *Discours*, in *Emile*, in the *Contrat social*, investing it with his own eloquent and contagious enthusiasm. At the same time, a number of publications revealed hitherto unknown glories of ancient art and architecture, while public interest was aroused by the discoveries at Pompeii.

The Greeks were not neglected. Socrates became one of the saints of the Enlightenment. Voltaire attempted to revitalize French tragedy by imitating the simplicity and tragic force of the Greek dramatists. But, given the bias in French education, it was natural that the Latin influence should predominate. Lucretius, Virgil, Plutarch, Sallust, Tacitus, and the Stoics were edited, translated, and provided with critical commentaries. Before 1789, Rome of the republican era was firmly established as a model state and words like 'vertu', 'patrie', 'citoyen', were certain to provoke an immediate emotional response.

It is this explosion of sentiment, typified by Mme Roland's tears at the thought of not having been born a Greek or

Roman, or Diderot's impassioned plea for 'La vérité, la nature, les anciens!' which distinguishes the cult of antiquity from classicism and neoclassicism. Much more was involved than the imitation of literary models recommended by Boileau. It was an attempt to recapture a style of life, to halt the decadence of an over-sophisticated and frivolous era by an appeal to the values of an imaginary golden age. The emphasis was on moral regeneration; hence the authors of classical antiquity whose influence was the most pervasive were the moralists and the moralizing historians who extolled the stern republican virtues of frugality, probity, loyalty, courage, and love of country.

Far from being merely a fashion, the enthusiasm for antiquity represents the culmination of some of the deeper trends of the century: sensibility, primitivism, and the rejection of Christian ethics in favour of *bienfaisance*. Since *Télémaque*, the 'return to nature' had usually meant the return to fundamental values and to a simpler, more virile existence. After the mid-century, one of the more persistent forms of primitivism, forcefully evident, for example, in Diderot's art criticism, was the reaction against the effeminate prettiness of the *style Louis XV* and in general against the softness and social hypocrisy of urban life. There seems to have been a universal desire to open the salon windows and let in a healthy gust of clean air. In the search for a new morality to replace the teachings of official Christianity, which sought to repress nature rather than perfect it, and which in any case was discredited by a record of dogmatic intolerance, the men of the eighteenth century turned instinctively to classical antiquity, with its familiar gods, myths, and heroes, and whose philosophers were more concerned with the practice of virtue than with personal salvation.

There is no doubt also that the long series of reverses sustained by the French in the Seven Years' War was a major contributing factor. England, long extolled as the model of a vigorous modern nation, a new Rome, as it were, cherishing its hard-won freedoms and honouring its great men, had triumphed; France had suffered a humiliating defeat. That the lesson was not lost is evidenced by the remarkable revival of French patriotism in the following decades.

'Patriotism', like 'republicanism', is a term which needs to be carefully defined, since it had a more general meaning in the eighteenth century than feelings of chauvinism or national pride. Jaucourt defined it in the *Encyclopédie* as 'l'amour des lois et du bonheur de l'état, amour singulière-ment affecté aux démocraties; c'est une vertu politique, par laquelle on renonce à soi-même, en préférant l'intérêt public au sien propre.'[16] Similarly, 'republicanism' was rarely used in the narrow sense of a political doctrine opposed to monarchy. Few political thinkers seriously considered the possibility of a genuinely republican form of government for France. The problem was how to put new life into the régime, not whether to depose the King. 'République' was in fact almost synonymous with 'patrie' and suggested a set of values rather than a rigidly defined system. In other words, republicanism implied concern for the laws and public welfare on the model of the Roman Republic. It was the antithesis, not of royalism, but of arbitrary despotism, and was indeed not infrequently used when referring to certain monarchies, such as those of England and Sweden.

'Virtue', significantly, lost its Christian connotations and took on a new, or rather ancient, meaning, closer to the Roman sense of courage, manliness, and good citizenship, coloured by the eighteenth-century concept of *bienfaisance*. 'Virtue', 'republicanism', and 'patriotism' were thus almost interchangeable terms referring to the same ideal.

It is possible therefore to speak of Voltaire's 'republican-ism' without suggesting that he was anything but a con-firmed royalist and a loyal subject of Louis XV. Contrary to popular opinion, he was not a servile flatterer of kings. Nor was he, for all his great social gifts, much of a success as a courtier, a profession for which he frequently expressed the utmost distaste. He cannot be said to have been a half-hearted courtier, because he never did anything half-

16. Art. 'Patrie'. See Denis J. Fletcher, 'Montesquieu's Conception of Patriotism', *SV*, LVI, 541–555.

heartedly, but he was certainly not happy at court. The correspondence betrays his malaise and one detects on occasion a rare note of self-disgust. The verses added in 1756 to the fourth *Discours en vers sur l'homme* are typical of many similar statements:

> J'ai vécu, je l'avoue, avec des souverains.
>
> . . . . . . . . . . . . . . . . . . . . . . . . . . . . . . . . . .
>
> . . . j'asservis au vain désir de plaire
> La mâle liberté qui fait mon caractère;
> Et, perdant la raison, dont je devais m'armer,
> J'allai m'imaginer qu'un roi pouvait aimer.
> Que je suis revenu de cette erreur grossière!
> A peine de la cour j'entrai dans la carrière,
> Que mon âme éclairée, ouverte au repentir,
> N'eut d'autre ambition que d'en pouvoir sortir.
> Raisonneurs beaux esprits, et vous qui croyez l'être,
> Voulez-vous vivre heureux, vivez toujours sans maître.
>
> (M. IX, 404)

In some of his earliest works, notably *Œdipe*, Voltaire was already protesting against the royalist mystique and asserting that the King is an ordinary mortal who should place the welfare of his subjects before his own ambitions and interest.[17] *La Henriade* provided the model in the person of Henri IV. These 'republican' leanings were confirmed by visits to Holland, and above all by his stay in England, which convinced him that the health of a society depends on the degree of liberty enjoyed by its citizens. 'All that is King or belongs to a King', he wrote to Thieriot, 'frights my republican philosophy, I wont drink the least draught of slavery in the land of liberty' (Best. D303). Precisely the same spirit animates the poem written thirty years later to celebrate his arrival in Geneva. In the meantime, he had produced the *Lettres philosophiques*, *La Mort de César*, and *Rome sauvée*. In spite of some illusions and

17. M. II, 66, 77, 79. A poem addressed to the Regent in 1716 includes the following couplet referring to Louis XIV (M. X, 234):
> De quelque nom sacré que l'opéra le nomme,
> L'équitable Français ne voit en lui qu'un homme.

misconceived attempts to compromise with autocracy, his fundamental attitude of sturdy independence never failed to reassert itself.

In some respects, Voltaire became more, rather than less, radical with age. The Ferney period saw the publication of the *Dictionnaire philosophique*, *Le Triumvirat*, *Les Scythes*, the *Idées républicaines*, the *Pensées sur le gouvernement*, and the campaign in favour of the Natifs of Geneva. In the year preceding his death, he made some amends to Montesquieu by praising the republican spirit of *De l'esprit des lois* (Best. 19649) and reversed his previous stand on the distinction between monarchy and despotism.[18]

While he never goes into detail, Voltaire's definition of a true republic seems to be a state in which the people, through representatives, have some say in the forming of policy and whose citizens are 'free' in the sense that they are all equal before the law.[19] The republican form of government is described as the most natural, not only because it accommodates man's desire for freedom and equality, but also because it is the one most likely to achieve a balance between each citizen's natural ambitions and interests. Hence Voltaire is led to contradict Montesquieu by affirming that a republic is not founded on 'virtue'; much more virtue is required, as he well knew, to 'dare to tell the truth' at court (M. XIX, 33); it is based rather on 'l'ambition de chaque citoyen, qui contient l'ambition des autres; sur l'orgueil, sur le désir de dominer qui ne souffre pas qu'un autre domine' (M. XXIII, 531). The first societies must have been republics. Why then are so few of them left? Voltaire's answer is that men are rarely worthy of self-government: 'C'est une société où des convives, d'un appétit égal, mangent à la même table, jusqu'à ce qu'il vienne un homme vorace et vigoureux qui prenne tout pour lui et leur laisse les miettes' (M. XXIII, 531). In its purest form, a republic

18. To Pierre Louis Claude Gin (Best. 19549): 'Je commence par avouer que *despotique* et *monarchique* sont tout juste la même chose dans le cœur de tous les hommes, et de tous les êtres sensibles. . . . Vous prouvez très bien que le gouvernement monarchique est le meilleur de tous; mais c'est pourvu que Marc Aurèle soit le monarque.'

19. 'La liberté consiste à ne dépendre que des lois' (M. XXIII, 526).

can only exist, precariously, in a small, relatively poor country protected from predatory neighbours by natural features: small, because republicanism requires a tightly knit community in which each citizen is acutely aware that his own interest depends on the welfare and security of the state; poor, because wealth leads inevitably to inequality and thirst for power.

Voltaire was a royalist, not by conviction, but for purely pragmatic reasons. He felt that a monarchy was the only practicable form of government for such a large, well-populated, and well-developed country as France. He refused, however, to accept the idea of a divinely appointed monarch or of pure despotism.[20] The King should have sufficient power to suppress dangerous factionalism, to control the Church and ensure civil peace and tolerance, but he should be himself subject to the law. The important thing in any case is not the name one cares to give to a government—monarchies are included in his list of republics—but whether it is genuinely republican in spirit, whether the individual enjoys dignity and freedom, whether each citizen is equal before the law and whether the laws are respected.

It is no paradox therefore to conclude that Voltaire, who has rightly been called a 'great humanitarian patriot,'[21] was republican and democratic in outlook, notwithstanding his realistic appraisal of the weaknesses inherent in actual republics and the fact that, like Rousseau, he had no time for a 'gouvernement de la canaille'. Of all his political statements, the one which has the most convincing ring is the following passage from *L'ABC*:

> Etre libre, n'avoir que des égaux, est la vraie vie, la vie naturelle del 'homme; tout autre est un indigne artifice, une mauvaise comédie, où l'un joue le personnage de maître, l'autre d'esclave, celui-là de parasite, et cet autre d'entremetteur. Vous m'avouerez que les hommes ne peuvent être descendus de l'état naturel que par lâcheté et par bêtise.

20. 'Le pur despotisme est le châtiment de la mauvaise conduite des hommes' (M. XXIV, 413).
21. Constance Rowe, *Voltaire and the State* (New York, 1955), p. 191.

> Cela est clair: personne ne peut avoir perdu sa liberté
> que pour n'avoir pas su la défendre. Il y a eu deux mani-
> ères de la perdre: c'est quand les sots ont été trompés
> par des fripons, ou quand les faibles ont été subjugués par
> les forts. (M. XXVII, 348)

One can believe him when he writes to Cramer, 'Pour moi
si je reviens jamais au monde, je veux renaître républicain'
(Best. 10815). His republicanism was less a matter of intellectual preference than of feeling, of 'cette sensibilité
touchante qui contraste avec l'insolence du despotisme'.[22]

It is evident in his descriptions of the three modern
'republics' which which he was personally acquainted:
Holland, England, and Geneva. A shrewd and clear-eyed
observer of men and manners, Voltaire was perfectly conscious of the fact that he was dealing with real, not ideal,
societies. Undoubtedly he conceals some embarrassing coun-
ter-evidence; undoubtedly one of his motives is to draw
attention to deficiencies in the French régime; nevertheless,
the enthusiasm is genuine, and few would deny its impact on
successive generations of enlightenment intellectuals up to
and including the Revolution.

Voltaire's references to Holland are uniformly eulogistic.
Occasionally, they take on a Utopian tinge.[23] He seems to
have had a particular fondness for a hard-working people
who had had the courage to defy Philip II and had used their
freedom to forge a commercially prosperous nation. In the
*Essai sur les mœurs*, after comparing the Dutch rebels to
the ancient Spartans and dwelling on the relation between
their frugal manners and their drive for independence,
he adds that The Hague eventually became 'un séjour
agréable' and that Amsterdam 'fut, par le commerce seul,
une des plus florissantes villes de la terre'.[24]

22. The reference is to *Les Scythes*, as reported by Despréaux de la
Condamine in *Soirées de Ferney ou Confidences de Voltaire, recueillies
par un ami de ce grand homme* (Paris, 1802), p. 165.
23. Writing to the marquise de Bernières in 1722 (Best. D128), he
describes the region between The Hague and Amsterdam as 'un paradis
terrestre'. See also the *Princesse de Babylone* (M. XXI, 406).
24. *Essai sur les mœurs*, ed. R. Pomeau, II, 450.

Voltaire's prolonged love-affair with England is well known. He detailed the reasons for his admiration point by point in *L'ABC* (M. XXVII, 386–387): a humane jurisprudence; a King whose power is restricted to doing good; equality of every citizen in the eyes of the law. The key to this enviable social progress is freedom: 'L'homme est né libre: le meilleur gouvernement est celui qui conserve le plus qu'il est possible à chaque mortel ce don de la nature' (M. XXVII, 388). It is no coincidence that he was attracted to Roman themes during and immediately after his stay in England. He found literary models in Shakespeare's *Julius Caesar* and Addison's *Cato*, but the general atmosphere of English society, which seemed to him to revive the great days of Greece and Rome, was the real source of inspiration.[25] Innumerable references, in the correspondence and elsewhere, show that his republican temperament had found its spiritual home.

Voltaire's relations with the authorities of his adopted republic of Geneva were not always idyllic by any means. Like the 'citoyen de Genève' himself, he had harsh words to say on occasion, and close contact brought progressive disenchantment. Yet he more than repaid the hospitality he received by a number of glowing tributes. An earlier, more theoretical assessment of Helvetic republicanism appeared in the chapter on Switzerland in the *Essai sur les mœurs*, which begins, 'De tous les pays de l'Europe, celui qui avait le plus conservé la simplicité et la pauvreté des premiers âges était la Suisse', and develops into a eulogy of the Swiss spirit of independence and equality ('le partage naturel des hommes') and of the courage displayed in defending its stronghold against all odds. Again, there is the

25. In *La Mort de Mlle Lecouvreur* (1730), he praises England in these terms:

> Quiconque a des talents à Londre est un grand homme.
> L'abondance et la liberté
> Ont, après deux mille ans, chez vous ressuscité
> L'esprit de la Grèce et de Rome (M. IX, 370).

In the *Lettres philosophiques*, he concedes that the 'horrible madness' of internal religious war was unknown to the Romans; on the other hand, civil war led to freedom in England, to despotism in Rome (M. XXII, 102–103).

comparison with ancient Sparta; again, early primitivism, which made the preservation of liberty possible, is found to be not inconsistent with the eventual development of civilized amenities: 'On est parvenu en quelques endroits à joindre la politesse d'Athènes à la simplicité de Lacédémone.'[26]

Neither Switzerland, nor Holland, nor even England could really be compared with France; Voltaire was not suggesting that their institutions were exportable. He was, however, implying, particularly in such works as the *Lettres philosophiques* and *Les Scythes*, that there was a lamentable lack of freedom, justice, and vigorous public spirit in his native country. This generally critical attitude, together with his cosmopolitanism and his supposed 'betrayal' of France by deserting the court of Louis XV for that of Frederick, has been taken by some of his compatriots, in the nineteenth century especially, as proof that he was 'unpatriotic'. The accusation makes little sense in the context of the eighteenth century and in the light of Voltaire's own definition of the term.

'Qu'est-ce que la patrie?' he asks in the *Dictionnaire philosophique*, and replies:

Ne serait-ce pas par hasard un bon champ, dont le possesseur, logé commodément dans une maison bien tenue, pourrait dire: Ce champ que je cultive, cette maison que j'ai bâtie, sont à moi; j'y vis sous la protection des lois, qu'aucun tyran ne peut enfreindre? Quand ceux qui possèdent, comme moi, des champs et des maisons, s'assemblent pour leurs intérêts communs, j'ai ma voix dans cette assemblée; je suis une partie du tout, une partie de la communauté, une partie de la souveraineté: voilà ma patrie. (M. XX, 182)

A man will be a patriot if he has a genuine stake in the country he inhabits and a say in its affairs and if the laws are obeyed. In other words, patriotism is inseparable from a

26. *Essai sur les mœurs*, ed. R. Pomeau, II, 14.

measure of democracy. It is difficult to be patriotic in a monarchy,[27] impossible under despotic rule.

Hence 'le véritable et solide amour de la patrie consiste à lui faire du bien, et à contribuer à sa liberté autant qu'il nous est possible' (M. VIII, 352). On the basis of this definition, Voltaire was certainly a most active patriot. One feels, however, as one commentator has noted, that there is an unresolved conflict between this concept of patriotism and *bienfaisance*, which is concerned with humanity in general; that is, between two facets of his sensibility.[28] The combination of self-interest and civic virtue makes for a powerful and prosperous state, which may seek to further promote its power at the expense of its neighbours. Ancient Rome and its nearest modern equivalent, imperialist England, were obvious examples. Always inclined to be at his most pessimistic on the subject of war, Voltaire could see no answer to this dilemma.

Although he detested cultural chauvinism—had he not done more than any other Frenchman to popularize Locke, Newton, Shakespeare, and Milton?—and never confused patriotism with 'l'amour aveugle de la patrie',[29] it is untrue to say that Voltaire was unpatriotic. When he could have been excused for taking refuge in indifference and the enjoyment of private freedom, he devoted his energies to an incessant propaganda attack on the forces obstructing his vision of a dynamic but humane French society. He poured scorn on 'les Welches', but was strangely upset by similar criticism from outsiders and anxiously followed the news of French military engagements.[30] Moreover, Voltaire was the

27. 'Un républicain est toujours plus attaché à sa patrie qu'un sujet à la sienne, par la raison qu'on aime mieux son bien que celui de son maître' (M. XXIII, 527).

28. Denis J. Fletcher, 'Montesquieu's Conception of Patriotism', *SV*, LVI, 544.

29. Hence his dislike of De Belloy's tragedy, *Le Siège de Calais* (1765), which owed its short-lived success to its patriotic fervour, but which was also an attack on *la philosophie* from a narrow royalist standpoint.

30. According to one British visitor in 1757 he could, on occasion, be 'as arrant a Frenchman as the most illiterate of his nation' ('Voltaire's British Visitors', ed. Sir Gavin de Beer and A. M. Rousseau, *SV*, XVIII, 239). The same year, Voltaire wrote to d'Argental (Best. 6792): 'Je ne m'intéresse à aucun événement que comme français. Je n'ay d'autre intérest et d'autre sentiment que ceux que la France m'inspire. J'ay en France mon bien et mon cœur.'

French poet who produced the most stirring and quotable verses on the subject[31] and who, in *Adélaïde du Guesclin*, referred to patriotism as a mysterious voice, like that of 'nature', which speaks directly to the heart (M. III, 93). Delisle de Sales called him 'le premier qui dans *Adélaïde, Zaïre,* et *Tancrède* ait fait parler avec succès les héros de la France'.[32]

Voltaire's most important role, however, in the development of the complex of merging trends which went to make up the 'republicanism' of the declining years of the century was undoubtedly his pioneering activity in promoting the cult of antiquity, largely, but not exclusively, through the Roman tragedies. It was certainly a feature of his work which his contemporaries, and later the men of the Revolution, found particularly striking. Jean Louis de Poilly hailed him as 'le Salluste de nos jours' (Best. 18843). *Rome sauvée* moved Condorcet to exclaim, 'L'énergie républicaine et l'âme des Romains ont passé tout entières dans le poète' (M. I, 227). Leclerc de Montmerci considered that he had brought back to the theatre

> Cette noble simplicité
> Qu'en foule au Théâtre d'Athène
> Admirait en pleurant la docte Antiquité.[33]

Voltaire became familiar with the works of the Latin moralists during his schooldays at the college of Louis le Grand and it is perhaps significant that the study of Roman history was the highlight of the Ingénu's programme of education.[34] The sympathy for Roman primitivism evident

31. e.g. 'Passion des grands cœurs, amour de la patrie' (M. VIII, 383); 'A tous les cœurs bien nés la patrie est chérie' (M. V, 526); 'Le devoir le plus saint, la loi la plus chérie, / Est d'oublier la loi pour sauver la patrie' (M. V, 253).

32. J. B. Delisle de Sales, *Essai sur la tragédie* (1772), p. 322.

33. *Voltaire, poème en vers libres* (1764), p. 23.

34. 'Les beaux siècles de la république romaine le rendirent quelque temps indifférent pour le reste de la terre. Le spectacle de Rome victorieuse et législatrice des nations occupait son âme entière. Il s'échauffait en contemplant ce peuple qui fut gouverné sept cents ans par l'enthousiasme de la liberté et de la gloire' (M. XXI, 276).

in the early *Ode sur les malheurs du temps* obviously owed a great deal to the influence of his Jesuit teachers. It was not, however, until he had experienced the exhilaration of 'English liberty' and had seen for himself the effect of Shakespeare's *Julius Caesar* and Addison's *Cato*, whose hero he described as 'un des plus beaux personnages qui soient sur aucun théâtre',[35] that he became seriously attracted to the theme of republicanism and initiated the cult of the great men of Rome which culminated in his strong intellectual and emotional attachment to Cicero.

Through Cicero he rediscovered the Stoics, whose doctrine he had at first associated with Jansenist puritanism. His mature attitude is one of profound admiration. In fact, apart from its 'insensibilité' and excessive disdain for harmless pleasure, Stoicism as a philosophy had much to commend it to Voltaire. The Stoics cultivated reason, believed in God and emphasized the need for social involvement and abnegation. Voltaire saw their philosophy as a difficult but noble ideal, superior to the egoism of the Epicureans.[36] Numerous references show that he was familiar with their writings and regarded the great figures—Marcus Aurelius, Epictetus, the Antonines, Cicero, Cato, Julian—as god-like examples of virtue.[37] The article 'Philosophie' in the *Dictionnaire philosophique* contains the following tribute: 'Quel est le citoyen parmi nous qui se priverait, comme Julien, Antonin et Marc-Aurèle, de toutes les délicatesses de notre vie molle et effeminée? qui voudrait s'imposer leur frugalité? qui marcherait comme eux à pied et tête nue à la tête des armées, exposé tantôt à l'ardeur du soleil, tantôt aux frimas? qui commanderait comme eux à toutes ses passions? Il y a parmi nous des dévots; mais où sont les sages? où sont les âmes inébranlables, justes et tolérantes?' Such a passage, it is

35. *Lettres philosophiques*, M. XXII, 155.
36. 'Si les épicuriens rendirent la nature aimable, les stoïciens la rendirent presque divine' (M. XXVI, 90).
37. 'Julien était stoïcien, de cette secte ensemble philosophique et religieuse qui produisit tant de grands hommes, et qui n'en eut jamais un méchant, secte plus divine qu'humaine, dans laquelle on voit la sévérité des brachmanes et de quelques moines, sans qu'elle en eût la superstition: la secte enfin des Caton, des Marc-Aurèle, et des Epictète' (*Examen de milord Bolingbroke*, M. XXVI, 283).

hardly necessary to add, could not have been written by a champion of luxury and opponent of primitivism.

Voltaire's attitude to the Roman historians who glorified the golden age is ambivalent. He criticized them as historians, since the purpose of history, as he saw it, is not primarily to edify but to get as close as possible to the truth. He found too much rhetoric and too little concern for fact in Livy (M. XXVII, 252) and 'plus d'utilité morale que de vérité historique' in Plutarch (M. XIV, 421). He did not condemn their message; he simply considered it out of place. Tragedy, which is, among other things, 'une école de vertu', is a different matter. The dramatic poet is not concerned with historical exactitude but with emotion, imagination, and inspiration. He has the right, even the duty, to modify history in order to move the public by presenting examples of *grandeur d'âme*. The historian's cautious approach was therefore temporarily set aside during the composition of *Rome sauvée*. The play was completed in a week after extensive readings in Plutarch, Sallust, and Cicero (Best. 3433). It is clear from this and other Roman tragedies that what Voltaire particularly admired in the Stoics, in the Romans of the Republic, and in their nearest modern equivalents was their devotion to the cause of freedom and equality and their feeling for moral greatness.

Voltaire's views on freedom require no elaboration. The necessity for free thought and expression, the dangers of arbitrary despotism, the right of every citizen to conduct his life as he sees fit, subject only to reasonable laws, are recurring themes. Along with civilization, freedom is one of the two great underlying motifs of the *Essai sur les mœurs*. Voltaire traces their slow and fragile development throughout modern history, their sudden flowering and equally sudden disappearance. But if it is necessary to choose between them, he makes it clear where he stands: '[Il vaut] encore mieux être libre que civilisé.'[38]

He was almost as assiduous in promoting the closely related idea of equality, by which, of course, he did not mean that all men are the same or that differences in incomes

38. *Essai sur les mœurs*, ed. R. Pomeau, I, 809.

and conditions should be abolished. 'Chaque homme, dans le fond de son cœur, a droit de se croire entièrement égal aux autres hommes' (M. XVIII, 477), but since men differ widely in physical and intellectual endowment and since many are by nature ambitious and domineering and even more are lazy and servile, absolute equality is an absurd pipe-dream. He meant something more attainable: the same justice for all classes and individuals. 'Il n'y a pas de pays dignes d'être habités', he wrote in the *Essai sur les mœurs*, 'que ceux où toutes les conditions sont également soumises aux lois.'[39] With this restriction, Voltaire was one of the most effective egalitarian propagandists of the age. Some of his statements have a decidedly Rousseauistic flavour, as for example the following: 'Les hommes naissant tous égaux, la violence et l'habileté ont fait les premiers maîtres; les lois ont fait les derniers' (M. XX, 23). The very popular *Nanine* is full of references to the injustice of social distinctions not based on merit. The tragedies contain verses which could be, and indeed were deliberately intended to be, quoted as slogans, such as this couplet from *Les Scythes*:

Nous sommes tous égaux sur ces rives si chères,
Sans rois et sans sujets, tous libres et tous frères,[40]

or this from *Mahomet*:

Les mortels sont égaux: ce n'est pas la naissance,
C'est la seule vertu qui fait leur différence. (M. IV, 114)

What Voltaire deplored most about his own age was its appalling heartlessness and its mediocrity, which was due, he felt, to a general unwillingness to take important matters seriously enough. It is curious that he should be so often accused of flippancy and superficiality when he was, in fact,

39. *Essai sur les mœurs*, ed. R. Pomeau, II, 21. See also *Poème sur la loi naturelle* (M. IX, 459):
La loi dans tout Etat doit être universelle:
Les mortels, quels qu'ils soient, sont égaux devant elle.
40. M. VI, 278. The first Paris edition (1767) contains the following instruction: 'Détachez ce morceau, et enflez un peu la voix'.

incensed by precisely this attitude on the part of his contemporaries, and particularly of his compatriots. He constantly
criticized what he saw as a common tendency of Frenchmen
to be fascinated by trifling pleasures while remaining
callously indifferent to suffering and deaf to the call of
greatness. His countrymen are depicted in the *Princesse de
Babylone* as 'des enfants à qui l'on prodigue les jouets pour
les empêcher de crier. Si on leur parlait des horreurs qui
avaient, deux siècles auparavant, désolé leur patrie, et des
temps épouvantables où la moitié de la nation avait massacré
l'autre pour des sophismes, ils disaient qu'en effet cela
n'était pas bien, et puis ils se mettaient à rire et à chanter
des vaudevilles.'[41] Elsewhere they are described, even less
flatteringly, as 'Romains du Bas Empire', 'Arlequins
anthropophages', 'singes devenus tigres'. France is 'un pays
fait pour les jeunes femmes et les voluptueux ... le pays
des madrigaux et des pompons' (Best. D1253), 'une nation
aussi barbare que frivole' (Best. 9596), a country where
public spirit is unknown.[42]

Disparaging comments on contemporary France are frequently accompanied by nostalgic references to the great
days of Rome. One of the few critics to accord full importance
to this facet of Voltaire's thinking has pointed out that in
spite of his intellectual disapproval of Louis XIV's policy
of prestige and conquest, Voltaire could not help admiring
the feeling for national excellence which characterized the
reign of the Sun King and comparing it with the petty
preoccupations of the succeeding age. 'Voltaire', concludes
Professor Adam, 'n'est pas tout à fait de son siècle.'[43] He was
indeed in some respects the forerunner of a more heroic
epoch.

All these related themes—patriotism, freedom, equality,
and republican heroism—are given particularly forceful
expression in the theatre. Not being easily related to the

41. *Princesse de Babylone*, M. XXI, 418.
42. Best. D1722. See M. VIII, 472–473; X, 344–349; XX, 535; Best.
5838, 9137, 11179, 13191, 14050, 14824, 14885, 15302, 15780, 16179,
17943, 18227, 18738, 18858.
43. A. Adam, 'Voltaire et les lumières', *Europe*, 361–362 (mai-juin
1959), p. 17.

stereotype of Voltaire, the Roman tragedies have been something of an embarrassment to critics, who have tended to go to one of two extremes, interpreting them either as manifestations of political republicanism, hence difficult to reconcile with their author's known monarchist views and his supposed preference for enlightened despotism, or as exercises in rhetoric devoid of any real political significance. It is true that Voltaire was not writing dramatized pamphlets; he was attempting to produce successful plays aimed at a specific audience and limited by the conventions of a specific genre, whose subject-matter was normally drawn from antiquity. Characters, if they are to be convincing, must express feelings and ideas appropriate to their historic role and particular dramatic situation. Nevertheless, it is not impossible to assess the probable effect of a play, particularly a play by Voltaire, and the prefaces, commentaries, and remarks in the correspondence leave little doubt as to his intentions.

The precise influence of the Roman tragedies over a long period is another matter. It is certain that it was considerable. In H. N. Brailsford's words, 'A republican sentiment declaimed by an actor in a toga moved all Paris more profoundly than did any oration by Danton in later days.'[44] However unfashionable his tragedies may be today, Voltaire's enormous prestige in his own century was based primarily on his achievement in the theatre. *Œdipe*, not the *Lettres philosophiques*, first brought him to the attention of a wide public and he was famous as the author of *Zaïre* and *Mérope* long before *Candide* and the *Dictionnaire philosophique* were written. His remarkable success in using the framework of classical tragedy as a vehicle for the discussion of a 'republicanism' which was to become part of the revolutionary mystique helps to explain the rather surprising fact that it was not the *drame bourgeois* which was the real opposition theatre at the close of the century but a genre which was aristocratic by definition and which had

44. *Voltaire* (London, 1935), p. 23. See also L. Fontaine, *Le Théâtre et la philosophie au dix-huitième siècle* (Paris, 1878), p. 7.

earlier shown signs of decay.[45] It would be logical to conclude, even if contemporary evidence did not confirm it, that if a writer is to be singled out as the one who led French intellectuals back to ancient Rome as a source of republican inspiration, that writer is Voltaire.

*Brutus*, first performed in 1730 and revived with success in 1742,[46] is not a tract in favour of political republicanism, but rather a debate which reflects some of Voltaire's doubts and reservations. Liberty is possible in a monarchy (M. II, 331), which is 'affreux sous un tyran, divin sous un bon roi' (M. II, 360). Revolution always involves terrible risks and may simply mean changing one master for a 'hundred tyrants'. On the other hand, 'Qui naquit dans la pourpre en est rarement digne' (M. II, 347). The king who breaks his oath by disregarding established law has forfeited his right to govern (M. II, 330).

But the play, both in its early and somewhat different later versions, is thoroughly republican in a more general sense. What interests Voltaire is the moral effect of political liberty. Significantly, it is Arons, the eloquent defender of the monarchic system, who makes the comparison between a courtier and a free man:

> Crois-moi, la liberté, que tout mortel adore,
> Que je veux leur ôter, mais que j'admire encore,
> Donne à l'homme un courage, inspire une grandeur,
> Qu'il n'eût jamais trouvés dans le fond de son cœur.
> Sous le joug des Tarquins, la cour et l'esclavage
> Amollissaient leurs mœurs, énervaient leur courage.
>
> (M. II, 334)

Even Titus, who betrays the Republic in a moment of weakness, acknowledges that his greatest passion is freedom (M. II, 337, 343). *Brutus* is animated by a patriotic fervour more

45. G. V. Plekhanov discusses this point in *Art and Social Life* (London, 1953), pp. 149–150. The social contradictions of France, he argues, could not be resolved by preaching morality. The enemies of the old order felt the need for an appeal to heroism and civic virtues and these could best be sought in antiquity.
46. See Best. D2625.

appropriate to the early revolutionary period than to the age of Louis XV. It is full of inspiring and easily detachable maxims: 'l'homme est libre au moment qu'il veut l'être' (M. II, 341); 'Dieux! donnez-nous la mort plutôt que l'esclavage' (M. II, 371); or the final line: 'Rome est libre: il suffit . . . Rendons grâces aux dieux.' And dominating the action is the towering central figure of Junius Brutus, legendary example of Roman firmness, who places public welfare even before parental feeling.

Of *La Mort de César*, outlined in England and published in 1736, the author himself remarked, 'Il est aisé d'apercevoir . . . le génie et le caractère des écrivains anglais, aussi bien que celui du peuple romain. On y voit cet amour dominant de la liberté, et ces hardiesses que les auteurs français ont rarement' (M. III, 310). Like *Brutus*, it is not an attack on royalism but an analysis of various attitudes to political power and an endorsement of republican philosophy.

Caesar is an ambitious man, a despot in the making, who plays on the fear that freedom will lead to anarchy in order to further his own designs. Yet he is not unsympathetic: he believes in a policy of clemency and is opposed to the brutal misuse of power. As in *Brutus*, it is the proponent of autocracy who pays homage, in spite of himself, to republican ideals:

> Soit qu'étant né Romain, la voix de ma patrie
> Me parle malgré moi contre ma tyrannie,
> Et que la liberté que je viens d'opprimer,
> Plus forte encore que moi, me condamne à l'aimer.
> Te dirai-je encor plus? Si Brutus me doit l'être,
> S'il est le fils de César, il doit haïr un maître.
> J'ai pensé comme lui dès mes plus jeunes ans;
> J'ai détesté Sylla, j'ai haï les tyrans.
> J'eusse été citoyen si l'orgueilleux Pompée
> N'eût voulu m'opprimer sous sa gloire usurpée.
> Né fier, ambitieux, mais né pour les vertus,
> Si je n'étais César, j'aurais été Brutus. (M. III, 324)

Brutus, like Junius Brutus, is portrayed as a fiery idealist.

but unlike his namesake he allows his sensibility to encroach on his stern principles, to the extent of shedding 'Stoic tears'. When virtue becomes 'féroce', he hesitates. To oppose tyranny is one thing; the cold-blooded murder of a man one knows, loves, and respects is another. Voltaire's humanity would never allow him to condone regicide, much less parricide.

The two other principals, Antony and Cassius, are extremists with whom Voltaire obviously has very little sympathy: Antony, the cynical absolutist, whose simple solution to the problem of government is naked tyranny based on fear; Cassius, the demagogue and heartless conspirator. It is notable that none of the characters has any illusions about the behaviour of the populace; the play is concerned with republican rather than democratic ideals.

In the case of *Rome sauvée*,[47] Voltaire's purpose is quite clear. The subject, 'peu fait pour les mœurs, pour les usages, la manière de penser, et le théâtre de Paris', is itself a rebuke to his compatriots. It is intended as an appeal to youth, an attempt 'de faire connaître Cicéron aux jeunes personnes qui fréquentent les spectacles' (M. V, 205).

In the play, Catilina, whose undeniable personal qualities have been corrupted by ambition, egoism, and an avid desire for novelty and luxury—one of the 'vices of the age'—is the leader of a group of factionists who refer to patriotism contemptuously as 'le fanatisme usé des siècles antiques'. Against them are ranged the two heroic figures, Cicero and Cato. Cicero in particular, the great man who makes no apology for pursuing fame based solidly on merit and love of virtue, becomes the author's spokesman and alter ego. He calls for a return to the austerity, abnegation, and noble devotion to freedom of the 'siècles héroïques' in a couplet which heralds the beginning of a new republican era:

O grandeur des Romains! ô majesté flétrie!
Sur le bord du tombeau, réveille-toi, patrie! (M. V, 257)

47. Performed privately in 1750; first performed at the Comédie Française in 1752.

*Le Triumvirat* (1764), a gloomy sequel to *Rome sauvée*, might well have been called *Rome perdue*. It describes what happens when mediocre, cynical men, motivated solely by ambition—Octavius, Antony, Lepidus—replace the Ciceros and Catos. Provided with lengthy historical notes, often more interesting than the play itself, *Le Triumvirat* documents the beginning of the decline of the great days of Rome as the aftermath of civil war and the ignoble schemes of petty tyrants.

*Les Scythes* (1767), while not a Roman play, was also a vehicle for Voltaire's republicanism. Among the many themes of this strange allegorical 'tragedy' is a comparison between the Scythians, who resemble the Swiss, and the Persians, representing the French. Despite reservations and the explicit statement that 'Scythian' institutions are not transferable, Voltaire leaves the spectator in no doubt as to his own feelings of admiration for their liberty, equality, and fraternity, especially when the author himself makes his entry in the role of Sozame and pays this tribute to Swiss hospitality:

> Bientôt dans vos forêts, grâce au ciel parvenu,
> J'y trouvai le repos qui m'était inconnu.
> J'y voudrais être né. Tout mon regret, mon frère,
> Est d'avoir parcouru ma fatale carrière
> Dans les camps, dans les cours, à la suite des rois,
> Loin des seuls citoyens gouvernés par les lois. . . .
>
> (M. VI, 284)

Voltaire never for a moment hinted, in his plays or elsewhere, that the French monarchy should be abolished. What he did say, over and over again, with all the poetic force at his command, was that the only life worth living is that of a free man who is equal to his fellow-citizens in the eyes of the law, and that the best way to transcend the petty mediocrity of modern life is to recapture something of the spirit symbolized by the heroes of republican Rome. Inevitably, his distinction between political and moral republicanism was sometimes ignored. His critics and enemies did not hesitate to accuse him of antimonarchist tendencies.[48]

*Brutus* was too far ahead of its time to provoke much immediate public reaction, but it undoubtedly helped prepare the way and set the tone for later developments. 'Il me semble', wrote Shuvalov in his *Lettre à Voltaire*, 'que jamais l'esprit républicain des Romains, leur grandeur d'âme, leur sublime patriotisme, leur caractère décidé, n'ont été peints avec plus de vérité, de force et de noblesse, que dans les Tragédies de *Brutus* et de *Rome sauvée*.'[49] M. J. Chénier's blunt affirmation may well be close to the truth:

> Tes tragiques pinceaux des demi-dieux du Tibre
> Ont su ressusciter les antiques vertus;
> Et la France a conçu le besoin d'être libre
> Aux fiers accens des deux Brutus.[50]

One reliable guide to the extent of this influence is the great popularity of Voltaire's plays during the Revolution. We have the word of Napoleon, who detested Voltaire,[51] that the author of *Brutus* dethroned Racine and Corneille.[52] Press listings show that there were no fewer than 984 performances of nineteen plays by Voltaire between 1789 and 1799, with *Brutus* as the most popular and the years 1791 to 1793 as the period of greatest favour.[53] At the opening night of *Brutus* on 17 November 1790, the line 'Dieux! donnez-nous la mort plutôt que l'esclavage' was wildly applauded and had to be repeated several times.[54]

48. e.g. Nonnotte, *Les Erreurs de Voltaire* (Lyon, 1770), II, 184: 'Ne semble-t-il pas que M. *de Voltaire* ait voulu inspirer de l'horreur pour la Monarchie?'; letter to the *Journal de Trévoux*, May 1731 (Best. D410).

49. A. P. Shuvalov, *Lettre à Voltaire* (Amsterdam, 1779), p. 15.

50. *Hymne sur la translation des cendres de Voltaire au Panthéon français*, le 2 juillet, 1791 (*Œuvres* [Paris, 1824], III, 348).

51. Napoleon's hostility is natural enough. He would hardly have appreciated Voltaire's views on such subjects as war and freedom or the numerous portraits of cynical, ambitious, and insensitive tyrants in the tragedies. Cf. Musset's remark: 'Napoléon ne pouvait pas tenir compte à l'auteur d'*Œdipe* des efforts admirables qu'il a entrepris pour faire goûter à une société dépravée et blasée les fruits sauvages de l'antiquité' (*Œuvres complètes en prose*, ed. M. Allem [Paris, 1960], p. 914).

52. Quoted by Moland, I, xlii.

53. Phyllis S. Robinove, 'Voltaire's Theater on the Parisian Stage, 1789–1799', *FR*, 32 (May 1959), pp. 534–538.

54. Robinove, p. 536.

After the final curtain, the actors were obliged to bring out a bust of Voltaire and keep it on the stage during the entire performance of the second play.[55]

A week before this event, a play was performed containing the following passage in the preface: 'Voltaire, si tu vivais, quel ascendant ne donnerais-tu pas à la scène française, aujourd'hui qu'elle est dégagée de son ancien esclavage! ... Jeunes auteurs, à qui ce grand homme a légué ses pinceaux, c'est à vous de consacrer les principes si longtemps oubliés des mœurs, de civisme et de la liberté sur tous nos théâtres.'[56] The advice was followed, not only by playwrights, but by journalists and politicians. One has only to glance through a few samples of the impassioned oratory produced by the Revolution to rediscover the accents, attitudes, and vocabulary of Voltaire's noble Romans, their Stoic pride, their rallying cries and also their sensibility, which sometimes masked a rigidity and cruelty which Voltaire would have been the first to condemn.

It is appropriate that when the remains of the author of *Rome sauvée* were transferred to Paris at the height of the Revolution, David should have designed classical costumes and a 'char antique' for the occasion.

55. J. Hérissay, *Le Monde des théâtres pendant la Révolution (1789–1800) d'après des documents inédits* (Paris, 1922), p. 86.
56. Quoted by Henri Welschinger, *Le Théâtre de la Révolution 1789–1799*, Slatkine Reprints (Geneva, 1968), pp. 369–370.

CHAPTER 4

# The Critic

It is often said that Voltaire was a radical philosopher and an
ultraconservative in matters of taste. In fact, his esthetic
principles are closely related to his moral, political, and
religious views. His conception of esthetic judgment is not
unlike his theory of moral law. The highest taste is an
instinct, but one which must be strengthened and cultivated
by education, experience, and exposure to great examples.
Essentially the same everywhere and at all times, it permits
us to evaluate and compare; yet local customs differ widely
and must be taken into account. Rules imposed upon the
arts are similar to 'positive laws' governing nations and
provinces: it is impossible to do without them, but many are
absurd, arbitrary restrictions on freedom. Dogmatic critics
'sont des tyrans qui ont voulu asservir à leurs lois une nation
libre, dont ils ne connaissent point le caractère' (M. VIII,
305). England is the liberating model in poetry as in politics:
'Quelle profusion d'images chez les Anglais et chez les
Italiens! Mais ils sont libres, ils font de leur langue tout ce
qu'ils veulent. O liberté, il n'y a point de biens sans toy
en aucun sens' (Best. D1047). In art, as in other contexts,
Voltaire castigated the contemporary vices of pettiness,
pretentious mediocrity, and affectation, admiring Vauvenargues' 'grand goust, dans un siècle où tout me semble un
peu petit, et où le faux bel esprit s'est mis à la place du
génie' (Best. 2845). He expressed the same distaste for the
narrow, rigid mind preoccupied with dogma and advocated
the same tolerance in culture as in religion and politics.
He was consistent also in according primacy to feeling over
reason, however essential the role of the latter. And, as
usual, for all his caution, he was in many ways far in advance
of his age, a revolutionary in effect, if not always in intention.

Voltaire's basic esthetic doctrine was outlined in the *Essai sur la poésie épique* (1733), preceded in 1727 by the more openly relativistic and less typical English version of the same work. His ideas were not completely original, since several of his major theses had already been expounded by Saint-Evremond and Dubos. Nevertheless, the *Essai* introduced to a wide French public a conception of literature which struck at the foundations of conventional classicism and which was not to be fully developed until the beginning of the nineteenth century.

The *Essai* opens with an uncompromising attack on petty rules, the majority of which are dismissed as 'useless and false'. Excessive deference to them has led to a sterile and static view of art. The final criterion for judging a work is not some preconceived and artificial yardstick, but feeling: 'Pour juger des poëtes, il faut savoir sentir, il faut être né avec quelques étincelles du feu qui anime ceux qu'on veut connaître' (M. VIII, 319). Voltaire goes on to argue for greater tolerance in matters of taste and for a more enlightened understanding of the particular historical and social conditions which to some extent determine the form of any work of art. Speaking of the epic, he says that although certain essential and universal requirements must be met, 'Tout ce qui dépend de la tyrannie de la coutume et de cet instinct qu'on nomme goût, voilà sur quoi il y a mille opinions, et point de règles générales' (M. VIII, 309). It is thus useless, for example, to blame Homer for depicting the men and gods of his day.

Voltaire does not condemn all rules or affirm that taste is purely relative. He takes a moderate stand by establishing a distinction between universal taste, which makes judgments possible, and local taste, concerned with 'details'. One may admire Homer and Milton as writers of towering genius, while at the same time condemning the 'bizarre' and 'barbarous' elements in their poems which prevent them from measuring up to universal standards.

The difficulty, of course, lies in defining the latter. To Voltaire, they were as self-evident as the tenets of natural law. To modern readers of his critical works they look suspiciously like the principles of neoclassicism. In spite of this reintroduction of classical reason by the back door, the implications of the *Essai* are sufficiently far-reaching to justify calling it a landmark in the development of the esthetics of eighteenth-century sensibility. Sentiment is stated to be primary; rules, however indispensable, are secondary. There are no recipes for the production of master-pieces and the rationalist approach to art is dismissed as totally inadequate.[1] Moreover, Voltaire goes some way to-wards the romantic conception of genius. Milton is described as the supreme example of the 'bizarre'; yet he frequently reaches sublime heights and 'does as much honour to England as the great Newton', surely the highest praise the author could bestow. By calling attention to the extrava-gances of Milton, and later of Shakespeare, Voltaire undoubt-edly helped to foster the tendency to identify genius with the strange and monstrous. Finally, however hedged in with reservations, his moderate relativism was a significant step in the direction of the literary cosmopolitanism of Mme de Staël. Readers, especially of the English version, were left in no doubt that the French had much to learn from the barbarians to the North.

This basic statement was modified and elaborated and occasionally contradicted; there were frequent changes of emphasis, usually due to circumstances of the moment or to polemical necessity; but on the major principle of the over-riding importance of sentiment, Voltaire never varied. Intellectualism, he was convinced, inevitably leads to an arid and sterile form of art. The writer who draws his inspiration exclusively from the mind will quickly find him-self banished from the Temple of Taste:

Malheur à qui toujours raisonne,
Et qui ne s'attendrit jamais!
Dieu du Goût, ton divin palais
Est un séjour qu'il abandonne. (M. VIII, 580)

---

1. 'Ceux qui ne peuvent pardonner des fautes d'Homère en faveur de ses beautés sont la plupart des esprits trop philosophiques, qui ont étouffé en eux-mêmes tout sentiment' (M. VIII, 319).

Critics who take an intellectual approach are not much better. Preferring to toy with theories rather than trust their feelings, they isolate themselves from the general public and are likely to miss the total impact of an individual work: 'Ceux qui ont trop scrupuleusement recherché les principes d'un art, se tirent quelquefois tellement du vulgaire, qu'ils ne peuvent plus juger de l'effet qu'un ouvrage fera sur le commun des hommes, car à force de méditation on ne sent plus, et on ne peut plus par conséquent deviner le sentiment des autres.'[2]

This preference for sentiment over reason is evident in Voltaire's attitude to the major poets of French classicism. He praised the *Art poétique* for the soundness of its technical advice and placed Boileau alongside Racine as one of the great masters of the French language. Yet his final verdict is not very different from that of the romantics. Lacking the one essential attribute of the true poet—sensibility—Boileau is judged to be 'correct' but 'cold'.[3] According to Voltaire, he was not a truly creative artist but an imitator who wrote polished but pedestrian verse and was incapable of attaining the sublime. A poem addressed to Helvétius in 1740 makes the point:

> Le ciel vous anima de ces flammes secrettes,
> Que ne sentit jamais Boylau l'imitateur
> Dans ses tristes beautez si froidement parfaites.
> Il est des baux esprits; il est plus d'un rimeur;
> Il est rarement des poètes.
> Le vrai poète est créateur.
> Peut être je le fus, et maintenant vous l'êtes.
>
> (Best. D2147)

2. *Voltaire's Notebooks*, ed. Theodore Besterman. *The Complete Works of Voltaire*, vol. 81, p. 348.

3. 'Boileau, correct auteur de quelques bons écrits' (M. X, 397). Coldness was for Voltaire the one unforgivable sin, far more serious than any infringement of the rules: 'L'abbé d'Aubignac écrivit contre l'*Œdipe* de Corneille; il y reprend plusieurs fautes avec lesquelles une pièce pourrait être admirable: fautes de bienséance, duplicité d'action, violation des règles. D'Aubignac n'en savait pas assez pour voir que la principale faute est d'être froid dans un sujet intéressant, et rampant dans un sujet sublime' (M. XXXII, 158).

Voltaire never forgave Boileau for despising Quinault, whom he tended to overrate by contrast, seeing in him the symbol of the poet whose appeal is exclusively to sensibility.

His frequently expressed preference for Racine over Corneille was based on the same premise that the true domain of poetry, especially dramatic poetry, is the heart and not the mind. The reason given in *Le Siècle de Louis XIV* for the former's superiority is that he is 'toujours élégant, toujours correct, toujours vrai, qu'il parle au cœur, et que l'autre manque trop souvent à tous ces devoirs' (M. XIV, 548). Even Racine is somewhat too cold for Voltaire's taste. If there is one thing, he says, that is open to criticism in his treatment of love in tragedy, 'c'est de s'être quelque-fois contenté de l'élégance, de n'avoir que touché le cœur, quand il pouvait le déchirer' (M. XXXII, 297). Voltaire idolized Racine as the very model of poetic excellence; there is no question whatever about the sincerity of his admiration. And yet, beneath the superlatives, one detects a certain reserve, as though Racine represented an immaculate but distant deity rather than a familiar spirit.[4] Voltaire was more interested in the overt manifestations of sensibility and in passions that 'tear the heart' than in subtle analysis of feeling.

One form of intellectualism to which he was strongly opposed was the 'esprit géométrique' of the early eighteenth century. A group of writers, of whom Lamotte was the most prominent, influenced by Cartesianism and by the current vogue for science, demanded that the same criteria of truth, clarity, and reason be applied to art as to philosophy. Voltaire saw this as an example of misplaced rationalism, constituting a menace to art in general and to poetry in particular, and sounded the alarm. In his view, the 'géomètres', by confus-ing the truth of philosophy with the truth of art, and poetry

---

4. Raymond Naves makes this observation: 'Les vrais textes poétiques de Racine, Voltaire les connaît bien, mais il ne les cite que dans des morceaux composés et non dans ses lettres; Racine paraît donc être plutôt son champion que son ami; c'est que probablement cette psycho-logie ne répondait pas à la sienne et ne lui offrait ni la morale aimable ni la sensibilité naturellement tendre qu'il trouvait chez Virgile et chez Horace' (*Le Goût de Voltaire* [Paris, 1938], p. 171).

with rhymed prose, were hastening the decadence already evident in the arts since the glories of the age of Louis XIV. However sympathetic to the rapid spread of enlightenment, he was not prepared to countenance its invasion of literature at the expense of feeling. 'Les vers ne sont guère à la mode à Paris', he wrote to Cideville in 1735. 'Tout le monde commence à faire le géomètre et le phisicien. On se mêle de raisoner. Le sentiment, l'imagination et les grâces sont bannis. Un homme qui auroit vécu sous Louis 14 et qui reviendroit au monde ne reconoîtroit plus les français. Il croiroit que les Allemans ont conquis ce pays cy. Les belles lettres périssent à vue d'œil. Ce n'est pas que je sois fâché que la philosofie soit cultivée, mais je ne voudrois pas qu'elle devint un tiran qui exclût tout le reste' (Best. D863).

Even less to his liking was the high value placed on 'wit'. Despite his latter-day reputation, Voltaire was no admirer of wit, except in its proper place, namely in the polite conversation of the salons or in the minor genres. He detested affectation and insincerity in any form of literature. Hence his severe criticism of Fontenelle's 'bergeries'. 'Je veux que le cœur parle', he wrote, referring to the latter, 'ou que l'auteur se taise' (M. X, 378).

Voltaire, as the author of a recent study of his literary criticism has stated, 'remained immovably opposed to the eighteenth century trend to a more consciously intellectualized literature'.[5] In this respect, he was in basic agreement with another pioneer in the field of esthetics, the abbé Jean Baptiste Dubos, whose *Réflexions critiques sur la poésie et sur la peinture*, published in 1719, he described as the most useful work ever written in any nation on these matters (M. XIV, 66). This book, intended as a defence of the values of poetry against the onslaught of the 'géomètres', marked a radical change in critical theory and may be said to have provided the theoretical justification for the literature of sensibility.

Dubos' views, like those of Voltaire, are linked to a general theory of man. Following Locke and the sensationalists,

5. David Williams, *Voltaire: Literary Critic, SV*, XLVIII (Geneva, 1966), p. 97.

he accords primacy to feeling rather than reason. Passion
and feeling are forces making for good as well as evil.
Sensibility, in fact, is the foundation of society. We are born
*sensibles*, he argues, 'afin que ceux qui ont besoin de notre
indulgence ou de notre secours pussent nous ébranler avec
facilité'.[6] Thus for Dubos, as for Voltaire, *bienfaisance* is the
essential instinct which makes social life possible.

Dubos' originality lies in his attempt to transfer this
philosophy of feeling to the realm of literature and art,
identifying the latter with pathos and strong emotions. Art,
for Dubos, is fundamentally an escape from boredom. In
order to make life bearable, we instinctively seek whatever is
susceptible of exciting passion, and the function of art is
to convey the excitement while divesting it of the pain
and risk inevitably associated with genuine passion. Falling
into the same error as later exponents of sensibility, including
Voltaire, Dubos concludes that the most powerful passions
are the most artistic. Thus the theatre, and in particular
tragedy, is the highest form of literature, since it affects our
senses most acutely and portrays the most violent emotions.
He seems to see tragedy as something akin to melodrama:
a succession of tableaux 'qui nous conduisent, comme par
degrés, à cette émotion extrême, qui fait couler nos larmes'.[7]

Since art gives pleasure through emotion, the only reliable
judge is feeling; reason has the secondary function of telling
us why a given work repels or attracts. This spontaneous
judgment is a kind of extra sense, a nonconscious process
quite independent of any preconceived rules. It is similar
to, although not identical with, the Voltairean conception
of taste. Like Voltaire, Dubos tends to be rather more
conservative in practice than his theory would suggest.
While maintaining that the final verdict of the public is
infallible, since it is founded on feeling, he reduces the
public to an élite because of the need for discerning comparison which can only come from long experience.

The same might be said of his relativism, which is more

6. Jean Baptiste Dubos, *Réflexions critiques sur la poésie et sur la
peinture*, 7e éd. (Paris, 1770), I, 40.
7. *Réflexions*, I, 424.

impressive in theory than in application. He does, however, insist on the importance of environmental and historical factors, thus taking the first decisive step away from the abstract classical concept of universal man. Moreover, he anticipates Voltaire by noting that there is much in English literature that is estimable and that English tragedy, with its greater emphasis on spectacle and action, compares favourably in some respects with the French classical theatre.

That Voltaire was an admirer of Dubos' ideas is hardly surprising.[8] As David Williams has pointed out, 'It was . . . Dubos's emphasis on the "sentimental" nature of aesthetic appreciation, and his consequent liberation of criticism from the artificial criteria of the seventeenth century, that appealed most of all to Voltaire.'[9] Dubos must be given full credit for blazing the trail. Yet one might plausibly argue that Voltaire's contribution to the development of an esthetics of sensibility was ultimately much more important. Paradoxically, Dubos himself was far from being a typical *homme sensible*. Voltaire was not only a theorist of sensibility, he was a living example. Moreover, as he complained, with some exaggeration, Dubos was no stylist; his own critical commentaries were much more readable and influential. Finally, Voltaire was a creative artist as well as a critic and one concrete artistic success, as Dubos himself would have been logically forced to admit, is worth more than volumes of abstract reasoning on esthetics.

Why then does Voltaire have the reputation of being an ultraconservative critic and a rather narrow purist? The answer possibly lies in a misunderstanding of his admittedly complex conception of taste. Notwithstanding isolated pronouncements made in the heat of controversy, his theory is consistent. The man of good taste is, first and foremost, *un homme sensible*, one of the outstanding examples being Vauvenargues. Taste is a spontaneous feeling, an immediate reaction, not a product of reflection and reason (M. XIX, 270).

8. According to Alfred Lombard, *L'Abbé Dubos, un initiateur de la pensée moderne (1670–1742)* (Paris, 1913), p. 332, 'Voltaire est en somme, de tous les grands écrivains de son siècle, celui qui a le mieux rendu justice à Du Bos.'

9. *Voltaire: Literary Critic*, p. 151.

Nor is it the exclusive property of one particularly favoured nation or epoch. It has nothing to do with global judgments based on some critical formula, however sensible and carefully thought out; great art is too much like life to be confined within neat, static boundaries.

Voltaire therefore carefully distinguishes taste from the application of rules. Not that he felt that rules should be rejected or ignored. Used with discretion, certain well-established principles of poetic art can provide a useful guide. But they are essentially negative: at best, they forestall errors in technique. The sublime artist obeys higher rules which are beyond the reach of pedestrian reason and common sense.

Properly speaking, beauty is relative, yet there must be a distinction between good and bad taste; otherwise there would be no difference in value between a popular song and the *Aeneid*. While maintaining that the public must be the ultimate judge of all art, Voltaire, like Dubos, restricts the public to those capable of making valid comparisons, in other words to an élite with the advantage of a good education and long exposure to varied examples of artistic excellence. Mob rule appealed to him even less in esthetics than in politics.

'Le grand goût' is concerned with what is essential in the production of a masterpiece, that is with form rather than content: 'Il ne faut pas disputer des goûts, c'est à dire il faut permettre d'être plus touché de la passion de Phèdre que de la situation de Joas, d'aimer mieux être ému par la terreur que par la pitié, de préférer un sujet romain à un grec. Mais quand il s'agit de savoir si un sujet est bien traitté, bien écrit, etc. c'est alors qu'il ne peut y avoir qu'un goust qui soit bon.'[10] This he defines as 'le sentiment prompt d'une beauté parmi des défauts et d'un défaut parmi des beautés' (M. XIX, 278). Hence he could appreciate Shakespeare under the first heading and criticize Corneille under the second. If he tended rather to dwell on the faults of the writers he admired, as for example in the *Commentaires sur*

10. *Notebooks*, ed. Theodore Besterman. *The Complete Works of Voltaire*, vol. 82, p. 456.

*Corneille*, this is not due to author's jealousy or timid purism—compared with the majority of his contemporaries, Voltaire is singularly free of these vices—but rather to a lofty conception of the critic's responsibilities, which included education of the public taste and providing guidance for the new generation of writers, and to his realistic view that even the greatest masterpieces are necessarily flawed and are much more likely, by the very fact that they are master-pieces, to lead young authors astray than are second-rate works.

Voltaire thus arrives, not at a rejection of relativism and impressionism, but at a compromise. Taste is basically relative but necessarily governed by certain universal prin-ciples; it should be comprehensive and tolerant, yet selective and exacting; it is spontaneous, yet it reflects social conditions and must be perfected by training.

When all allowances have been made for the conservative aspect of his esthetic ideas, Voltaire remains one of the most important innovators of the eighteenth century. The *Essay on Epic Poetry* is revolutionary in its implications. It is astonishing to find, at this date, a French author, and a passionate admirer of the age of Louis XIV, establishing by examples that 'there is such a Thing as a National Taste' and expressing such relativistic sentiments as the following: 'But it is not with the Inventions of Art, as with the Works of Nature. The same Fancy which hath invented Poetry, changes every Day all its Productions, because it is liable itself to eternal Vicissitudes. The Poetry and Musick of the Persians, differ as much from ours, as their Language. Even a Nation differs from itself, in less than a Century. There are not more Revolutions in Governments, than in Arts. They are shifting, and gliding away from our Pursuit, when we endeavour to fix them by our Rules and Defini-tions.'[11]

It would be unjust to conclude that because he later found himself obliged to defend the threatened values of French tradition his early views can be dismissed as simply a

11. Florence D. White, *Voltaire's Essay on Epic Poetry, a Study and an Edition* (New York, 1915), p. 82.

means of promoting his epic poem in England. 'J'aime passionnément', he once wrote, 'à faire valoir dans ma patrie les chefs-d'œuvre des étrangers' (Best. D1608). Judging by his success, one can hardly question the sincerity of this statement. His record as a pioneer of literary cosmopolitanism is a remarkable one, especially if one takes into account the formidable barriers of prejudice which still existed in the early eighteenth century. Voltaire's aim was to tear them down without at the same time destroying 'le grand goût', an extremely delicate operation involving a combination of bold attacks with numerous tactical retreats.

He continued to maintain that a work of art must be considered in relation to its epoch, its environment and the intentions of its author. But some epochs and some intentions are obviously more important than others and even genius can only partly transcend the disadvantages of an unfavourable environment. He saw Homer, the Greek writers of tragedy, Milton, Shakespeare, even Corneille, as great pioneers living in relatively uncivilized periods, whose work was bound to be grossly imperfect. 'Leurs fautes', he says of the Greeks, 'sont sur le compte de leur siècle, leurs beautés n'appartiennent qu'à eux' (M. II, 27). We should therefore admire the beauties of these works and acknowledge the genius of their authors, but the connoisseur must judge them in the last resort by the exacting standards of the highest taste. Voltaire's shortcomings as a critic are not the result of his basic assumptions, which are defensible, but of his inability to appreciate fully certain ages and certain authors; which amounts to saying that he was human and therefore to a great extent the prisoner, like everyone else, of his own environment.

Champion of 'le grand goût' at a time when the hegemony of French culture was undisputed, Voltaire nevertheless kept an open mind on foreign literature. No work, he felt, should be excluded because it does not conform to a Frenchman's idea of artistic excellence; and no work should be hailed as a masterpiece simply because it is bizarre and exotic. He was in favour of equality, but in the case of art this could only mean equality before the law of taste. In keeping with this principle, he was prepared not only to welcome, but to publicize, whatever he considered to be of outstanding interest from any source, particularly if he thought that there was any chance of thereby infusing a little more life and vigour into contemporary French literature.

It is hardly surprising that he cultivated the great writers of ancient Greece and Rome, although taking care not to fall into the 'superstition' of blindly preferring the ancients to modern writers, regardless of true merit.[12] Nor is it strange that he was well versed in Italian literature, for which he showed a fine and discriminating appreciation. More important from the point of view of the development of sensibility is the key role he played in the genesis of Anglomania which, perhaps more than anything else, precipitated a radical change in esthetic as in other values.

Whatever regrets he expressed in later years after witnessing some of the less desirable effects of the English vogue, Voltaire always insisted, with evident and justifiable pride, that he was the most important pioneer. He claimed this title as early as 1736.[13] Forty years later, in the midst of the Shakespeare controversy, he vigorously maintained in the *Lettre à l'Académie* that he was 'le premier parmi vous qui apprit la langue anglaise, le premier qui fit connaître Shakespeare, qui en traduisit librement quelques morceaux en vers (ainsi qu'il faut traduire les poëtes), qui fit connaître Pope, Dryden, Milton; le premier même qui osa expliquer les éléments de la philosophie du grand Newton, et qui osa rendre justice à la sagesse profonde de Locke' (M. XXX, 351).

It is possible, on the basis of strict historical accuracy to dispute this statement. English literature and ideas were

12. 'En un mot, admirons les anciens, mais que notre admiration ne soit pas une superstition aveugle: et ne faisons pas cette injustice à la nature humaine et à nous-mêmes, de fermer nos yeux aux beautés qu'elle répand autour de nous' (M. VIII, 313).

13. Referring to himself in the third person, he wrote: 'Il traduisit en vers, il y a quelques années, plusieurs morceaux des meilleurs poëtes d'Angleterre, pour l'instruction de ses amis, et par là il engagea beaucoup de personnes à apprendre l'anglais; en sorte que cette langue est devenue familière aux gens de lettres. C'est rendre service à l'esprit humain, de l'orner ainsi des richesses des pays étrangers' (M. III, 309).

by no means totally unknown in France before the publication of the *Lettres philosophiques*. Locke's *Essay Concerning
Human Understanding* had been translated by Coste and
published in 1700. Muralt, in his *Lettres sur les Anglais*
(1725), praised precisely those qualities in the English
tragic theatre—force, action, and spectacle—which appealed
most to Voltaire. Careful research has unearthed a few
earlier French references to Shakespeare, the most notable
by far being Prévost's comment in the *Mémoires d'un homme
de qualité* (1728). None of these is of any great importance
compared with the wave of interest stimulated by Voltaire's
*Lettres philosophiques*, his *Essai sur la poésie épique*, the
prefaces to his tragedies, and other writings. We may sum
it up by saying that before Voltaire a few intellectuals had
begun to show interest in English philosophy and literature;
Shakespeare was virtually unknown. After Voltaire there
was general enthusiasm among a wide public for anything
English; Locke, Milton, Dryden, Pope, Addison, and Swift
were names almost as familiar as Descartes, Corneille, and
Racine. As for Shakespeare, Paul Van Tieghem has summarized Voltaire's role thus: 'Voltaire fut l'introducteur de
Shakespeare, non seulement en France, mais sur le continent;
son rôle à cet égard ne peut être comparé qu'à celui de Mme
de Staël introductrice de la littérature allemande auprès
de plusieurs nations qui n'apprirent que par elle à connaître
cette littérature.'[14] Mme de Staël herself stated flatly that
'Ce n'est que depuis Voltaire que l'on rend justice en France
à l'admirable littérature des Anglais'.[15] Chateaubriand[16] and
Voltaire's contemporaries agreed.

One may therefore conclude, with E. Preston Dargan, who
has investigated the question of Voltaire's primacy, that
'He really was the first to promote to any extent the vogue
for English literature and philosophy in eighteenth-century
France'.[17] Even more important, such was Voltaire's influence

14. Paul Van Tieghem, *Le Préromantisme; Etudes d'histoire littéraire
européenne* (Paris, 1924–30), III, 19.
15. Quoted by Williams, *Voltaire: Literary Critic*, p. 298.
16. *Œuvres complètes* (Paris, 1839–61), VI, 385.
17. E. Preston Dargan, 'The Question of Voltaire's Primacy in
establishing the English Vogue', in *Mélanges offerts à Fernand Baldensperger* (Paris, 1930), I, 198.

on the whole of eighteenth-century Europe, that he set the tone. His judgments and comments were repeated everywhere. One of the most significant statements on English literature, and one which provided preromantic and romantic criticism with its central image, appeared in the *Lettres philosophiques*, where Voltaire compares the cold formality of French classicism with the spontaneity and vigorous irregularity of English genius: 'Le génie poétique des Anglais ressemble, jusqu'à présent, à un arbre touffu planté par la nature, jetant au hasard mille rameaux et croissant inégalement avec force. Il meurt si vous voulez forcer sa nature, et le tailler en arbre des jardins de Marly.' [18] Here, in germ, is the contrast between the natural and the artificial, between the free flight of genius and the cramped mediocrity of the merely correct.

The overriding importance of genius, seen as 'quelque chose d'inspiré et de divin' (M. XIX, 431) which transcends all rules and artistic conventions, is a theme which recurs frequently in Voltaire's criticism. 'Tel est le privilège du génie d'invention: il se fait une route où personne n'a marché avant lui; il court sans guide, sans art, sans règle; il s'égare dans sa carrière, mais il laisse loin derrière lui tout ce qui n'est que raison et qu'exactitude' (M. VIII, 318). It is a crime, he says, 'en fait de beaux arts de mettre des entraves au génie. Ce n'est pas pour rien qu'on le représente avec des aîles: il doit voler où il veut et comme il veut' (Best. 16438). In the theatre, no amount of rational discussion is worth one scene of genius, as is evident from an examination of the plays of Corneille:

Cette habitude de faire raisonner ses personnages avec subtilité n'est pas le fruit du génie. Le génie peint à grands

18. M. XXII, 156. Voltaire repeats this image elsewhere, e.g. M. X, 307–308:

> Jardins plantés en symétrie,
> Arbres nains tirés au cordeau,
> Celui qui vous mit au niveau
> En vain s'applaudit, se récrie,
> En voyant ce petit morceau:
> Jardins, il faut que je vous fuie;
> Trop d'art me révolte et m'ennuie.

traits, invente toujours les situations frappantes, porte la terreur dans l'âme, excite les grandes passions, et dédaigne tous les petits moyens: tel est Corneille dans le cinquième acte de *Rodogune*, dans des scènes des *Horaces*, de *Cinna*, de *Pompée*. Le génie n'est point subtil et raisonneur: c'est ce qu'on appelle *esprit* qui court après les pensées, les sentences, les antithèses, les réflexions, les contestations ingénieuses. Toutes les pièces de Corneille, et surtout les dernières, sont infectées de ce grand défaut qui refroidit tout. L'esprit dans Corneille, comme dans le grand nombre de nos écrivains modernes, est ce qui perd la littérature. Ce sont les traits du génie de ce grand homme, qui seuls ont fait sa gloire et montré l'art. (M. XXXII, 38)

In this respect, Voltaire was in accord with a fundamental tendency of eighteenth-century criticism. For Helvétius, as for Voltaire, the writer of genius is distinguished by the intensity of his emotions; he produces works which are 'sublime' rather than conventionally beautiful, and which often contain an element of terror. Genius is defined in the *Encyclopédie* as 'l'étendue de l'esprit, la force de l'imagination et l'activité de l'âme'. It has no necessary connection with taste:

Le goût est souvent séparé du génie. Le génie est un pur don de la nature; ce qu'il produit est l'ouvrage d'un moment; le goût est l'ouvrage de l'étude et du temps; il tient à la connaissance d'une multitude de règles, ou établies ou supposées; il fait produire des beautés qui ne sont que de convention. Pour qu'une chose soit belle selon les règles du goût, il faut qu'elle soit élégante, fine, travaillée sans le paraître: pour être de génie, il faut quelquefois qu'elle soit négligée; qu'elle ait l'air irrégulier, escarpé, sauvage. Le sublime et le génie brillent dans Shakespear comme des éclairs dans une longue nuit, et Racine est toujours beau: Homère est plein de génie, et Virgile d'élégance.

Voltaire indicated his approval in his own article on the subject in the *Dictionnaire philosophique*. He too makes the

distinction between genius and taste: 'On peut être totale-
ment dépourvu de génie et avoir beaucoup d'esprit et de
goût' (M. XXIV, 218) and vice versa. The most conspicuous
example in Voltaire's view was, of course, Shakespeare, a
genius whose work he considered to be devoid of the slightest
vestige of taste. While he maintained that the loftiest artistic
achievements are invariably the result of a happy fusion of
genius and taste, Voltaire's order of priority is clear enough:

> Mais je préfère, avec raison,
> Les belles fautes du génie
> A l'exacte et froide oraison
> D'un puriste d'académie.[19]

Like Diderot, Voltaire associated genius with inspiration,
enthusiasm, and imagination. His own definition is simply
'imagination d'invention dans les arts' (M. XIX, 431). The
inventive imagination is not opposed to judgment; on the
contrary, 'elle ne peut agir qu'avec un jugement profond'
(M. XIX, 431). The article on 'Imagination' in the *Dictionnaire philosophique* enlarges on this point. As a sensationalist,
Voltaire believed that all ideas are derived from the senses
and are originally images. The imagination is therefore 'le
seul instrument avec lequel nous comprenons des idées, et
même les plus métaphysiques'. He sees two types of imagination: the passive imagination, not unlike the Id, independent
of the will and determining it, 'espèce d'imagination servile,
partage ordinaire d'un peuple ignorant', which inspires the
worst kind of enthusiasm—fanaticism and the belief in
magic; and the active imagination, which permits reflection,
combination, and comparison. Strictly speaking, the so-called
'creative mind' does not create, since all images are imposed
on the senses from outside, but it arranges them to form a
significant or striking pattern. The rare inventive imagination functions therefore in basically the same way as reason,
but at a much deeper level. In some mysterious way, its
operation is spontaneous, instinctive, and immediate: 'Il
faut avouer que dans les arts de génie tout est l'ouvrage de

19.  *Epître au prince royal de Prusse*, 1738 (M. X, 307).

l'instinct' (Best. 17250). The task of the reflective reason is to draw up the plan of a work; imagination and enthusiasm then take over. 'Comment le raisonnement peut-il gouverner l'enthousiasme? C'est qu'un poëte dessine d'abord l'ordonnance de son tableau; la raison alors tient le crayon. Mais veut-il animer ses personnages et leur donner le caractère des passions; alors l'imagination s'échauffe, l'enthousiasme agit: c'est un coursier qui s'emporte dans sa carrière; mais sa carrière est régulièrement tracée' (M. XVIII, 554). This is a reversal of the 'emotion recollected in tranquillity' formula, but the important thing is that imagination and emotion are no less primary for Voltaire than for Wordsworth.

It goes without saying that genius cannot exist without extreme sensibility: 'Quiconque est vivement ému voit les choses d'un autre œil que les autres hommes. Tout est pour lui objet de comparaison rapide et métaphore: sans qu'il y prenne garde, il anime tout, et fait passer dans ceux qui l'écoutent une partie de son enthousiasme' (M. XVIII, 514). It goes without saying also that genius, as the offspring of sensibility, is necessarily virtuous.[20]

Perhaps the best way to summarize Voltaire's esthetic ideas, and at the same time put them in their proper perspective, is to establish his priorities. The rational processes, including obedience to the rules, are relegated to a secondary, albeit useful and even essential, role. There are two categories of taste: on the less important level, it is relative and concerns matters on which one can agree to disagree, but without 'le grand goût' no work can be truly beautiful when judged by the highest universal standards. Above even taste, however, is genius. If totally uncontrolled, it is likely to be led astray into the bizarre; but only genius provides the divine fire which enables an artist to attain the sublime. The lowest place is reserved for 'intellectual' literature, for formally correct but uninspired productions which follow

20. See M. X, 384:
> Le souffle du génie et ses fécondes flammes
> N'ont jamais descendu que dans de nobles âmes;
> Il faut qu'on en soit digne, et le cœur épuré
> Est le seul aliment de ce flambeau sacré.
> Un esprit corrompu ne fut jamais sublime.

the rules but are not motivated by genuine feeling, and for mere displays of wit.

Voltaire's critical practice is in general conformity with these principles and represents, on the whole, a remarkable achievement. A cautious traditionalist in some respects, he was by no means free of personal prejudice or of the assumptions of his time. His most vivid and spontaneous critical assessments often appeared in polemical pieces in the form of replies or protests, with tone and emphasis dependent upon the circumstances. It would not be difficult to 'prove' his inconsistency by making a selection of them taken out of context. But when due allowance has been made for these factors, Voltaire emerges as a moderate but forward-looking critic, much more a man of feeling than a dogmatic classicist.

He was, of course, a fervent admirer of the artistic achievement of the age of Louis XIV. His judgments on his great predecessors of the classical school may lack originality —originality was not, in fact, what he was seeking—but they are sensitive, apt, and generally just. For Voltaire, the late seventeenth century in France had the distinction of being one of the four great periods of cultural excellence in the history of humanity. He was convinced that such an unusual flowering of genius and talent could only be followed by a period of decadence, as though nature had exhausted itself. This view is expressed, to use Dr. Besterman's phrase, 'with despairing emphasis' in the *Notebooks*, but it occurs frequently elsewhere, notably in the *Siècle de Louis XIV*:

> Il ne s'éleva guère de grands génies depuis les beaux jours de ces artistes illustres; et, à peu près vers le temps de la mort de Louis XIV, la nature sembla se reposer.
>
> La route était difficile au commencement du siècle, parce que personne n'y avait marché; elle l'est aujourd'hui, parce qu'elle a été battue. Les grands hommes du siècle passé ont enseigné à penser et à parler; ils ont dit ce qu'on ne savait pas. Ceux qui leur succèdent ne peuvent guère dire que ce qu'on sait. Enfin une espèce de dégoût est venue de la multitude des chefs-d'œuvre. (M. XIV, 552)

The danger inherent in this position is obvious. 'Le siècle à ses débuts est dominé par l'idée stérélisante que la perfection de l'âge classique ne peut être suivie que d'une décadence. D'où cette timidité qui, par angoisse de dégénérer, condamne les écrivains à l'imitation servile des grands modèles.'[21] Such, however, is far from being Voltaire's conclusion. His conception of decadence at the close of the seventeenth century is related to his attack on the 'géomètres'; it is thus, in part, an expression of his antirationalist sensibility. He saw, correctly, that the eighteenth century was developing into an age when enlightenment would make rapid progress at the expense of poetry. While applauding the advance of reason and philosophy—was he not himself a pioneer and a leader?—he never ceased deploring the 'barbarous' invasion of art by the mathematical mind:

La lumière, il est vrai, commence à se répandre;
Avec moins de talents, on est plus éclairé;
Mais le goût s'est perdu, l'esprit s'est égaré.
Ce siècle ridicule est celui des brochures,
Des chansons, des extraits, et surtout des injures.
La barbarie approche: Apollon indigné
Quitte les bords heureux où ses lois ont régné. . . .

(M. X, 386)

He saw equally clearly that with the disappearance of the cluster of outstanding talent which had produced poetry of unmatched elegance and noble simplicity, mediocre successors were tending to go to one of two extremes by resorting either to sterile formulas or to the 'bizarre'. An examination of much of what passed for literature in the eighteenth century, especially in the 'higher' genres, shows that his pessimism was amply justified.

In one respect, Voltaire remained a traditionalist to the end. For him, literature consisted principally of tragedy, comedy, the epic, and other forms of poetry. The other genres, including the novel, were forms of entertainment

21. André Monglond, *Histoire intérieure du préromantisme français, de l'abbé Prévost à Joubert* (Grenoble, 1929), I, 52.

or means of disseminating opinions, propaganda, and useful information. He failed to grasp, or perhaps refused to grasp, the fact that formal barriers in literature were breaking down, that the classical hierarchy was doomed to disappear and that the rigid distinction between literature and philosophy was no longer valid. To the extent that he was aware of them, he deplored these trends, while paradoxically contributing to their success by his innovations in the theatre and by the excellence of his own performance in the so-called 'minor' genres.

He therefore accepted decadence as a fact without realizing that the greatness of eighteenth-century literature resided in those unclassifiable productions of which he himself was a master. Given his critical assumptions, he could not be expected to suggest a solution. Genius cannot be produced at will, nor does it emerge from a careful study of models. Voltaire never recommended the slavish imitation of either ancient or modern classics, knowing full well that this can only result in the production of lifeless copies. The best one can do is to avoid their faults and try to recapture something of the spirit which inspired them. In David Williams's words, 'He was not trying to re-establish classicism; he was trying to revive the greatness behind it.'[22]

Voltaire's treatment of Corneille has often been cited as evidence for the view that he was a fault-finder and a rigid purist, or worse, rather than a true critic. As in so many other respects, it is difficult to reconcile Voltaire's reputation with his intentions. The kind of detailed analysis which makes up much of the *Commentaires sur Corneille* is indeed somewhat negative, especially if detached from the passages expressing genuine admiration. Voltaire was the first to agree that this form of criticism has its limitations: 'Tous ceux qui s'érigent en critiques des écrivains célèbres compilent des volumes. J'aimerais mieux deux pages qui nous fissent connaître quelques beautés: car je maintiendrai toujours, avec tous les gens de bon goût, qu'il y a plus à profiter dans douze vers d'Homère et de Virgile que dans toutes les

22. *Voltaire: Literary Critic*, p. 347.

critiques qu'on a faites de ces deux grands hommes.'[23] He saw himself as a critic who took the positive approach of the creative artist. Yet in the same *Lettres philosophiques*, he suggested that the Académie Française should publish the works of the great writers of the seventeenth century 'épurés de toutes les fautes de langage qui s'y sont glissées.'[24]

Voltaire saw no contradiction. This project, like the examination of Corneille's 'faults', was based on the belief that the errors of the great are more likely to be copied than those of lesser writers.[25] Severity, therefore, with Voltaire, often indicates admiration. His attitude is well expressed in the *Temple du Goût*: 'je connus alors que le dieu du Goût est très-difficile à satisfaire; mais qu'il n'aime point à demi. Je vis que les ouvrages qu'il critique le plus en détail sont ceux qui en tout lui plaisent davantage' (M. VIII, 579–580). In any case, he was convinced that unless accompanied by a *feeling* for greatness, the analysis of faults is mere carping criticism and a waste of time. Understanding and appreciation precede critical dissection; only if there is something to appreciate is the latter worth while.

Voltaire's treatment of the writers considered by the eighteenth century as 'primitives' reveals, in its most acute form, the perpetual conflict in his mind between the claims of taste and those of genius. It also marks an important stage in the development of eighteenth-century romanticism, with Shakespeare as the key figure.

It would be absurd to censure Voltaire for not showing the same kind of respect for Shakespeare as a modern critic, conditioned by two centuries of bardolatry. What is truly astonishing is that he should have felt such a strong and permanent attraction. Voltaire was born in France in the seventeenth century; nothing in his educational and cultural background prepared him to appreciate the merits of Shakespeare. As a playwright himself, whose ambition was to

23. *Lettres philosophiques*, M. XXII, 150.
24. *Mélanges*, Pléiade, pp. 103–104.
25. 'C'est sur les imperfections des grands hommes qu'il faut attacher sa critique; car si le préjugé nous faisait admirer leurs fautes, bientôt nous les imiterions, et il se trouverait peut-être que nous n'aurions pris de ces célèbres écrivains que l'exemple de mal faire' (M. II, 35).

become a worthy successor of the dramatists of the age of Louis XIV, he considered Racine to be the supreme model of tragic art.

Generally speaking, Voltaire's views on Shakespeare's 'faults' are not very different from those expressed by English critics of the time. His most violent and frequently quoted criticisms were made late in his career. They do not constitute a personal vendetta against Shakespeare, whom he continued to refer to as a genius, but an attempt to stem the growing tide of 'barbarism' among certain of his contemporaries who were using Shakespeare as a rallying-cry. If he overstepped the mark by using such terms as 'Gilles de la Foire' and 'sauvage ivre', he was more than repaid by those outraged English critics who felt it to be their patriotic duty to accuse him of the basest motives.

It is easy to exaggerate the importance of this type of polemic, common enough in the eighteenth century. Of much greater interest is Voltaire's overall judgment of Shakespeare, which was consistent. Having described him in the *Lettres philosophiques* as a great genius totally lacking in taste, he never departed from his conviction. More than that, he cited Shakespeare as the supreme example of a writer who, by natural gifts alone, reached the heights of the sublime, who painted with 'broad strokes' scenes of such gripping interest that 'nos déclarations d'amour et nos confidentes' seemed trivial in comparison (Best. D940); yet whose plays were monstrously irregular.

Voltaire did more than publicize Shakespeare's name; he produced the first reasonably accurate translation of some scenes, far superior to the timid adaptations which appeared later. His aim, of course, was not to make Shakespeare's plays acceptable to Frenchmen; on the contrary, he wanted to shock his compatriots, as he had been shocked, by showing how far Shakespeare went in flouting the rules of taste and common sense, while at the same time conveying something of his strange power and fascination. The fact remains that besides introducing Shakespeare to the French public and popularizing the notion of a great natural genius owing little to art, he provided an authentic glimpse of his work. Paul

Van Tieghem is surely correct in suggesting that Voltaire played a key role in the evolution of the 'preromantic' concept of genius: 'Dès ces premiers jugements se pose assez nettement l'antithèse *goût-génie*, qui sera reprise à propos de Shakespeare pendant un siècle, et qui forme un des axes principaux du préromantisme européen; c'est la forme littéraire de l'antithèse, plus générale encore, *esprit-cœur*, qui oppose aux *rationaux* les *sensibles*.'[26]

One might go further and question the prevalent view that Voltaire was blind to Shakespeare's real qualities, particularly his rare understanding of human beings and their motives, his naturalism, and his poetry. It is true that Voltaire's borrowings are comparatively slight and superficial. He himself said that he took the idea of using subjects from national history from Shakespeare (M. II, 542). As a dramatist with a keen eye for effective novelty, he seems to have been most impressed by the possibility of introducing more action and spectacle and by Shakespeare's 'republican' eloquence: precisely those elements which he felt could add life and vigour to French tragedy without destroying it entirely. It would be unrealistic to expect more. The more closely one examines Voltaire's numerous references to Shakespeare, however, the more one feels that his admiration was genuine and that it went beyond externals. He constantly praises Shakespeare's imaginative power, the 'belles scènes', the 'morceaux si grands et si terribles'. On Shakespeare's feeling for character, he has this to say: 'Son grand mérite, à mon avis, consiste dans des peintures fortes et naïves, de la vie humaine' (Best. 9526). Even at his most critical, in the *Appel à toutes les nations*, he is careful to point out that one finds in Shakespeare 'de la vérité, de la profondeur, et je ne sais quoi qui attache, et qui remue beaucoup plus que ne ferait l'élégance' (M. XXIV, 203).

Writing to David Garrick in 1755, Claude Patu reported a discussion he had had with Voltaire on the merits of Shakespeare:

Je n'ai pas manqué de lui dire ce que je pensais de ses expressions si fausses, si peu réfléchies au sujet de Shake-

26. *Le Préromantisme*, III, 28.

speare. Il est convenu de bonne foi que c'était *un barbare aimable, un fou séduisant*; ce sont ses propres termes: le grand article qui le met de mauvaise humeur est l'irrégularité des plans de cet illustre poète, irrégularité dont vous êtes bien loin d'être le défenseur. Quant au naturel, à la chaleur, aux idées admirables répandues dans les pièces de Shakespeare, il est tombé d'accord, et convient en riant que si vous nous preniez moins de vaisseaux et ne *piratiez* pas ainsi sur l'océan, il aurait plus ménagé le créateur de votre théâtre. (Best. 5900)

This anecdote is interesting for the light it throws on several aspects of the Voltaire-Shakespeare controversy: the ambivalence of Voltaire's insults ('barbare *aimable*', 'fou *séduisant*'); the fact that Garrick agrees with Voltaire on the subject of Shakespeare's irregularity; the joking reference to the influence of patriotic feeling, which contains a grain of truth; and Voltaire's recognition of Shakespeare's qualities.

It is no exaggeration to say that his lifelong interest amounted to a veritable obsession. Although he paid homage to Dryden and Addison, it was almost always Shakespeare he had in mind whenever he referred to the English theatre. One has the impression that he was fascinated in spite of himself to an extraordinary degree and deeply disturbed, perhaps more than he cared to admit, by this monstrous but hypnotic talent; that the man of impeccable taste, for all his scornful epithets, could not quite convince the intuitive poet-critic. Lamartine's assessment is probably closer to the mark than those of many subsequent commentators: 'Voltaire bien qu'il fût violemment choqué par l'étrangeté quelquefois barbare de cette scène shakespearienne, en sentit néanmoins la moelle humaine, les proportions gigantesques, l'audace politique, la profondeur, l'élévation, l'étendue.'[27]

Voltaire's critical comments on two other great 'primitives', Homer and Milton, fall into a similar pattern. Homer is full of 'fautes grossières', largely attributable to the age in which he lived, but also of 'beautés plus grandes que ces

27. *Cours familier de littérature*, XXVIII, 209.

fautes' (M. VIII, 317); he is 'plein de défauts mais sublime' (M. VIII, 320). While condemning Homer's crudity, Voltaire nevertheless makes of him a kind of symbol of the poetic values he was defending against the 'geometric' invasion. Homer was at least a true poet, at his best a sublime genius, in any case the opposite of a 'wit'. In poetry, coarseness is a serious fault but forgivable; intellectualism and affectation are not.

*Paradise Lost*, whose author, besides his artistic deficiencies, had the added demerit of being 'sombre et fanatique', is described as an 'amas de folies désagréables' (M. VIII, 358) and the prime example, after Dante's *Inferno*, of the 'bizarre' (M. XIX, 434). Yet Voltaire paid eloquent tribute to Milton's poetic genius and was chiefly responsible for the spread of his fame in France, and indeed Europe.[28]

Even the *Old Testament*, on the rare occasions when he was able to detach himself from religious controversy long enough to see it simply as a work of literature, evidently appealed to him as a crude but imaginatively powerful, sometimes singularly beautiful example of primitive art, on the same level as the *Iliad*. He praised its grandeur, its dramatic qualities and bold imagery in a review of Bishop Lowth's *De Sacra Poesi Hebræorum* (M. XXV, 201–208). His own translations are sufficient proof that he was not indifferent to the qualities of Hebrew poetry.

There are, of course, severe limits to Voltaire's literary primitivism. It would be as misleading to underrate the importance of taste in his critical judgment as to say that taste was his sole criterion. His ideal remained that rare combination of genius and taste exemplified in the best of Virgil and Racine. Yet 'natural' genius, if excluded from the inner Temple, was by no means neglected. The debt owed by the romantics to his popularization of Shakespeare and Milton was enormous and acknowledged.

Perhaps it would be fair to call him a 'moderate romantic'. As Raymond Naves says, he points the way to Chénier and

28. See J. M. Telleen's conclusion (*Milton dans la littérature française* [Paris, 1904], p. 42): 'Mais ce qui appartient à Voltaire, d'une façon incontestable, c'est l'honneur d'avoir travaillé mieux que personne à répandre le grand nom de Milton.'

Lamartine, 'c'est-à-dire à des romantiques tempérés qui conservent la noblesse et le goût dans les élans de leur inspiration'.[29] His contemporaries often saw him rather as a revolutionary critic who was clearly on the side of erratic genius, while some of his enemies condemned him as an irresponsible innovator. Sabatier de Castres, for example, complained that writers would learn from him 'à peu respecter les modeles, à déguiser leurs larcins, à violer les regles, à oublier les bienséances, à se déchirer, sans égard'.[30] J. M. B. Clément, a violently ill-disposed critic, was firmly convinced of his disastrous influence on the direction of French literature: 'Vous avez vu votre siècle suivre aveuglément vos décisions et former son goût sur le vôtre. Vous avez donc, par vos opinions littéraires, préparé cette révolution qui a été plus loin que vous ne pensiez'.[31]

The more sympathetic Mercier considered Voltaire himself to be 'above the rules'.[32] Aquin de Château-Lyon made a similar observation in his *Siècle littéraire de Louis XV*. After quoting Voltaire's maxim that 'il faut courir dans la carrière et non pas s'y traîner avec des béquilles', he adds in a note: 'Les traits merveilleux dont *Milton*, le grand *Corneille*, & M. de *Voltaire* étincellent, rachetent tous les defauts qu'on leur reproche.'[33] The wheel has come full circle. By the mid-century, Voltaire, like Milton and Shakespeare, had become, in the eyes of some critics, one of the unorthodox writers of genius whose sins against good taste are compensated by flashes of great beauty.

29. *Voltaire, l'homme et l'œuvre*, p. 107.
30. *Les Trois Siècles de la littérature française* (Amsterdam, 1774), III, 503.
31. *Première Lettre à Monsieur de Voltaire* (The Hague, 1773–1776), I, 33.
32. *L'An 2440*, p. 218, n.
33. Pierre Louis d'Aquin de Château-Lyon, *Siècle littéraire de Louis XV, ou Lettres sur les hommes celebres* (Amsterdam, 1753), II, 20.

# CHAPTER 5

# *The Poet*

Emile Faguet's assessment of Voltaire as a poet opens with an incredulous exclamation: 'Voltaire poète! Mais pouvons-nous bien parler ici de poésie? Véritablement, on pourrait avoir quelques doutes; c'est que, de l'aveu de tous, Voltaire n'a pas été ce qu'on appelle un poète. La critique contemporaine,—et cette tendance s'est répandue uniformément depuis 1820,—est unanime à ce sujet. On ne peut aller contre cette affirmation. Voltaire n'a pas été poète; c'est un fait.'[1] With all due respect to Faguet, Voltaire was indeed a poet, and in more than name. Unfortunately, he was 'the great poet of an age without poetry':[2] a great poet compared with contemporary versifiers, but the victim of the conventions of an age without poetry.

The period of the Enlightenment, with its fervent emotionalism, its emphasis on the senses and the passions, on feeling and sensibility, with its 'back-to-nature' philosophy, would seem to be ideally suited to the development of lyrical poetry. Instead, it produced some pleasant light verse and countless frozen imitations of what once had been the living art of the seventeenth century. It is a commonplace to say that if one is looking for poetry one is more likely to find it in the novel and in some of the genuinely original prose pieces than in verse.

Eighteenth-century France witnessed an intense intellectual ferment marking the transition to the modern world; yet outwardly it was a rigidly stratified, aristocratic society with

---

1. Emile Faguet, *Histoire de la poésie française de la renaissance au romantisme* (Paris, 1934), VII, 87.
2. Georges Ascoli, 'Voltaire. L'Œuvre poétique', *RCC*, 25[2] (15 juin 1924), 419.

artistic and social values similar to those of the preceding era. While the whole structure was being undermined from within, the façade appeared solid and imposing. The *bien-séances* were accorded the same kind of exaggerated respect in poetry as in the salon and even the most original minds, including Voltaire, continued to think of literature in hierarchical terms with the noble, poetic genres at the summit and various prose forms—comparatively unimportant and therefore open to innovation—at the base. Artistic liberation had to await the political revolution.

Poetry was frequently thought of as being in conflict with philosophy. Thanks to the rapid development of science during the latter part of the seventeenth century and the early decades of the eighteenth, the universe was beginning to lose some of its mystery. Poetry, it was felt, should reflect the triumph of clear reasoning and become a creation of the rational mind. Intellectuals such as the abbé Terrasson, imbued with the spirit of Cartesianism, advanced the view that poetry is little more than an ornament, a frosting on the cake of reason; its purposes were becoming more and more confused with those of prose. But if poetry is merely rhymed prose, it is difficult to see rhyme and metre as much more than essentially useless additions and so many obstacles to sense. At best, poetry is an amusement; at worst, by playing on the imagination of the reader at the expense of truth, it deals in illusions and poets are 'liars'. The abbé Trublet expressed the pious hope that 'Plus la raison se perfectionnera, plus le jugement sera préféré à l'imagination, et par conséquent moins les Poètes seront goûtés. Les premiers écrivains, dit-on, ont été Poètes. Je le crois bien, ils ne pouvaient être autre chose. Les derniers seront Philosophes.'[3]

This attitude was by no means confined to the 'géomètres'. Similar views were expressed by Montesquieu, Buffon, and Duclos. Even Diderot, in many ways the most romantic of eighteenth-century writers, saw the poet as inferior to the *philosophe*. 'Je ne peux souffrir', he wrote in the article 'Encyclopédie', 'qu'on s'appuie de l'autorité des auteurs

---

3. Quoted by Jean Jacquart, *L'Abbé Trublet critique et moraliste, 1697–1770* (Paris, 1926), p. 185.

dans les questions de raisonnement. . . . Point de vers, surtout; ils ont l'air si faibles et si mesquins au travers d'une
discussion philosophique.'[4] One can understand Voltaire's
pessimistic outburst: 'Oserai-je le dire? C'est que de toutes
les nations polies, la nôtre est la moins poétique' (M. VIII,
362).

Not that he himself was entirely unaffected by the trend
of his age, but he had a much surer grasp of the nature of
poetry than any of his contemporaries. He rejected absolutely the notion that reason by itself is capable of producing
poetry of any value. Rationalist intruders are described in
one of his earliest poems, *Le Bourbier* (1714), a satire directed
particularly against Lamotte, as

> ces esprits timides,
> De la raison partisans insipides,
> Qui, compassés dans leurs vers languissants,
> A leur lecteur font haïr le bon sens. (M. X, 76)

He even went so far as to accept the charge that poets are
'liars', if the truth they distort is simply the truth of logic.
'Nous osons même dire', he wrote in one of his 'l'art pour
l'art' moods, 'que la poésie, par sa nature, est plus favorable
au mensonge qu'à la vérité; car son but est de tout exagérer,
d'éveiller les passions, non de les calmer, et de troubler la
raison plutôt que de l'éclairer' (M. XXV, 202). True to his
general esthetic doctrine, he insisted that poetry is directed
to the feelings at least as much as to the intellect[5] and gave
precedence to genius over beauty: 'Tout ouvrage en vers,
quelque beau qu'il soit d'ailleurs, sera nécessairement ennuyeux . . . si la pièce n'a point ce charme inexprimable de la
poésie que le génie seul peut donner' (M. II, 165).

In many respects, Voltaire's ideas on poetry are astonishingly modern. He defined it—and Verlaine would not have
disagreed—as 'la musique de l'âme'; 'et surtout', he added

4. See Roland Mortier, 'Diderot au carrefour de la poésie et de la
philosophie', *Revue des Sciences humaines*, 28 (1963), 486–487.
5. 'La vraie poésie, c'est-à-dire celle qui est naturelle et harmonieuse,
celle qui parle au cœur autant qu'à l'esprit' (*La Princesse de Babylone*, M.
XXI, 419).

in the *Dictionnaire philosophique*, 'des âmes grandes et sensibles' (M. XX, 232). He saw it as something quite different from rhymed prose. The best poetry is more precise and says more in fewer words than the best prose and since the total meaning of a poem is conveyed not merely by the logical sense of the words but more subtly and effectively by their music, it is not translatable. 'Peut-on traduire de la musique?' (Best. 5172). Poetry is indeed a difficult art, perhaps made unnecessarily so by petty conventions, but the difficulties confronting the poet are not to be regarded as useless barriers to clear expression. 'Quiconque se borne à vaincre une difficulté pour le mérite seul de la vaincre est un fou; mais celui qui tire du fond de ces obstacles mêmes des beautés qui plaisent à tout le monde est un homme très-sage et presque unique' (M. II, 57). Hence his refusal to consider prose tragedy, or even the use of blank verse, as anything more than a 'soft option'. Voltaire's position in the prose-poetry controversy reflects, according to David Williams, 'a "modern" awareness of the enervating conventionalities and deficiencies of everyday speech and the relationship of this automaticized language to the creation of poetry'.[6] In this respect, he was a distant forerunner of Mallarmé.

Yet for all his admirably far-sighted grasp of essentials, Voltaire remained a willing prisoner of the classical tradition. Poetry is far more than versified prose; he never varied on this point. But he could not imagine a form of poetry which would not *also* possess all the qualities of good prose: precision, simplicity, clarity, and elegance. While protesting vigorously against the tyranny of unnecessary rules, he confined poetry within the bounds of a narrowly conceived taste, which excluded all obscurity, 'vulgar' diction, unusual imagery and anything which might be considered 'bizarre'. 'Tout ne doit pas être orné, mais rien ne doit être rebutant. Un langage obscur et grotesque n'est pas de la simplicité: c'est de la grossièreté recherchée' (M. XXII, 255). Thus, although fully aware of the kind of effect which only genuine poetry can achieve, he ensured that his own major poetic

6. David Williams, 'Voltaire and the Language of the Gods', *SV*, LXII, 63.

works would be cast in the obsolete mould of neoclassicism and effectively isolated himself from freedom of invention and originality of expression.

The prime example is his epic poem, *La Henriade*, which, along with the tragedies, was the foundation of his literary reputation. Voltaire was convinced that his real talent lay in the field of the epic.[7] To judge by the number of editions and by the great prestige enjoyed by this work, composed when Voltaire was in his twenties, his contemporaries agreed. Enthusiasm did not begin to wane until the latter part of the century, by which time *La Henriade* had become something of a national monument, highly respected, but considered somewhat cold and formal compared with the more direct and appealing emotionalism of the tragedies.[8] By 1788, Linguet could pronounce the following judgment: 'On admire les beaux vers qui s'y rencontrent souvent, surtout dans le genre tranquille, et descriptif: mais on n'est ni ému, ni attaché par les événemens.'[9]

Linguet's explanation of the poem's failure to retain its popularity is worth noting: 'La société, où il vivoit alors, étoit composée d'amis plus éclairés que sensibles, plus délicats que passionnés, livrés à une philosophie très-propre à perfectionner le goût, mais non à réveiller l'imagination.'[10] There is some truth in this. The features of the poem which were beginning to seem too patently artificial were precisely those which had satisfied the conservative taste of the preceding generation. Marais' delighted exclamation—'Je l'ai lu: c'est un ouvrage merveilleux, un chef-d'œuvre d'esprit, beau comme Virgile'—[11] was not untypical of the early reaction and few would have quarrelled with d'Argens' reference to the author as the 'French Virgil'. Voltaire, it was thought, had finally provided France with an epic worthy of the

7. 'L'épique est mon fait, ou je me suis bien trompé' (Best. D253).

8. O. R. Taylor discusses this decline in popularity in the preface to his edition of *La Henriade* (*SV*, XXXVIII, 205–208). All quotations from *La Henriade* refer to this edition, published as vol. XXXIX of *Studies on Voltaire and the eighteenth century*.

9. *Examen*, p. 51.

10. *Examen*, p. 64.

11. Mathieu Marais, *Journal et mémoires sur la régence et le règne de Louis XV (1715–1737)* (Paris, 1863–8), III, 89.

nation's history and one, moreover, which contained nothing to offend the taste of the refined public of the 1730s.

O. R. Taylor uses a strikingly appropriate comparison to suggest why *La Henriade* later became a museum-piece:

> Ni dans son style, ni dans son évocation du XVI<sup>e</sup> siècle, Voltaire n'atteint le sublime. Il n'y dépasse jamais une grandeur stylisée, une grandeur d'honnête homme, la seule vraiment à portée de son âge, trop raisonnable, trop civilisée. Sa *Henriade*, sur le plan poétique, correspond très exactement à ce que sont, dans la peinture, ces portraits de famille ou de parade qui campent de nobles personnages devant un champ de bataille de convention et les entourent de figures allégoriques.[12]

It would be difficult to disagree with this verdict. *La Henriade* is the masterpiece of a defunct artistic form. Yet its very real merits—the smooth, rapid, and logical unfolding of a fascinating story, the expert analysis of character and motive, the forceful presentation of a unified point of view— make it something more than an 'unreadable' literary curiosity.

It is possible to overstress the role played by political and artistic calculation in its composition. The Voltaire who wrote the first version, *La Ligue*, was a determined young man in search of fame and fortune, already an outstandingly successful publicist and highly sensitive to contemporary political factors and to the wishes of the public. But the poem is far from being the clever product of a detached mind. It deals with matters which were to engage Voltaire's passionate interest for the rest of his life: war, intolerance, the causes and effects of religious dissension, the definition of 'true' religion and its relationship to political power and ethics, patriotism, the nature of kingship, and the qualities of an authentic hero.

The underlying subject is fanaticism in both its political and religious manifestations, from the 'false zeal' of callous and hypocritical priests, who take advantage of mob ignorance and prejudice in order to defy legitimate authority, to the

12. *SV*, XXXVIII, 9–10.

horrors of uncontrolled 'enthusiasm' encouraged by weak, cynical, or corrupt leaders. *La Henriade* is much more akin to *Mahomet*, *Alzire*, or *Les Guèbres* than to the *Aeneid*. Whenever Voltaire touches on this question, he writes with an impassioned eloquence which goes beyond dignified rhetoric. The most famous example is the description of the Saint Bartholomew's Day massacre, but there are many others, such as the scenes of mob fanaticism (pp. 431 and 451–452), the attack on monasticism (pp. 444–445), the death of d'Ailly at the hands of his father (p. 520), the description of the Paris mob during the siege (pp. 562–568), or the portrait of a regicide (pp. 449–450).

The negative and critical aspect of Voltaire's message is made crystal clear in these passages, which are in striking contrast to the ideal of *bienfaisance* exemplified by the hero. Henri's principles of kingship are in conformity with the Fenelonian maxims of the early tragedies, *Œdipe* and *Mariamne*.[13] A king should be the father of his people, entirely devoted to their welfare (p. 498). He can only reign effectively by love, not fear. The chivalric virtues of courage, endurance, and skill in war are necessary, but may be useless or even dangerous unless tempered by compassion, justice, and a genuine concern for human happiness:

C'est peu d'être un Héros, un Conquérant, un Roi,
Si le Ciel ne t'éclaire, il n'a rien fait pour toi . . . .(p. 479)

Like the wise and just Louis XII (p. 490), Henri is portrayed as 'un roi bienfaisant, le modèle des Rois' (p. 567), sublime in his clemency and *grandeur d'âme*, as befits the representative and protégé of a beneficent deity (p. 530). As a man of action who is profoundly humane and *sensible*, he is close to being Voltaire's perfect hero. His character combines three ingredients of Voltairean sensibility: *bienfaisance*, enlightenment, and virtue in the republican sense of virile patriotism and self-sacrifice.[14] Voltaire admired Henri's

13. Like Fénelon, Voltaire expresses dislike of courtiers and court intrigue (p. 455), hatred of tyranny (p. 487), which he equates with rebellion (p. 434), but remains a royalist.

14. There is a similar portrait in the *Essai sur les mœurs* (ed. Pomeau, II, 533), in which Henri's *bienfaisance* is particularly stressed.

'éloquence du cœur' and his reforming activity more than his heroic qualities. As Michelet remarked, *La Henriade* may have disappeared, but not before the idealized image of its central character—'héros de clémence, d'humanité, d'un cœur facile et tendre'—had become firmly etablished in the minds of Frenchmen.[15] It was Voltaire's epic poem which made him one of the saints of the cult of sensibility.

As elsewhere in Voltaire's works, 'true' religion is defined both negatively and positively. It is not concerned with pomp or worldly power and therefore its ministers should have no political influence; it is totally devoid of fanaticism and hypocrisy and offers no support for tyrants. Religion should teach those virtues which God has engraved on all hearts (p. 484): benevolence, tolerance, and a willingness to suffer. The two references to the example set by the early Christians in this respect are no doubt intended to draw attention to the belligerence and worldliness of their successors, but they are also in keeping with the Stoic tendencies of the poem, for example the admiration for those Roman senators who

> Attendaient fièrement, sur leur siège immobiles
> Les Gaulois et la mort avec des yeux tranquilles. (p. 436)

The religious lesson of *La Henriade* is thus a peculiarly Voltairean mixture of deism, primitive Christianity, Stoicism, sentimental benevolence, and hostility to *l'infâme*.

For Voltaire, these were life-and-death issues, not abstractions. Unfortunately, the heavy hand of tradition, his own formal conservatism, his constant striving for dignified eloquence and anxiety to stay within the bounds decreed by convention conspire to give a superficial impression of coldness. The personifications of Discord, Religion, Fanaticism, and Love are ineffective substitutes for the classical deities. Most of the situations and many of the verses are too obviously derived from literary models, particularly Virgil, Racine, and Corneille. The young poet, consciously attempting to create the first great national epic according to the rules, was much too sensitive to criticism and too aware of the magnitude of his task to allow himself the luxury of originality.

15. *Histoire de France*, XIV, 384.

Nevertheless, Voltaire's sensibility is already apparent in his passionate denunciation of the evils wrought by zealots and in his fervent appeal for *bienfaisance*. It is latent in the outline of themes which will be more fully developed later when, with the change of taste, the man of feeling will be less rigidly inhibited. And in spite of appearances, in its psychology and conception of the hero, the poem has a certain romantic flavour. As Raymond Naves has noted, 'Si un tel poème n'est pas une épopée, les héros ont quelques parties du caractère épique que le romatisme développera.'[16]

For the modern reader, Voltaire's qualities as a poet are more apparent in the casual poems, the *stances*, the *épîtres*, the *poésies mêlées*, on which he seems to have placed little value. Free of the obligation to produce large quantities of noble, correct, and carefully controlled verses on a given model, he becomes completely himself: original, spontaneous, imaginative; in short, a poet. Unless one takes the narrow view that 'light' verses belong to a separate category, it is surely unjust to refuse to accept as poetry the many exquisite short lyrics hidden away in the Moland edition of the complete works; poems such as the *Epître des vous et des tu*, a little masterpiece of its kind, addressed to a former mistress who has become a respectable and unapproachable *grande dame*, in which the poet, by the simple but effective device of alternating the formal and familiar second person pronouns, contrasts the carefree happiness of youth with the changes wrought by time; or *Aux Mânes de M. de Genonville* on Voltaire's favourite theme of friendship, a poem which movingly conveys a sense of nostalgia and time's irreversibility and which reveals the character of the author at his best: a dedicated friend, a man of warm personality and deep feeling who did not always take himself seriously, who was disillusioned but not cynical and sentimental without being mawkish.

The subjects range from advice to kings to verses accompanying a soup recipe, and from expressions of love to personal invective, with a few frequently recurring themes, notably time, death, preference for the simple life, love of

16. *Voltaire, l'homme et l'œuvre*, p. 109.

freedom, and contempt for servility. Not all the poems are
'light'; some are serious in message and tone. They include
philosophical verses suggesting that virtue is more to be
prized than rank, flattery, or military fame (M. X, 244) and
a poignant comment on the forewarning of death (M. X,
246).

The *épître* entitled *L'Auteur arrivant dans sa terre, près
du lac de Genève*, which Lamartine admired, is a hymn to
new-found freedom ('Liberté! liberté! ton trône est en ces
lieux. . . .'), ending in an appeal to two Voltairean deities,
Friendship and Freedom, to join in presiding over his retreat:

> Descend dans mes foyers en tes beaux jours de fête.
>   Viens m'y faire un destin nouveau.
> Embellis ma retraite, où l'Amitié t'appelle;
> Sur de simples gazons viens t'asseoir avec elle.
> Elle fuit comme toi les vanités des cours,
> Les cabales du monde et son règne frivole.
> O deux divinités! vous êtes mon recours.
> L'une élève mon âme, et l'autre la console:
>   Présidez à mes derniers jours! (M. X, 366)

The poem is full of historical references and is philosophical
rather than lyrical, but the dominant note is one of infectious
enthusiasm. Although not classified as such, it is Voltaire's
only really successful ode.

The best of the *épîtres* and *stances* have the kind of
spontaneity and perfect marriage of form and content which
one finds in so many of Voltaire's personal letters. With no
classical censor at his elbow and no model to follow, he makes
excellent use of those inimitable turns of phrase which
came to him naturally and which surprise, amuse, and not
infrequently move the reader. He seems to be perfectly at
ease, commenting on whatever comes into his head or
whatever is preoccupying him at the moment, always leaving
the strong imprint of his personality. His sensibility is
evident in the muted romanticism of many of these poems,
but since it is balanced by his sense of humour, it never
degenerates into the sentimentality more characteristic of the
age.

The verse tales included in the collection entitled *Contes de Guillaume Vadé* (1764) are successful for the same reason. Voltaire's reputation as the French Virgil not being involved, he could afford to be himself. Although the philosopher and man of taste condemned fairy stories—'ces imaginations fantastiques, dépourves d'ordre et de bon sens' (M. XIX, 431)—the poet was clearly fascinated. The delightful *Ce qui plaît aux dames* concludes with a defence of the poet as a magician which is worth quoting in full:

O l'heureux temps que celui de ces fables,
Des bons démons, des esprits familiers,
Des farfadets, aux mortels secourables!
On écoutait tous ces faits admirables
Dans son château, près d'un large foyer.
Le père et l'oncle, et la mère et la fille,
Et les voisins, et toute la famille,
Ouvraient l'oreille à monsieur l'aumônier,
Qui leur faisait des contes de sorcier.
On a banni les démons et les fées;
Sous la raison les grâces étouffées
Livrent nos cœurs à l'insipidité;
Le raisonneur tristement s'accrédite;
On court, hélas! après la vérité:
Ah! croyez-moi, l'erreur a son mérite. (M. X, 19)

The *Education d'un prince* begins in similar vein:

Je veux au coin du feu vous faire un nouveau conte:
Nos loisirs sont plus doux par nos amusements.
Je suis vieux, je l'avoue, et je n'ai point de honte
De goûter avec vous le plaisir des enfants. (M. X, 20)

Voltaire is not seriously proposing a new departure in poetry, but he is obviously enjoying himself. It is surprising that an author who is reputed to have had no sympathy for the Middle Ages was able to capture so perfectly the spirit of the medieval tale, and even more so that a man in his seventies should be capable of writing poems of this nature, remarkable for their youthful freshness and the author's delight in story-telling for its own sake.

Voltaire also excelled in another unexpected role: as translator of Old Testament poetry. He was particularly attracted to the book of *Ecclesiastes* by its poetic expression of the vanity of human aspirations and by the disillusioned but eminently sane philosophy of its maxims. 'Il montre le néant des choses humaines, il conseille en même temps l'usage raisonnable des biens que Dieu a donnés aux hommes: il ne fait pas de la sagesse un tableau hideux et révoltant; c'est un cours de morale fait pour les gens du monde' (M. IX, 484). His own version, the *Précis de l'Ecclésiaste*, composed originally for the marquise de Pompadour, who had become 'dévote', is a highly successful transmutation of Biblical wisdom into eighteenth-century philosophical poetry. Without betraying the spirit of the original, Voltaire stresses themes which occur elsewhere in his own work: man's profound ignorance (M. IX, 485); the advantages of the simple and natural life ('Mais mon goût s'émoussait en fuyant la nature: / Il n'est de vrais plaisirs qu'avec de vrais besoins' [M. IX, 486]); and the ultimate nothingness of the things of this world: 'tout se corrompt, tout se détruit, tout passe' (M. IX, 490). The atmosphere of melancholy and lament for vanished youth is beautifully evoked in lines of Lamartinian simplicity and purity:

Je ne vous verrai plus, beautés dont la tendresse
Consola mes chagrins, enchanta mes beaux jours.
O charme de la vie! ô précieuse ivresse!
Vous fuyez loin de moi, vous fuyez pour toujours.

(M. IX, 491)

What lesson is to be drawn? 'Usez, n'abusez point', and above all practise *bienfaisance*:

Répandez vos bienfaits avec magnificence;
Même au moins vertueux ne les refusez pas;
Ne vous informez point de leur reconnaissance:
Il est grand, il est beau de faire des ingrats. (M. IX, 493)

Incredibly, the poem was condemned in 1759 to be burnt by the public executioner.

Voltaire was even more impressed by the *Song of Songs*: 'c'est le poëme le plus tendre, et même le seul de ce genre, qui nous soit resté de ces temps reculés. Tout y respire une simplicité de mœurs qui seule rendrait ce petit poëme précieux' (M. IX, 496). Its dramatic construction, using dialogue and chorus, reminded him of Greek tragedy. His comments on the poem are particularly interesting because they contain his most powerful plea for a better understanding of 'primitive' forms of literature, too readily dismissed as barbarous by French men of letters who insult antiquity from the depths of their ignorance and presume to judge everything according to the petty standards of the Paris opera (M. IX, 498). He has nothing but contempt for critics whose prejudices prevent them from appreciating the universal beauty of a great poem: 'Ils ne connaissent que nos petits amours de ruelle, ce qu'on appelle des conquêtes; ils ne peuvent se faire une idée des temps héroïques ou patriarcaux; ils imaginent que la nature a été au fond de l'Asie ce qu'elle est dans la paroisse de Saint-André des Arts ou des Arcs, et dans la cour du Palais' (M. IX, 497). The genuine passion of the *Song of Songs*, he concludes, is infinitely more poetic than French 'galanterie'.

The *Précis du Cantique des cantiques* and the *Précis de l'Ecclésiaste* are related to *Rome sauvée* and *Tancrède*. Voltaire is attempting to point up, by means of contrast, the mediocrity, artificiality, and petty concerns of contemporary society. On the literary level, he would like to see a more vigorous and natural use of language and less fear of *le mot juste*: 'D'où vient notre délicatesse? C'est que plus les mœurs sont dépravées, plus les expressions deviennent plus mesurées. On croit regagner en paroles ce qu'on a perdu en vertu. La pudeur s'est enfuie des cœurs, et s'est réfugiée sur les lèvres. Les hommes sont enfin parvenus à vivre ensemble sans se dire jamais un seul mot de ce qu'ils sentent et de ce qu'ils pensent; la nature est partout déguisée, tout est un commerce de tromperie' (M. IX, 499). It is therefore the height of hypocrisy for a corrupt age to criticize the *Song of Songs* for its supposed indecency: 'Rien de plus naturel, de plus ingénu, de plus vrai que le *Cantique des cantiques*'

(M. IX, 499). His own translation, he adds, is not obscene but 'tendre' and 'noble', like the original. Voltaire's *Précis* is indeed the work of a sensitive and perceptive poet-critic; it could not have been written by a literary bigot.

At a higher level in the Voltairean hierarchy, and correspondingly farther removed from the modern conception of what poetry should be, are the philosophical poems. While they are perhaps best described as 'distinguished', with all that this adjective implies, rather than immediately appealing, one cannot help but feel that Voltaire has been the victim of a certain amount of prejudice against the genre itself. Undisguised didacticism and philosophizing in verse is out of fashion, but it is not impossible that when the current exclusive vogue for a particular form of lyricism has run its course, Voltaire's virtues as a poet will be more widely recognized.

Some of these are in evidence in the long *Discours en vers sur l'homme* (1734–1737). Inspired by Pope's *Essay on Man*, it is by no means an inferior pastiche. The verses are smooth, balanced, elegant, illumined by intellect rather than feeling, and include such well-known maxims as 'La liberté dans l'homme est la santé de l'âme' (M. IX, 391). On the whole, the poem is an expertly rhymed moral tract, although Voltaire's poetic inspiration is stimulated, as is often the case, by the theme of friendship (M. IX, 405; 423). Contemporary readers were nevertheless inclined to regard it as a significant contribution to the literature of sensibility, if Condorcet's reaction is any guide: 'La variété des tons, *une sorte d'abandon, une sensibilité touchante, un enthousiasme* toujours noble, toujours vrai, leur donnent un charme que l'esprit, l'imagination et le cœur, goûtent tour à tour: charme dont Voltaire a seul connu le secret; et *ce secret est celui de toucher*, de plaire, d'instruire sans fatiguer jamais, d'écrire pour tous les esprits comme pour tous les âges.'[17]

Voltaire's two best-known philosophical poems, the *Poème sur la loi naturelle*, composed in 1752, and the *Poème sur le désastre de Lisbonne*, written three years later, are often cited as examples of the alternation of optimism and pessi-

17. M. I, 216–217. My italics.

mism and of the decisive effect on Voltaire's outlook of the
Lisbon disaster. There is, undeniably, a marked difference
between them, but this is less a matter of philosophical
principles than of mood and emphasis.

The *Poème sur la loi naturelle* is a resounding affirmation
of Voltaire's positive deism. God exists; his law is made known
to men through the voice of conscience; it reveals itself in
the benevolent actions of those who follow nature and in the
remorse which men who are not totally depraved feel for
their crimes. The poem does not, however, proclaim that
God's purposes are fully comprehensible or that all is well
with the world. On the contrary, the most trenchant passage,
culminating in a strikingly sombre Pascalian image, describes
man's wretchedness:

> dans nos jours passagers de peines, de misères
> . . . . . . . . . . . . . . . . . . . . . . . . . . . . . . . . . . . .
> Je crois voir des forçats dans un cachot funeste,
> Se pouvant secourir, l'un sur l'autre acharnés,
> Combattre avec les fers dont ils sont enchaînés.
>
> (M. IX, 456)

Many other verses could be cited to show that philosophical
purpose does not automatically banish poetry, notably the
attack on fanaticism (M. IX, 454) and the final prayer. The
*Poème sur la loi naturelle* is one of Voltaire's most eloquent
pleas for humanitarian sensibility. At the same time, it is
undeniably a long didactic work concerned with issues which
have lost their urgency. As with all poems of its type, it
suffers from a tendency to prosaism, which can easily degener-
ate into chatty banality or pompous sermonizing. One cannot
help thinking that a thesis of this nature is better expounded
in prose. Yet the general effect is not simply that of a well-
written pamphlet. It is elegant, clear, and persuasive, but
it is also sufficiently close to some of Voltaire's deepest
concerns to at least touch the fringes of what he called the
'sublime'.

The *Poème sur le désastre de Lisbonne* is quite different.
It is not a discussion in verse of the relationship between

philosophy, morality, and religion, but the immediate, anguished reaction of a humane and sensitive man to the suffering of thousands of human beings. Lisbon was a long way from Geneva by the contemporary scale of distance and Voltaire had no particular affection for a city notorious for the activities of the Inquisition. But the opening description of scenes of destruction and terror in the wake of an earthquake have all the vivid actuality of experience or of a nightmare which cannot be conjured away. Voltaire is there, among the ruins, uttering a cry of horror and compassion:

> Ces débris, ces lambeaux, ces cendres malheureuses,
> Ces femmes, ces enfants, l'un sur l'autre entassés,
> Sous ces marbres rompus ces membres dispersés;
> Cent mille infortunés que la terre dévore,
> Qui, sanglants, déchirés, et palpitants encore,
> Enterrés sous leurs toits, terminent sans secours
> Dans l'horreur des tourments leurs lamentables jours!
>
> (M. IX, 470)

The poem is lyrical in inspiration rather than reflective. It is didactic in the sense that *Candide* is didactic, and indeed it makes its point in the same way, by contrasting the real horror of the human condition with the complacent abstractions of optimistic philosophers. The long description of misery and destruction is interrupted periodically by the calm voice of a smug theorist proclaiming that 'tout est bien': 'Dieu s'est vengé, leur mort est le prix de leurs crimes'; 'Tout est bien, et tout est nécessaire'; 'Tous vos maux sont un bien dans les lois générales'. As in *Candide*, the reader is constantly jerked back to earth and forced to look at life as it is.

The key verse is 'Je respecte mon Dieu, mais j'aime l'univers', followed by two equally significant lines:

> Quand l'homme ose gémir d'un fléau si terrible
> Il n'est point orgueilleux, hélas! il est sensible.
>
> (M. IX, 471)

This is certainly true of the author. If the poem has a thesis, it is simply that the voice of the heart is much closer to the essential *human* truth than the constructions of ingenious minds. Our itch to rationalize experience, to find solutions for insoluble metaphyical problems leads us away from the only thing that matters, compassion.

> Vous criez 'Tout est bien' d'une voix lamentable.
> L'univers vous dément, et votre propre cœur
> Cent fois de votre esprit a réfuté l'erreur. (M. IX, 474)

It is a further tribute to Voltaire's sensibility that in the conflict between his deism and his humanitarian instincts, the latter take precedence. He does not reject God, or even Providence—'Humble dans mes soupirs, soumis dans ma souffrance, / Je ne m'élève point contre la Providence'—but he rejects the notion that God's nature is amenable to human explanation. The *philosophe sensible* can only worship and hope; he cannot justify the ways of God to men.

Since Voltaire's sensibility is so immediately involved, the verses are more original, more 'Voltairean', than those of the *Poème sur la loi naturelle*. The unforgettable line, 'Vous criez "Tout est bien" d'une voix lamentable', is reminiscent of *Candide*; 'Atomes tourmentés sur cet amas de boue' of *Micromégas* and *Zadig*. The juxtaposition of elements not normally associated constantly jolts the reader. And who but Voltaire would have thought of the comparison between Bayle and Samson?

> Assez sage, assez grand pour être sans système,
> Il les a tout détruits, et se combat lui-même:
> Semblable à cet aveugle en butte aux Philistins,
> Qui tomba sous les murs abattus par ses mains.
>
> (M. IX, 477)

# CHAPTER 6

# *Tearful Tragedy*

Voltaire's interest extended over a broad range of poetic forms. His marked preference, however, was for the theatre, and particularly for tragedy.[1] He considered himself to be first and foremost a serious dramatist and was content to base his literary reputation on *Mérope*, *Zaïre*, *Alzire*, *Mahomet*, and *Tancrède*. To his contemporaries, he was the worthy successor of Racine. His plays enjoyed a critical esteem and public favour which placed him far ahead of any other eighteenth-century dramatist. They drew more spectators and aroused more comment than those of his distinguished predecessors of the seventeenth century.[2] They were translated and produced throughout Europe, including England, where they attained a peak of popularity during the third quarter of the century.[3]

Of Voltaire's total dramatic production, some thirty-one tragedies were publicly performed and many of these were frequently revived. Since most of them, whatever their official designation, clearly belong to the 'genre larmoyant', their author must be considered, on this score alone, as an outstanding figure of eighteenth-century sensibility. That he has not been generally recognized as such is presumably to be attributed partly to the tenacity of the myth concerning

1. 'Je ne vois pas comment on peut égaler une épître, une ode, à une bonne pièce de théâtre' (M. XXIV, 226).
2. Madeleine Fields's study of 'Voltaire et le *Mercure de France*' (*SV*, XX, 210) shows that during the period 1717–1766 Voltaire was mentioned in the *Mercure* 250 times, compared with 210 times for Racine, 127 for Corneille.
3. H. L. Bruce, 'Period of Greatest Popularity of Voltaire's Plays on the English Stage', *MLN*, 33 (January 1918), 23.

his views and character[4] and partly to the fact that his plays are no longer acted or read. If Voltaire could return to survey the graveyard of his favourite children, he would no doubt be moved to add further stanzas to his poem on the vanity of human wishes and the nothingness of all things. From the point of view of the literary historian, however, there is no question as to the importance of Voltairean tragedy in any assessment of the tendencies in French drama which led from *Athalie* to *Hernani*.

Even before *Athalie*, the theatre was beginning to evolve in the direction of melodrama. Corneille regarded tragedy as a 'machine à créer l'émotion' and was not above using complicated plots and sensational incidents, especially in his later tragedies, in order to stimulate the spectator's curiosity or anguish. These external obstacles, rather than the hero's struggle to overcome them by an extraordinary effort of the will, seem to have captured the interest of the dramatists and public of the early eighteenth century. The essential qualities of Racine were similarly ignored if one is to judge by the frequent use of the word 'tendre' to describe his plays: strange misunderstanding of an author who explored the depths of human passion with a harsh clarity which has never been equalled.

Before the turn of the century, Campistron was producing tragedies such as *Andronic* (1685) and *Tiridate* (1691), in which the hero was a passive victim of destiny. La Fosse in his *Manlius* (1698), the first French tragedy to show a definite English influence, followed his example by portraying the love of one of his characters as a touching weakness rather than as the source of destructive passion. Crébillon, whose early tragedies were hailed as works of genius and who later became Voltaire's only serious rival, extracted maximum dramatic effect by concentrating on surprise and horror. Another author of the transitional period, La Grange-

4. The discrepancy between the stereotype Voltaire and tendencies evident in the tragedies has led to some strange judgments, e.g. N. M. Bernardin's comment on *Zaïre*: 'Faire triompher à la scène une tragédie religieuse et tendre, quand on n'a soi-même ni religion dans l'âme ni presque aucune tendresse dans le cœur, c'était assez joli, déjà' ('Le Théâtre de Voltaire. *Zaïre*', RCC, 22 [20 juin 1914], 668).

Chancel, whose black and white characters and startling situations remind one of the novel of adventure, 'had in him the makings of a Romantic dramatist', according to H. C. Lancaster.[5]

The first real example of a *drame larmoyant* in neoclassical disguise was Lamotte's *Inès de Castro*. Voltaire, who was present at the first performance in 1723, was able to judge the effect on a public which was becoming more interested in 'la douceur de pleurer' than in genuine tragedy. 'J'ai vu aujourd'huy Ines de Castro', he wrote to the marquise de Bernières, 'que bien des gens condamnent, et voient pourtant avec plaisir. . . . On joue Ines deux fois la semaine et tout y est plein jusqu'au cintre' (Best. D154).

The classical ideal was rapidly losing ground to a type of theatre appealing more directly to the senses. Or perhaps it would be more accurate to say that French tragedy was reverting to something closer to the norm, since Corneille and Racine were exceptions of genius rather than typical seventeenth-century dramatists. What was new was not so much the manipulation of complicated intrigues as the emphasis on sentiment, on passivity rather than will, on the sufferings of virtue. It was this type of 'tragédie tendre' which Voltaire was to develop and perfect.

None of these plays had a clear-cut moral or philosophical aim, but the idea was very much in the air at the beginning of the century. That literature should teach a moral lesson was, of course, a commonplace of classical theory. Fénelon gave it a new twist by suggesting that the French theatre should imitate the moral seriousness of Greek tragedy 'sans y mêler cet amour volage et déréglé qui fait tant de ravages',[6] but substituting Christian morality for pagan myths. In his *Dissertation critique sur l'Iliade* (1715), the abbé Terrasson contended that the majority of people are more likely to be influenced by maxims concretely embodied on the stage than by those declaimed from a pulpit, while the abbé de Saint-Pierre took this argument to its logical conclusion in an

5. H. C. Lancaster, *A History of French Dramatic Literature in the Seventeenth Century* (Baltimore, 1929–1942), pt. 4, I, 384.
6. *Lettres à M. Dacier sur les occupations de l'Académie* (1714), in *Œuvres complètes* (Paris, 1850), VI, 633.

article published in the *Mercure* of April 1726 and recommended that authors be deliberately encouraged, by the award of titles and pensions, to produce plays beneficial to the state: 'Je suis de l'avis de ceux qui pensent que les bons Citoyens, dans leurs belles Pieces serieuses, peuvent inspirer, entretenir, et fortifier l'amour pour la Patrie, et des sentiments de courage, de justice et de *bienfaisance*'.[7]

The theoretical basis for a theatre of sentiment, first elaborated by Dubos, was supported by Lamotte, who stated in his *Discours* of 1730 that the true aim of tragedy is to make the audience weep and that the best way of doing this is to create a series of varied tableaux, to introduce more realism, more pathos, more spectacle, and above all more action, as exemplified in the works of the English playwrights.

Voltaire added little that was really new. Precedents can be found for most of the views expressed in his major pronouncements on tragedy. His achievement was to combine the various strands into a coherent doctrine and to provide highly successful examples of what was in effect a new genre.

The one essential principle governing Voltaire's theory and practice of the theatre is the necessity for strong emotional appeal. A play is defined as 'une expérience sur le cœur humain' (M. XXXI, 194); it must therefore be directed to the feelings, not primarily to the intellect. In all his writings on the theatre—prefaces, critical works, articles, incidental comments in the correspondence and elsewhere—he returns again and again to this central thesis:

C'est au cœur qu'il faut parler dans une tragédie. (M. XXXI, 338)

Le théâtre, soit tragique, soit comique, est la peinture vivante des passions humaines. (M. II, 323)

Il faut plus que de la beauté. Il faut se rendre maître du cœur par degrés, l'émouvoir, le déchirer. (M. XVII, 406)

Tout ce qui n'est point fait pour remuer fortement l'âme n'est pas du genre de la tragédie: le plus grand défaut est d'être froid. (M. XXXII, 191)

Ce sont les passions qui font l'âme de la tragédie. Par

7. 'Mémoire pour rendre les Spectacles plus utiles à l'Etat', *Mercure* (avril 1726), p. 715.

conséquent un héros ne doit point prêcher, et doit peu raisonner. Il faut qu'il sente beaucoup et qu'il agisse. (M. XXXII, 348)

Si vous ne frappez pas le cœur du spectateur par des coups toujours redoublés au même endroit, ce cœur vous échappe. (M. XXXII, 168)

Heureuses les pièces où tout parle au cœur, qui commencent naturellement, et qui finissent de même! (M. XXXII, 361)

Si vous avez versé quelques larmes à Zaïre ou à Alzire, vous n'avez point trouvé parmi les défauts de ces pièces là l'esprit d'analyse, qui n'est bon que dans un traité de philosophie, et la sécheresse, qui n'est bonne nulle part. (Best. D1697)

Point de milieu entre s'attendrir et s'ennuyer.

(M. XXXII, 349)

Je n'ai consulté que mon cœur; il me conduit seul; il a toujours inspiré mes actions et mes paroles. (M. V, 295)

Nothing should be cold or insipid. The dramatist's first task is to find a subject that will 'tear the heart'; it is then his business to maintain emotion at the highest pitch. The great weakness of French tragedy, in Voltaire's view, is that it is deficient in this kind of emotional intensity: 'Il nous a presque toujours manqué un degré de chaleur; nous avions tout le reste' (M. XXIV, 219). Even Racine is not excepted, especially in those tragedies where too often elegant conversation takes the place of passion. Corneille, however, is the chief offender. He rarely succeeds in moving audiences to tears (M. XXXI, 532). 'La pitié et la crainte, les deux pivots de la tragédie, ne subsistent plus. Corneille a souvent oublié ces deux ressorts du théâtre tragique. Il a mis à la place des conversations dans lesquelles on trouve souvent des idées fortes, mais qui ne vont point au cœur' (M. XXXII, 160–161). This is the main reason why his tragedies, with all their outstanding qualities, are inferior to those of Racine: 'Corneille raisonnait plus qu'il ne sentait, au lieu que Racine sentait plus qu'il ne raisonnait: et au théâtre il faut sentir' (M. XXXI, 202).

Naturally enough, Voltaire was attracted by the possibility

of dramatizing historical events, but he was the first to admit that historical subjects must be combined with the depiction of passion if they are to be successful on the stage. The type of discussion which is entirely appropriate in a work of history makes for dull theatre. Hence the relative unimportance of the historical background in *Adélaïde du Guesclin*: 'Si j'avois baucoup parlé des guerres civiles, Adelaïde ne toucheroit pas tant. Il ne faut jamais perdre un moment son principal sujet de vue' (Best. D675).

Nor is it sufficient to rely on the epic stature of the hero to inspire emotion. 'Ce genre de tragédie', he says of Corneille's *Nicomède*, 'ne se soutenant point par un sujet pathétique, par de grands tableaux, par les fureurs des passions, l'auteur ne peut qu'exciter un sentiment d'admiration pour le héros de la pièce. L'admiration n'émeut guère l'âme, ne la trouble point. C'est de tous les sentiments celui qui se refroidit le plus tôt' (M. XXXII, 94). Strength of character is, however, an admirable quality in a tragic hero providing it is associated with sensibility, since 'les âmes fortes ont des sentiments bien plus violents que les autres quand elles sont tendres'.[8]

Obviously the only certain way to gauge the success of the kind of theatre that Voltaire had in mind is to observe the emotional reaction of the spectators. If they weep, it has fulfilled its purpose; if they remain dry-eyed, it can hardly be called tragic, for 'qu'est-ce qu'une tragédie qui ne fait pas pleurer?' (Best. 9437). The ultimate test of excellence in composition and performance is therefore quite simple: one counts handkerchiefs. In a letter praising Mme Denis' acting ability, Voltaire suggests that the Ferney production of a play is not necessarily inferior to that of the Comédie Française: 'Je voudrais qu'on pût compter les larmes qu'on verse à Paris et chez nous, et nous verrions qui l'emporte.'[9]

8. *L'Ingénu*, M. XXI, 302.
9. Best. 8505. This seems to have been the general view in the eighteenth century. In one of Marmontel's short stories, *La Bonne Mère*, a mother who has to decide between two equally desirable candidates for son-in-law, takes them both to the theatre and opts for the one who bursts into tears at the pathetic moment in the drama. Tears not only gave a clear indication of the quality of a play, but also of the moral character of the spectators.

Voltaire's primary concern with emotional effect helps to explain his apparently contradictory attitude to the role of sexual love in tragedy. Throughout his career he was tempted by the idea of writing a successful tragedy with no love interest whatever, an ambition which he achieved in *Mérope*. It was not so much a question of fundamental opposition to love in tragedy as of his intense dislike of the French habit, as he saw it, of replacing genuine passion by 'long amorous conversations'. He distinguished between 'l'amour tragique' and 'la galanterie', that is, love treated for its own sake and therefore more suited to comedy. 'Il n'y a point de sujets tragiques', he wrote, 'qui souffrent que l'amour y soit introduit. Il faut qu'il y soit nécessaire; qu'il en soit la base; qu'il en soit l'âme unique. Furieux, terrible, auteur des crimes accompagnés de remords, il est tragique: ainsi dans *Phèdre*, dans *Roxane*, dans *le Cid*; mais, étranger dans la pièce, il devient galant et froid.' [10] One is reminded of Diderot's views on the place of love in the novel.[11]

In theory, Voltaire preferred tragedy based on other, even stronger emotions—maternal love, for example, 'le sujet le plus touchant et le plus vraiment tragique qui ait jamais été au théâtre' (M. IV, 192–193)—but he was too sensitive to public preference to consider total exclusion. Moreover, *Zaïre* convinced him that he had a flair for depicting passionate love in tragedy and that he was right to allow himself to be dominated by his feelings:

> *Zaïre* est la première pièce de théâtre dans laquelle j'ai osé m'abandonner à toute la sensibilité de mon cœur; c'est la seule tragédie tendre que j'aie faite. Je croyais, dans l'âge même des passions les plus vives, que l'amour n'était point fait pour le théâtre tragique. Je ne regardais cette faiblesse que comme un défaut charmant qui avilissait l'art des Sophocle. . . . Il faut de la tendresse et du sentiment; c'est même ce que les acteurs jouent le mieux. . . . Il a donc fallu me plier aux mœurs du temps, et commencer tard à parler d'amour (Best. D517).

10. *Sottisier*, p. 126.
11. See Georges May, *Diderot et 'la Religieuse'* (Paris, 1954), p. 9.

He finally compromised by saying that other passions are perhaps more suited to tragedy but the treatment of love is permissible if it is genuinely tragic and if it remains the centre of interest.[12]

In spite of his stated aim of defending good taste, Voltaire was less a 'literary' dramatist than an eminently practical man of the theatre with audience reaction uppermost in his mind. He drove actors to despair by insisting on correcting and rewriting in the course of production, always with the aim of extracting the maximum possible emotion. His motto was not 'frapper juste' but 'frapper fort'. He thought of a play as something quite different from any other kind of poem.[13] All poetry should appeal first to the emotions, but an ode or an epic is usually read privately in tranquillity; it can be analysed, pondered, re-read at leisure. A play is not intended for the study but for the stage; the literary qualities of the printed version are therefore secondary.[14] Voltaire was much more interested in whether a play acted well than whether it read well: 'La situation est théâtrale; elle attache malgré la réflexion. Une invention purement raisonnable peut être très-mauvaise. Une invention théâtrale, que la raison condamne dans l'examen, peut faire un très-grand effet. C'est que l'imagination, émue de la grandeur du spectacle, se demande rarement compte de son plaisir' (M. XXXI, 563).

Hence his relative lack of concern for the depiction of well-rounded characters, for the logical unfolding of plot, and for considerations of probability. An emotional recognition scene, a surprising reversal of events, a spectacular tableau,

12. 'L'amour doit régner seul . . .; il n'est pas fait pour la seconde place' (M. IV, 9).

13. 'There is one kind of poetry of which the judicious readers and the men of taste are the proper judges. There is an other that depends upon the vulgar, great or small. Tragedy and comedy are of these last species. They must be suited to the turn of mind and to the ability of the multitude and proportion'd to their taste' (Voltaire to Sir George Lyttleton, 17 May 1750 [Best. 3577]).

14. To d'Argental on the subject of L'Enfant prodigue: 'Je peux la corriger pour les lecteurs, mais ce que j'y ferais est inutile pour le théâtre. Je vous demande donc en grâce qu'on la joue telle que je vous la renvoie; et quand il s'agira de l'impression, vous serez si sévère qu'il vous plaira' (Best. D1052).

an ingenious and striking coup de théâtre can be counted on
to compel the spectator to suspend his disbelief, at least for
the duration of the performance.[15] On the other hand,
a tragedy which fails to move the audience for which it is
written, however carefully composed according to the rules
of good taste and probability, is nothing. Voltaire could be
quite frank on the subject: 'Pour qu'une tragédie ait du
succès il faut qu'elle soit tendre. Ce n'est pas le bon qui
plaît, c'est ce qui flatte le goût dominant' (Best. 4980).
One should beware, however, of mistaking this frankness
for cynicism. The conflict here is between culture and
instinct, between the 'honnête homme' and the man of
the theatre. Voltaire was a dramatist who calculated his
effects, but he was no cold sentimentalist like Dubos or La
Chaussée. He knew what the public wanted and he knew
that he was particularly suited by temperament and dramatic
gifts to supply it.

Ironically, while satisfying the growing public taste for
sentiment and melodrama, and thus making the decisive
break with classicism, Voltaire managed to convince himself
that he was upholding the French tradition. He saw himself
as a moderate reformer, a liberal-minded conservative rather
than a revolutionary. There was no question in his mind of
tampering with the basic doctrine of Boileau. Although
willing to concede that the bienséances are 'always a little
arbitrary', he considered the unities to be absolutely necessary, pointing to the fact that the epochs when playwrights
of genius, such as Lope de Vega and Shakespeare, were
ignorant of them, were now universally regarded as barbarous (M. II, 48–49). His idea of a liberal interpretation of the
unity of time was to extend it to one day instead of three
hours; of the unity of place, to permit the action to unfold in
'plusieurs endroits contigus que l'œil puisse voir sans peine'.
He was careful to qualify recommendations for more action
and greater attention to spectacle by adding that a descriptive

---

15. 'Un vraisemblable froid et glaçant', he wrote, referring to the
bizarre tomb scene in Sémiramis, 'ne vaut pas un colin maillard vif et
terrible. . . . Le public s'accoutumera bien vite au colin maillard du
tombeau, quand il sera touché du reste' (Best. 3347).

passage written by Racine is superior to any theatrical action and that four beautiful verses are worth more than a 'regiment of cavalry'. The real value of a tragedy as a work of literature lies in the quality of its poetry, and here Racine, along with Corneille at his best, are the undisputed models.

As Voltaire saw it, the one serious charge which could be brought against classical French tragedy was its lack of warmth. To remedy this, he prescribed a judicious admixture of the features which appealed to him most in the tragedies of the ancient Greeks and the English. His often-quoted witticism at the expense of the former—'Comment trouvez-vous ces tragédies grecques?—Bonnes pour des Grecs'—[16] should not be taken too seriously. He found Greek tragedy to be crude, static, and lacking in the qualities of a well-made play; the Greeks had no conception of the use of suspense in drama and too often mistook horror for terror; but their redeeming qualities of simplicity, force, and passion made their modern French counterparts seem pale and superficial by comparison. Voltaire agreed with Diderot that the Greek playwrights, unlike the French, knew how to 'tear the heart'. Above all, he admired their high conception of tragedy as a solemn religious spectacle on a vast scale: 'Les véritablement grandes tragédies, les représentations imposantes et terribles, étaient les mystères sacrés qu'on célébrait dans les plus vastes temples du monde, en présence des seuls initiés: c'était là que les habits, les décorations, les machines, étaient propres au sujet; et le sujet était la vie présente et la vie future' (M. XXIV, 212).

The virtues and defects of the English stage are described as somewhat similar. Even more barbarous and inclined to monstrous scenes of horror and carnage, it is also vital, spectacular, and imaginative, and excites emotions of an intensity unknown to French spectators, accustomed to polished conversational dialogue. Would it not be possible, he asks, to make some of these situations, which now seem 'horrible and disgusting', acceptable to French audiences by

16. *L'Ingénu*, M. XXI, 279.

moderating their violence and presenting them in regular and beautiful verse?[17]

The great advantage of the English theatre over both the Greek and the French, according to Voltaire, is its preference for 'action'. As his use of the term clearly indicates, he had in mind not only the depiction of actual events as opposed to poetic description, but also a kind of visual effect such as those which had so profoundly impressed him at performances of Shakespeare's *Julius Caesar*.[18] As an example of what could be achieved in France, he praised the 'natural' style of acting in the performance of his *Oreste* and *Sémiramis*:

> Qui aurait osé, avant Mlle Clairon, jouer dans *Oreste* la scène de l'urne comme elle l'a jouée? qui aurait imaginé de peindre ainsi la nature, de tomber évanouie tenant l'urne d'une main, en laissant l'autre descendre immobile et sans vie? Qui aurait osé, comme M. Lekain, sortir, les bras ensanglantés, du tombeau de Ninus, tandis que l'admirable actrice qui représentait Sémiramis se traînait mourante sur les marches du tombeau même? Voilà ce que les petits-maîtres et les petites-maîtresses appelèrent d'abord des postures, et ce que des connaisseurs, étonnés de la perfection inattendue de l'art, ont appelé des tableaux de Michel Ange. C'est là en effet la véritable action théâtrale. Le reste était une conversation quelquefois passionnée. (M. VI, 268)

One may be forgiven for observing that this description inevitably calls to mind wild-eyed melodrama rather than Michelangelo. Voltaire himself pointed out the resemblance between his idea of action and what Diderot was advocating for the *drame*: 'Je prie mon cher frère [Damilaville] de dire au frère Platon [Diderot], que ce qu'il appelle pantomime, je l'ai toujours appelé action'; adding, 'J'ai toujours songé autant que je l'ai pu à rendre les scènes tragiques pittoresques'

17. M. II, 318–319. This suggestion prompted Flaubert to exclaim, 'Singulier pronostic: Voltaire pressentait-il le romantisme dont on pourrait dire que théâtralement il fut une des origines?' (*Le Théâtre de Voltaire*, ed. Theodore Besterman, *SV*, L, 33).

18. 'Au reste, quand je parle d'une action théâtrale, je parle d'un appareil, d'une cérémonie, d'une assemblée, d'un événement nécessaire à la pièce' (M. IV, 500).

(Best. 9599). It seems likely that this taste for striking and pathetic tableaux owed less to the Greeks or Shakespeare than to the sentimental tragedies and melodramas which were popular at the time of his stay in England.[19]

In any case, Voltaire's attempt to rejuvenate French tragedy, strongly influenced by his personal preference for emotional drama, was in effect a rejection of classicism in favour of a new kind of play which was tragedy in name only. It was designed to appeal to a public whose taste inclined to the romanesque rather than to psychological insight, to sentiment rather than to intellectual analysis.[20] Its essential element was *l'intérêt*, another favourite term, generally used in the sense of strong emotional and dramatic effect produced by heart-rending situations, regardless of whether these are capable of surviving cold analysis by the rare 'censeurs éclairés'. 'La religion combatue par les passions', he wrote to the sceptical Frederick, explaining why *Zaïre* and *Alzire* were so successful, 'est un ressort que j'ay employé, et c'est un des plus grands pour remüer les cœurs des hommes. Sur cent personnes, il se trouve à peine un philosophe, et encor sa philosophie cède à ce charme et à ce préjugé qu'il combat dans le cabinet. Croyez moy sire, tous les discours politiques, tous les profonds raisonnements, la grandeur, la fermeté sont peu de choses au téâtre, c'est l'intérest qui fait tout, et sans luy il n'y a rien' (Best. 3374).

To Voltaire, the success of a play depended as much on the choice of the subject as on the treatment.[21] Eighteenth-century critics praised the great variety which he introduced to the French stage, especially his comparisons of different civilizations: Christian and Mahometan in *Zaïre*, Tartar and Chinese in *L'Orphelin de la Chine*, Greek and Scythian in *Les Lois de Minos*, American and European in *Alzire*. Always in search of novelty, Voltaire was proud of the fact that he had widened the geographical and historical

19. See H. Fenger, *Voltaire et le théâtre anglais* (Copenhagen, 1949), pp. 260, 262–263.

20. Best. D1879; M. XXXI, 386.

21. 'Le mérite est de bien conduire et de bien écrire mais le bonheur est le choix du sujet' (*Notebooks*, ed. Theodore Besterman. *The Complete Works of Voltaire*, vol. 82, p. 453); 'Mon dieu ce que c'est que de choisir un sujet intéressant!' (Best. D515).

horizons of French tragedy; justifiably so, for he may certainly
be said to have made a substantial contribution to the development of exoticism and local colour.

Basically, however, he was attracted to two types of subject, the first dealing with matters of political and historical
importance—revolution, republican ideals, the example of
great men—the other, best exemplified by *Zaïre* and *Alzire*,
stressing 'tenderness' associated with love, family affection,
or *bienfaisance*. They correspond, as has already been noted,
to two equally important trends in eighteenth-century
sensibility. Like many later exponents of sentimental
literature, Voltaire inclined now to one now to the other.
He sometimes contrasted them, claiming that while his own
preference was for Roman idealism, the French public,
dominated by feminine influence, generally preferred 'tender' subjects. 'Le public', he complained, in his justification
of *Le Triumvirat*, 'semble n'aimer que les sentiments
tendres et touchants, les emportements et les craintes des
amantes affligées. Une femme trahie intéresse plus que la
chute d'un empire. J'ai trouvé dans cette pièce des objets qui
se rapprochent plus de ma manière de penser et de celles de
quelques lecteurs qui, sans exclure aucun genre, aiment les
peintures des grandes révolutions ou plutôt des hommes qui
les ont faites' (M. VI, 178). Yet he admitted that he was
ideally suited to write *tragédies tendres* in the style of
*Zaïre*: 'Vous vous serez aperçu, en essayant dans votre
imagination les sujets que vous vous proposiez, qu'il y en a
toujours un qui se fait faire malgré qu'on en ait. Le goust
se détermine tout seul vers le sujet pour le quel on se sent
plus du talent' (Best. D536). Voltaire's taste, as well as
public demand, frequently directed him towards romanesque plots concerning star-crossed lovers.

Whether cast in the heroic or sentimental mould, Voltaire's tragedies are expressions of eighteenth-century optimism, idealism, and confidence in the goodness of man. The
subject in both cases is virtue: virtue in distress but ultimately
triumphant or virtue in the Latin sense. Both types appealed
strongly to audiences in the second half of the century.

He was therefore justified in calling his theatre a 'school

of virtue'.[22] He never disguised his moralizing intentions; on the other hand, he agreed with Dubos that the dramatist's main purpose is to give pleasure by arousing emotion, and disliked the idea that a play might be confused with a sermon. What he meant by 'a school of virtue' is suggested by such statements as 'on doit le plus qu'on peut mettre les maximes en sentiment'. The question of whether he considered the aim of tragedy to be esthetic or moral has very little significance. For Voltaire and his contemporaries, the two could hardly be separated. The eighteenth-century theatre of sensibility was by definition a means of conveying morality through feeling, the most satisfying feeling being that which arises from the contemplation of acts of benevolence or *grandeur d'âme*.

M. J. Chénier sums up the theory succinctly by saying that 'L'homme est essentiellement sensible. Le poète dramatique, en peignant les passions, dirige celles du spectateur.'[23] It was a universally accepted commonplace that since the dramatist is concerned with emotion, and since emotion rather than reason dictates conduct, his obligation to raise moral standards is even greater than that of the philosopher. According to the *Encyclopédie*, 'Les poètes dramatiques dignes d'écrire pour le théâtre ont toujours regardé l'obligation d'inspirer la haine du vice, et l'amour de la vertu, comme la première obligation de leur art.'[24] The general opinion in the eighteenth century was that Voltaire had admirably fulfilled this mission and that he, more than any other writer, was responsible for converting the stage into a school of morality. La Harpe's tribute may be taken as typical:

22. e.g. M. IV, 505; II, 457; V, 299; XXII, 247. The strongest statement occurs in Best. 8722, in which he claims that the theatre has made converts and that his own plays are dramatized moral tracts.

23. *Œuvres*, IV, 347.

24. Art. 'Tragédie'. The writers and critics of the seventeenth century had said much the same, but with a different emphasis. The eighteenth century was less concerned with the negative lesson than with the positive teaching of *bienfaisance*. Hence Jaucourt's definition of the aim of poetry in the art. 'Poésie': 'Le but de la poésie est de plaire, & de plaire en remuant les passions; mais pour nous donner un plaisir parfait & solide, elle n'a jamais dû remuer que celles qu'il nous est important d'avoir vives, & non celles qui sont ennemies de la sagesse.'

Le Théâtre, agrandi sous son brillant pinceau,
Offrit des Nations le mobile tableau,
Fit passer sous les yeux les rapides images
Des préjugés, des mœurs, des loix & des usages.
Le cœur toujours ému, de plaisir transporté,
S'ouvrant au sentiment, reçut la vérité.
Ainsi, des passions que le Théâtre exprime,
Voltaire sut tirer la morale sublime,
Et ne se bornant pas à de stériles pleurs
Attendrit les humains pour les rendre meilleurs.[25]

No doubt there is a distinction to be drawn between moral and philosophical propaganda in Voltairean tragedy, but it is as difficult to establish as that between its moral and esthetic aims. Voltaire deliberately confused them, partly because he sincerely believed *philosophie* and *bienfaisance* to be practically synonymous and partly because his claims to morality were a form of insurance against the censor. When he protested, in a letter to Mle Quinault, 'Je n'ai pourtant fait aucun ouvrage dont la religion et les mœurs ne fussent le fondement' (Best. D1209), he was obviously putting his own interpretation on the words 'religion' and 'mœurs'; but from his point of view the statement was strictly accurate.

Voltaire's dramatic theory is thus a mixture of tradition and novelty. He thought that he was effectively safeguarding the former by insisting on obedience to the basic classical rules and on preserving the harmonious elegance and noble decency of a poetic style modelled on that of Racine. It is clear, however, with the hindsight of two centuries, that these features were in effect a *trompe-l'œil* concealing the rapid evolution of tragedy towards a form of theatre not very different from Diderot's *drame*, with sentiment, 'action', and an eighteenth-century conception of moral purpose as the main pivots. The similarity has been noted by Norman Torrey: 'The essential differences between the two men in regard to the theatre resolve themselves into relative degrees of courage and common sense. Diderot

25. La Harpe, *Les Muses rivales, ou l'Apothéose de Voltaire* (Paris, 1779), p. 18.

displayed the greater courage and his ideas were destined for the future. Voltaire realized in a more practical way the difficulties involved in breaking with the past; and his plays were the more successful.'[26] The last point is worth emphasizing. Voltaire was not only two decades in advance of Diderot; as the century's most successful dramatist, he had a much greater following and influence. It was thanks largely to his prestige that the framework of neoclassical tragedy survived into the nineteenth century. But this framework was nothing more than an irrelevant and anachronistic shell. His real importance as theorist and playwright lies in his contribution to the fundamental transformation of the French theatre which began in the 1730s.

If Professor Pomeau is correct, the end of the era of French tragedy and the beginnings of melodrama may even be said to date from the performance of Voltaire's first tragedy, Œdipe, in 1718.[27] 'Plein de la lecture des anciens', and inspired by the supremely tragic situation of the third and fourth acts of Œdipus Rex, Voltaire was already attempting to remedy the coldness of his predecessors by presenting a 'civilized' version of the terrible events dramatized by Sophocles. The result is a play equally far removed from the spirit of both Greek and classical French tragedy.

The unity and tragic force of Œdipus Rex lie in the gradual unfolding of a situation which is clear to the spectators from the opening scene. Voltaire manipulates the plot in order to create suspense. The emphasis is no longer on Œdipe's growing awareness of the full horror of his position, but on the identity of the murderer of Laïus. Moreover, by insisting on the innocence of the principal characters, Voltaire converts a religious myth into a humanist protest against a hostile and unjust destiny. The tragedy ends on a note of defiance more reminiscent of Alfred de Vigny or Thomas Hardy than of Sophocles:

> . . . au milieu des horreurs du destin qui m'opprime,
> J'ai fait rougir les dieux qui m'ont forcée au crime.
>
> (M. II, 111)

26. 'Voltaire's Reaction to Diderot', PMLA, 50 (1935), 1126.
27. Religion de Voltaire, p. 89.

Apart from Œdipe's Fenelonian conception of kingship, there is little in the play which could be called sentimental. There is no trace of conflict between Jocaste's rigid conception of duty and her feelings for Philoctète. *Mariamne* (1724), on the other hand, shows unmistakable signs of Voltairean sensibility and is Voltaire's first attempt to put into practice his precept that the theatre should teach virtue. After an initial failure, he produced a second and much more successful version by following suggestions in Elijah Fenton's play on the same subject.[28] Mariamne becomes a tender and forgiving wife whose concern for the welfare of her subjects brings the tyrant Herod to the realization of the advantages of *bienfaisance*:

> Ma rigueur implacable,
> En me rendant plus craint m'a fait plus misérable.
> Assez et trop longtemps sur ma triste maison
> La vengeance et la haine ont versé leur poison.
>
> (M. II, 197)

This 'most unlikely candidate of all for the title of the Man of Feeling'[29] is the first of a long line of characters similarly directed towards repentance by virtuous example.[30]

On his return from England, Voltaire gave the Comédie Française a series of tragedies which established beyond any doubt his reputation as the foremost French dramatist. English influence is manifest in *Brutus* (1730), filled with 'cette force et cette énergie qu'inspire la noble liberté de penser' (M. II, 311), and in *La Mort de César*.[31] Both plays

28. K. H. Hartley, 'The Sources of Voltaire's *Mariamne*', *AUMLA*, 21 (1964), 5–14.

29. Hartley, p. 12.

30. Desfontaines particularly admired this conception of the character of Herod: 'Rien n'affecte plus vivement que les retours d'*Hérode* sur lui-même. Devenu son propre accusateur, il touche par la peinture de ses crimes & des vertus de *Mariamne*; ces deux objets ainsi réunis, réveillent toute la tendresse des spectateurs' (*Veritez litteraires sur la tragedie d'Herode et de Mariamne adressées à M. de Voltaire* [Paris, 1725], p. 17).

31. Composed in 1731, performed privately in 1733 and at the Comédie Française in 1743.

are remarkable for their impressive visual effects[32] and the substitution of action for description.

*La Mort de César* is particularly interesting as an early example of the duality of Voltairean sensibility and the fusion of its 'masculine' and 'feminine' aspects in the same play, and indeed in the same character. In general, Voltaire's truncated version follows the outline of Shakespeare's *Julius Caesar*. The most significant change is in the relationship between the two principal characters. In *La Mort de César*, interest is focused on the fact that Brutus is Caesar's son; the subject of the play is therefore not only political assassination but parricide. Voltaire's Brutus is a fiery idealist, 'toujours indépendant, toujours citoyen', a fanatic of freedom who exclaims, 'Qu'il est beau de périr dans des desseins si grands!' (M. III, 338). At the same time, he is unmistakeably a man of feeling for whom the voice of nature is stronger even than the call of patriotic duty. Voltaire's comments indicate that this internal conflict was intended to compensate for the lack of 'interest' inevitable in a play dealing exclusively with political matters:

> C'est même cette circonstance terrible, et ce combat singulier entre la tendresse et la fureur de la liberté, qui seul pouvait rendre la pièce intéressante; car de représenter des Romains nés libres, des sénateurs opprimés par leur égal, qui conjurent contre un tyran, et qui exécutent de leurs mains la vengeance publique; il n'y a rien là que de simple; et Aristote (qui après tout était un très grand génie) a remarqué avec beaucoup de pénétration et de connaissance du cœur humain, que cette espèce de tragédie est languissante et insipide. (Best. D1034)

*Eriphyle* (1732), with its theme of maternal love, its lugubrious setting and its ghost—a rather clumsy imitation of Hamlet's father—was a bold attempt by Voltaire to demonstrate the possibility of combining 'l'élégance moderne' with 'la force antique' (M. II, 459). The *Mercure*

32. In *Brutus*, the assembly of senators, lictors, and slaves; in *La Mort de César*, the gatherings of senators and conspirators, the 'people' on stage, the exhibition of Caesar's body.

called it 'une Tragedie dans un gout entirement nouveau'.
It is particularly notable for the introduction of a new type
of female character, very different from the classical heroine.
As an accomplice in the murder of her first husband, Eriphyle
is guilty of a crime for which she is eventually punished by
being killed (in error, as so often in Voltairean tragedy) by
her own son. Yet she is portrayed as *sensible*, and therefore
fundamentally virtuous and open to remorse. Her crime is
attributed to the impetuosity and inexperience of youth:

> C'est cet âge fatal et sans expérience,
> Ouvert aux passions, faible, plein d'imprudence;
> C'est cet âge indiscret qui fit tout mon malheur.
>
> (M. II, 466)

Voltaire is thus able to exploit one of his favourite themes—
the repentant sinner—while arousing the audience's sympathy for virtue in distress.

*Brutus* and *Eriphyle* were only moderately successful,
while *La Mort de César* was not considered suitable for
production at the Comédie Française until 1743. It was
the veritable flood of tears provoked by the enormously
popular *Zaïre* (1732) which convinced Voltaire that he had
at last found the perfect formula for a theatre of sensibility:
an innocent, ardent, and charmingly feminine heroine endowed with 'extreme tenderness' and exciting pity rather
than admiration; characters who are virtuous victims of
chance or passion; a melodramatic plot offering ample
opportunity for tearful recognition scenes, pathos, and coups
de théâtre; a 'vieillard sensible'; a crime which is followed
immediately by remorse; and an exotic or unusual setting,
in this case the colourful background of the Crusades. Everything in the play is calculated to awaken sentiment, including
a dialogue heavily laced with exclamations. Even that
favourite device of later popular melodrama, 'la croix de ma
mère', makes its appearance. The fact that the play hinges
on the improbable misreading of a letter, that the psychology
is often false and the characterization shallow is secondary;
what matters is the effect produced in the theatre, and on this

score Voltaire had good reason to be satisfied.[33] *Zaïre* played to enthusiastic audiences throughout the eighteenth century and, like his other highly successful sentimental dramas, *Alzire* and *Tancrède*, was equally popular during the heyday of romanticism.

*Adélaïde du Guesclin* (1734), *Alzire* (1736), and *Zulime* (1740) followed a similar pattern with varying success. *Adélaïde* was even provided with the happy ending which would seem to be the logical outcome of plays based on an optimistic assessment of human nature. Vendôme, 'tendre mais emporté', orders the death of Nemours, his brother and rival for the affections of Adélaïde. When the firing of a cannon indicates that the execution has been carried out, 'nature' re-establishes its rights. In an agony of remorse, he bitterly reproaches himself:

Ennemi de l'Etat, factieux, inhumain,
Frère dénaturé, ravisseur, assassin,
Voilà quel est Vendôme! (M. III, 130)

Fortunately, the execution has not taken place. Vendôme rushes to his brother to wash away the memory of his perfidy in a flood of tears:

Ah! c'est trop me montrer mes malheurs et ma perte!
Mais vous m'apprenez tous à suivre la vertu.
Ce n'est point à demi que mon cœur est rendu. (M. III, 135)

Voltaire makes the best of both tragic worlds. The audience is offered the double pleasure of experiencing the horror of fratricide, followed by ecstatic and tearful reconciliation.

*Alzire* is perhaps an even more typical example of Voltairean tragedy than *Zaïre*, since in addition to the features

33. The marquise de Pompadour's reaction is typical: 'Cette piece est un chef-d'œuvre; elle nous convient surtout, car c'est celle des ames sensibles' (*Lettres de Mme la marquise de Pompadour* [Londres, 1772], 3ᵉ partie, p. 42). La Harpe said of it, 'Si l'on s'en rapporte aux effets du théâtre si souvent et si vivement manifestés depuis plus de cinquante ans, si l'on consulte l'opinion la plus générale dans toutes les classes de spectateurs, je crois ne pas trop hasarder en assurant que *Zaïre* est la plus touchante de toutes les tragédies qui existent' (*Lycée*, IX, 147).

mentioned it has a clearly defined moral and philosophical thesis, outlined in the *Epître à Mme du Châtelet*: 'J'ai essayé de peindre ce sentiment généreux, cette humanité, cette grandeur d'âme qui fait le bien et qui pardonne le mal; ces sentiments tant recommandés par les sages de l'antiquité, et épurés dans notre religion; ces vraies lois de la nature, toujours si mal suivies' (M. III, 377). Voltaire had no difficulty in depicting these feelings; he had only to consult his own heart: 'J'ose vous dire que les sentimens vertueux qui sont dans cette pièce, sont dans mon cœur' (Best. D1000).

Stated bluntly, his aim is to teach Christians the real significance of Christianity. True religion, he says, 'est de regarder tous les hommes comme ses frères, de leur faire du bien et de leur pardonner le mal' (M. III, 379). It has little to do with dogma or ritual and its commandments are inscribed, not in sacred books, but on the hearts of all men whose natural feelings have not been eroded by excessive self-interest. By situating his drama in South America at the time of the Spanish conquest, Voltaire provided himself with ample opportunity to emphasize the universality of moral law. The Americans have their own code of honour and are not subject to the European vice of hypocrisy. They are simple, courageous, and naturally virtuous, 'savage' only when reacting to Spanish cruelty. At the same time, he justifies his use of the term 'religious' in the more conventional sense to describe his tragedy by making the Spaniard Alvarez the representative of enlightened Christianity and by the repentance of Alvarez' son, Gusman, a hard-line imperialist and advocate of brute force.

The whole play, from the opening scene, in which Alvarez expounds his philosophy of tolerance and benevolence, to the last words of Gusman—'Tout vous est pardonné puisque je vois vos pleurs'—is an elaboration in dramatic form of the main tenet of Voltaire's sentimental religion: listen to the voice of the heart. Melodrama and morality effectively complement each other. Pathetic situations, recognition scenes, and sudden changes of heart had an irresistible appeal for spectators avid for new emotional experience. They were also absorbing the lesson that sensibility engenders virtue. Zamore's tears of recognition are sufficient proof for Alvarez of the soundness of his character:

> Ne cache point tes pleurs, cesse de t'en défendre;
> C'est de l'humanité la marque la plus tendre.
>
> (M. III, 399)

Gusman's conversion seems sudden and contrived to the modern reader; in the context of eighteenth-century drama it is adequately prepared by the simple statement that he is *sensible* (M. III, 421) in spite of all evidence to the contrary.

All the characters weep abundantly. In fact, one is left with the impression that they enjoy their grief. 'Ne puis-je voir enfin ces captifs malheureux', asks Alzire, 'Et goûter la douceur de pleurer avec eux?' (M. III, 408). Alzire is in tears even before she speaks (M. III, 392). Zamore, who represents the noble savage led astray by passion and the thirst for vengeance, is introduced as 'un jeune Américain, les yeux baignés de larmes' (M. III, 388) and breaks down at the thought of meeting Alzire (M. III, 409). Tearful comedy had little to offer in comparison with this inexhaustible flow. As Servières remarked, 'Aussi tendre que *Zaïre*, mais plus forte dans la tendresse, *Alzire* touche les cœurs les moins sensibles.'[34]

Enthusiastically received during its initial run and frequently revived, *Alzire* was quickly accorded a high place among Voltaire's tragedies. It was recognized by critics as highly original and not strictly in accordance with the rules, but undoubtedly a masterpiece of sentimental literature. Gresset epitomized the general reaction in verses which probably did not displease the author:

> Aux règles, m'a-t-on dit, la pièce est peu fidèle.
> Si mon esprit contre elle a des objections,
> > Mon cœur a des larmes pour elle:
> Le cœur décide mieux que les réflexions.[35]

34. *Mémoires pour servir à l'histoire de M. de Voltaire* (Amsterdam, 1785), II, 193.
35. Quoted M. III, 370.

*Mahomet ou le Fanatisme* (1741) is without doubt Voltaire's most powerful propaganda play, the subject of which is indicated in the sub-title. But it is also clear from his summary that he conceived it as a *drame larmoyant* with pathos and sensibility balancing and supporting the philosophical thesis:

> . . . un Séïde qui sût être à la fois entousiaste & tendre, féroce par fanatisme, humain par nature, qui sût frémir et pleurer; une Palmire animée, attendrie, effrayée, tremblante du crime qu'on va commettre; sentant déjà l'horreur, le repentir, le desespoir, à l'instant que le crime est commis; un père vraiment père qui en eût les entrailles, la voix, le maintien; un père qui reconnait ses deux enfans dans ses deux meurtriers, qui embrasse en versant ses larmes avec son sang; qui mêle ses pleurs avec ceux de ses enfans, qui se soulève pour les serrer entre ses bras, retombe, se penche sur eux; enfin, ce que la nature & la mort peuvent fournir à un tableau.[36]

In *Mahomet*, the negative and positive aspects of Voltaire's deism are presented with equal force, although in his desire to heighten the contrast between good and evil he confuses the philosophical issues by making Mahomet an ambitious scoundrel rather than a genuine fanatic. The conflict is between the unscrupulous self-interest of a man who despises 'nature' on the one hand, and justice and humanity on the other. 'L'intérêt est ton dieu', says Zopire to Mahomet, 'le mien est l'équité; / Entre ces ennemis il n'est point de traité' (M. IV, 127). Mahomet's influence is founded on error and fear; Zopire opposes reason to fanaticism and presents the case for 'nature' and feeling.

In the scenes between Zopire and his children, the 'voice of nature', that 'wonderful affection which near relations are supposed to conceive for one another, even before they know that they have any such connection',[37] is more than a

36. *Des divers changemens arrivés à l'art tragique* in *Contes de Guillaume Vadé* (Geneva, 1764), pp. 208–209.

37. Adam Smith, *The Theory of Moral Sentiments* (London, 1892), p. 326.

dramatic device to produce instant emotion; it is part of Voltaire's whole nature mystique and obviously related to the instinct variously known as the voice of the heart, conscience, or natural law, which guides the conduct of the man of feeling. Zopire does not know that Séide and Palmire are his children. The latter are equally unaware of their relationship to Zopire and have been so effectively indoctrinated by Mahomet that they are willing to murder the man who turns out to be their own father. Yet in their presence Zopire feels a mysterious attraction:

> Hélas! plus je lui parle, et plus il m'intéresse?
> Son âge, sa candeur, ont surpris ma tendresse.
> Se peut-il qu'un soldat de ce monstre imposteur
> Ait trouvé malgré lui le chemin de mon cœur?
>
> (M. IV, 140)

Séide, for his part, hesitates before striking Zopire, warned by a benevolent deity who is obviously not the god of Mahomet:

> Un autre dieu, peut-être, a retenu mon bras.
> . . . . . . . . . . . . . . . . . . . . . . . . . . . . . . . .
> A mon cœur éperdu l'humanité parlait. (M. IV, 146)

When the identity of Séide and Palmire is revealed, Zopire realizes that the voices of God, nature, and the heart, which are really one voice, have not deceived him:

> O mes fils! ô nature! ô mes dieux!
> Vous ne me trompiez pas quand vous parliez pour eux.
> Vous m'éclairiez sans doute. (M. IV, 153)

This is the kind of scene which Voltaire—and his audience —regarded as high tragedy: one in which the maximum of pathos is extracted from a situation both heart-rending and morally instructive. 'Pour moi', wrote one spectator, '*mes larmes coulent*, mon oppression plus vive n'a rendu ma pitié que plus touchante, je n'ai point cessé de frémir, et je pleure . . . *Situation délicieuse! état heureux d'un art divin!*'[38]

38. *Nouveaux amusements du cœur et de l'esprit* (1737–1749), XIV, 354. According to Gazon Dourxigné (*Ami de la vérité*, p. 39), 'Il faut avoir une ame forte pour supporter même la lecture de cette Piéce'.

In *Mérope* (1743), the voice of nature, in this case speaking through maternal love, is again associated with an ethic of *bienfaisance* and contrasted with the 'vil intérêt' of a cruel and selfish tyrant. The lesson is conveyed by the sentimental maxim which underlies Voltairean tragedy: 'Il ne faut consulter que le ciel et son cœur' (M. IV, 246).

This 'mélange inouï d'horreur et de tendresse' is another attempt to combine the simplicity, solemn spectacle, and power of Greek drama with French decency. Voltaire considered that he had finally realized his ambition of writing a thoroughly classical tragedy, composed strictly according to the rules, without sacrificing 'interest'. Even the most severe of contemporary critics agreed. *Mérope* was universally admired as an example of 'pure' tragedy. It does not, however, diverge significantly from the general pattern. The theme of maternal love is treated emotionally, not explored in depth. The melodramatic coups de théâtre, especially the scene in which Mérope utters her famous cry of anguish, 'Barbare! il est mon fils', were the parts most appreciated. Voltaire's prestige production was in fact a triumph of sensibility, as is evident from critical comment[39] and from the enthusiastic remarks of an expert on the subject, Mme de Graffigny: 'Il semble que l'intérêt ne puisse augmenter, et cependant c'est bien pis, car si l'on a pleuré au troisième acte, on s'arrache les cheveux au quatrième, on s'égratigne le visage au cinquième. . . .' (Best. D1686).

*Mérope* was followed by two other 'Greek' tragedies. *Sémiramis* (1748) is one of Voltaire's strangest plays. He called it 'cette espèce de drame, vraiment terrible et tragique' (M. IV, 501) and claimed once again to have created 'un nouveau genre de tragédie' (M. IV, 501). It contains many of the features which audiences had now come to expect: intensely dramatic situations provoking shock and anguish; a feverish recognition scene; and the intervention

---

39. 'C'est de toutes les Piéces de M. de Voltaire, celle qui fait verser le plus de larmes aux représentations, et qui attendrit le plus à la lecture' (Gazon Dourxigné, *Ami de la vérité*, p. 46). In Poinsinet's play, *Le Cercle ou la Soirée à la mode* (1764), one of the characters vows she will never go to see *Mérope*: 'Mais, fi donc! une femme ne sort de ce spectacle que les yeux gros de larmes et le cœur de soupirs.'

of the voice of nature, here referred to as 'une force incon-
nue', 'un pouvoir secret', and conceived as a divine instrument for inducing repentance.

Apart from its ambitious spectacle, this reworking of the
forgotten *Eriphyle* is chiefly remarkable for its oppressive
atmosphere of terror, violence, and the supernatural. The
murky climax occurs in the midst of tombs and underground
passages. Even the style has the 'graveyard' quality of
Young's *Night Thoughts*:

> Sémiramis, à ses douleurs livrée,
> Sème ici les chagrins dont elle est dévorée:
> L'horreur qui l'épouvante est dans tous les esprits.
> Tantôt remplissant l'air de ses lugubres cris,
> Tantôt morne, abattue, égarée, interdite,
> De quelque dieu vengeur évitant la poursuite,
> Elle tombe à genoux vers ces lieux retirés,
> A la nuit, au silence, à la mort consacrés;
> Séjour où nul mortel n'osa jamais descendre,
> Où de Ninus, mon maître, on conserve la cendre.
> Elle approche à pas lents, l'air sombre, intimidé,
> Et se frappant le sein de ses pleurs inondé. (M. IV, 508)

Not surprisingly, *Sémiramis* was one of Voltaire's most
popular plays during the preromantic period and continued
to be revived during the early nineteenth century.[40]

According to its author, *Oreste*, produced two years later,
is a play which retains the 'spirit' and 'substance' of
Sophocles' *Electra*. On the contrary, it is a perfect illustration
of the abyss which separates the sentimental optimism of
Voltairean melodrama from the tragic simplicity which he
admired so much in the Greeks. Sophocles' tragedy is not
devoid of pathos, but it contains no trace of tearful hysteria.
Voltaire's characters, with their ostentatious emotionalism,
their submission to an inner voice advocating reconciliation

---

40. In the *Anecdotes dramatiques* of 1775, *Sémiramis* is stated to be
'une des pièces de cet homme célèbre qui attire aujourd'hui le plus nombreux concours de spectateurs, et que l'on donne le plus souvent' (M. IV,
484). The figures given by Joannidès in *La Comédie-Française de 1680 à
1920* (Paris, 1921) confirm this.

or remorse, their total inability to act decisively, or indeed to do very much except weep in each other's arms, are little more than caricatures of the Greek originals. Electre is too *sensible* to hate her mother, in spite of her call for vengeance and in spite of the injustice she has suffered. 'Eh bien!' she exclaims,

> vous désarmez une fille éperdue.
> La nature en mon cœur est toujours entendue.
> Ma mère, s'il le faut, je condamne à vos pieds
> Ces reproches sanglants trop longtemps essuyés.
>
> (M. V, 99)

Clytemnestre, torn between self-interest and maternal feeling, fails to silence the voice of the heart. Oreste kills his mother by mistake and immediately puts the blame on the gods. As in *Eriphyle* and *Sémiramis*, chance, the overworked deity of Voltairean drama, is invoked to replace fatality and provide an improbable but morally acceptable solution.

It is interesting to note that Voltaire, who was by no means insensitive to the real greatness of Greek tragedy, could see in it, as a practical dramatist, only the pretext for a series of touching scenes of recognition and reconciliation.

The effect of sensibility on character is also blatantly evident in *L'Orphelin de la Chine* (1755). In this play, a supposedly bloodthirsty tyrant who has led the Tartar hordes into China is suddenly transformed into an even less likely man of feeling than Herod. The all-powerful Gengis-Kan, having fallen madly in love with the wife of a Chinese mandarin, becomes the pitiable victim of a guilty conscience. "Que tout pèse à mon cœur en secret tourmenté!' he exclaims. 'Ah! je fus plus heureux en mon obscurité' (M. V, 335).

In spite of its novel setting, surely the ultimate in exoticism, *L'Orphelin de la Chine* is closely related to the Roman tragedies. The mandarin Zamti is a Chinese Brutus who does not hesitate to sacrifice his son to the cause of patriotic duty. His wife, Idamé, no less virtuous and patriotic, nevertheless places 'nature' above love of country. She refuses to substitute her own child for the Emperor's son, whose life is in danger. Thus the tension between 'masculine' and 'feminine' sensibility is here appropriately symbolized by the different priorities of a man and a woman, both sympathetic characters and both models of virtue. Eighteenth-century audiences tended to identify Zamti's devotion to the state with fanatical royalism and opted for Idamé. 'On était accoutumé sur notre théâtre à voir des sujets immoler leurs enfants pour sauver ceux de leurs rois, et l'on fut étonné d'entendre dans *l'Orphelin* le cri de la nature.'[41]

A marked decline in Voltaire's talents as a dramatist is evident after the triumph of *Tancrède* in 1760. His subsequent productions added nothing to his reputation and several of them were not even performed. Generally speaking, Voltaire's chief concern during the Ferney period was philosophical propaganda. It is not true, however, that reason replaced sensibility, as Laharpe seems to suggest.[42] On the contrary, the later plays, with few exceptions, are even less like genuine tragedy and even closer to the sentimental, moralizing *drame*.

The author of *Les Scythes* (1767) and *Les Guèbres* (1769) has clearly abandoned all pretence of fidelity to classical principles. In a letter to d'Argental, he spoke of *Les Scythes* as a *drame* which the actors should perform in exactly the same style as *Le Philosophe sans le savoir*: 'Le contraste qui anime la pièce d'un bout à l'autre, doit servir la déclamation, et prête baucoup au jeu muet, aux atitudes théâtrales, à touttes les expressions d'un tableau vivant' (Best. 12793). *Les Guèbres* is a 'tragédie plus que bourgeoise', with important characters below noble rank. These include an old gardener who leads a simple, useful life far from dissolute courts and cities, and who strongly resembles Voltaire as seen by Voltaire. In these two plays and in *Les Lois de Minos* (1773), all the devices of theatrical sensibility are marshalled in support of a message of 'humanity' and primitivism. The

41. Note by the Kehl editors (M. V, 318).
42. 'Ce n'est plus cette philosophie naturelle, cette douce morale du cœur, sobrement ménagée dans le dialogue et habilement fondue dans le sujet: c'est la raison d'un vieillard, c'est-à-dire, le résultat de l'expérience mis à la place des passions et des caractères' (*Lycée*, X, 425).

fact that they have become mechanical and even further removed from anything resembling reality is no reflection on the sincerity of Voltaire's intentions. He had already passed into legend as the hero of sentimental *bienfaisance* and was simply dramatizing his real-life role.

It is evident from this brief summary that Voltairean tragedy is much more a product of the age of sensibility than of neoclassical tradition. It is 'classical' only in style and in its adherence to certain conventions. Even the unities are frequently, albeit tacitly, violated. Changes of scene are fairly common, while the action of such plays as *Mahomet*, *L'Orphelin de la Chine*, and *Rome sauvée* can scarcely be imagined as taking place in the course of a single day.

The underlying philosophy is optimistic. In the idealized world of Voltaire's dramas, human nature is basically good, although easily perverted by egoism and passion. All men possess a God-given instinct which infallibly leads them to benevolent action unless they have deliberately closed their minds to 'nature'. Even then, it may still operate through repentance, usually inspired by the spectacle of virtue. Tyrants are almost invariably the unhappy victims of a guilty conscience. Mahomet himself, the arch-villain of Voltaire's melodramatic imagination, feels pangs of remorse just before the final curtain.

Given the superiority of instinct as a guide to behaviour, it follows that spontaneity and intensity of feeling are more to be admired than will power. Voltaire's most appealing characters, especially his heroines, are passive victims of misfortune, conspicuous for their tender devotion and self-sacrifice rather than for their decisiveness in moments of crisis. They have a romantic conception of love as something sacred and eternal which compels fidelity, even when the object of it has proved unfaithful. A character who is in love is always a sympathetic figure, whatever crime he may commit. Orosmane and Zamore, both guilty of murder, evoke pity rather than condemnation.[43] The only real

---

43. Condorcet has this to say of Orosmane: 'Jamais un amour plus vrai, plus passionné, n'avait arraché de si douces larmes; jamais aucun poëte n'avait peint les fureurs de la jalousie dans une âme si tendre, si naïve, si généreuse' (M. I, 205).

villains—and they are rare, since tragedy is more often the result of mischance than misdeed—are cold schemers who persist in remaining deaf to the voice of the heart.

This preference for virtuous characters has been noted by most commentators, contemporary and modern. It accorded perfectly with the general eighteenth-century outlook. The article 'Tragédie' in the *Encyclopédie* is explicit: 'Le but de la *tragédie* étant d'exciter la terreur & la compassion, il faut d'abord que le poëte tragique nous fasse voir des personnages également aimables & estimables, & qu'ensuite il nous les représente dans un état malheureux. Commencez par faire estimer ceux pour lesquels vous voulez m'intéresser. Inspirez de la vénération pour les personnages destinés à faire couler mes larmes.'[44]

Linguet sees Voltaire's tragedies as possessing two outstanding qualities in addition to the great variety of subjects: 'Le premier c'est cette philosophie touchante et majestueuse à la fois, dont il a rempli ses bonnes pièces. L'autre c'est de n'y avoir admis aucun personnage vil, ni lâche, ni absolument odieux'. The passage which follows is even more revealing. It clearly indicates why Voltaire was regarded in his own time as the undisputed master of the theatre of sensibility: 'Il n'a point de ces caractères qui révoltent, de ces horreurs qui indignent même contre l'auteur: il remue l'ame; il intéresse; il donne des leçons utiles sans employer d'autre ressource que la peinture des malheurs dont une conscience pure ne sauve pas toujours les hommes, & des sentiments honnêtes que les passions peuvent quelquefois combattre, mais non pas éteindre dans les coeurs vertueux.'[45]

The reason for Voltaire's popularity may be summed up in one word: emotion. The one sure way of supplying it in the eighteenth century was to show virtue in distress. To alleviate the monotony of uniform virtue, the distress must be acute and maintained. Moreover, characters who are on the stage primarily to express extreme emotion and whose

44. See La Harpe's comment: 'M. de *Voltaire* a l'avantage d'avoir peint sur la scène des âmes pures et vertueuses plus souvent qu'aucun autre auteur' (*Commentaire sur le théâtre de Voltaire par M. de La Harpe* [Paris, 1814], p. 209).
45. *Examen des ouvrages de M. de Voltaire*, p. 93.

psychological interest is slight require a sensational plot. As Lanson justly remarked apropos of La Chaussée, 'Le public comprend du premier coup la violence des transports d'un personnage qui est victime d'un roman mélodramatique: il est infiniment plus délicat de lui faire comprendre qu'on peut ressentir extraordinairement des événements ordinaires.'[46] The eighteenth century generally preferred intensity to subtlety and Voltaire was applauded for emphasizing the former.[47]

Tragedies with a romanesque plot were, of course, common enough in the seventeenth and eighteenth centuries. Voltaire was simply using the well-worn stage devices of his immediate predecessors, although usually with considerably more skill. They seemed fresh to contemporary audiences because he combined them with the new sentimental outlook, and more than that with a consistent philosophy of sensibility. Any number of French dramatists before him had resorted to the 'voice of nature' to add an element of mystery to plots based on mistaken identity;[48] Voltaire invested it with a moral and religious significance which made it seem less of a theatrical trick and gave the impression of originality.

It is not difficult to see why Voltaire's serious plays were held in the highest esteem until the early years of the nineteenth century and have been neglected ever since. If tragedy is a poetic expression of the tragedy of existence itself; if it offers a glimpse of the evil as well as the greatness of human personality; then, obviously, they are not tragedies in any true sense of the word. They belong, as Voltaire and his critics never tired of saying, to a 'new genre', best defined as a literary form of melodrama.[49] They have quali-

46. Gustave Lanson, *Nivelle de La Chaussée et la comédie larmoyante* (Paris, 1887), p. 242.

47. 'Ce grand Poëte ... n'a point analysé les sentiments, n'a point fait parler à *Melpomene* une langue barbare, n'a point effleuré les passions, il les représente avec tous leurs désordres, toute leur impétuosité' (Aquin de Château-Lyon, *Siècle Littéraire de Louis XV*, II, 60–61).

48. Clifton Cherpack has traced the history of its use on the French stage in *The Call of Blood in French Classical Tragedy*.

49. Popular melodrama developed independently during the latter part of the eighteenth century. As its name indicates, it was originally a play interspersed with songs.

ties which are by no means negligible. Voltaire was a born man of the theatre who knew how to create an effective dramatic situation and how to exploit it. He must be given credit for pioneering a large number of significant innovations—the important role accorded to spectacle, the introduction of subjects taken from national history, the use of local colour and the supernatural, the development of the *pièce à thèse*—which had a marked influence on the course taken by French drama, especially in the romantic period. Individual scenes could be cited which have a touch of greatness and some of the verses are memorable. It seems highly unlikely, however, that even the best of these plays could be resurrected, except as historical curiosities.[50] Their failure to hold the stage is not due entirely to the fact that they are shameless melodramas, or even to the deficiencies of a derivative and generally colourless style. Voltaire set himself the task of appealing directly to the feelings of a particular audience and succeeded only too well, with the result that his theatre is the perfect reflection of a vanished epoch.

Like Diderot's *drames*, and much else that was written in the same vein, his tragedies are a prime example of the truth of Gide's dictum, 'C'est avec les beaux sentiments qu'on fait de la mauvaise littérature.' The proposition that human nature is basically good and that emotional display is an infallible measure of character now seems absurdly naïve. It is difficult to take seriously characters who loudly proclaim their virtue and simplicity or a Mahomet who is constantly discussing his own vices and failings. But it was precisely the

50. For a contrary opinion, see Virgil W. Topazio, *Voltaire: A Critical Study of His Major Works* (New York, 1967), p. 90. If Voltaire's tragedies may be said to survive at all, they survive in nineteenth-century Italian opera. Bernard Shaw once remarked that the chief glory of Victor Hugo as a stage poet was to have provided libretti for Verdi. The same might be said of Voltaire. His plays inspired many composers, including Bellini (*Zaïre*) and Rossini (*Mahomet, Tancrède, Sémiramis*). Verdi's *Alzira* and Rossini's *Semiramide* have recently been revived with considerable success. More important perhaps is their indirect influence via romantic drama. The most celebrated of all grand operas, Verdi's *Aïda*, with its exotic setting, its spectacle associated with religious ceremony, its theme of jealousy and self-sacrificing love, its heroine, portrayed as the tender victim of circumstances and torn between love and filial duty, its attacks on fanaticism, has a thoroughly Voltairean libretto.

'touching philosophy' which made such a great impression
on contemporaries. Tragedy was defined in terms of Voltairean practice. According to Marmontel, 'La sensibilité
humaine est le principe d'où part la tragédie', and Voltaire is
the author who best understood this: 'C'est lui qui le
premier a répandu dans la *tragédie* cet intérêt si doux de la
touchante humanité; c'est lui qui, sur la scène, a fait un
sentiment religieux de la bienfaisance universelle; c'est lui
qui a mis dans les sujets modernes toutes les tendresses du
sang; et quel pathétique il en a tiré!'[51] The same writer, in
the comments added to his play *Aristomène*, after describing
the work of the best Greek and French writers of tragedy,
has this to say of Voltaire:

> ... qu'il me soit permis de demander quel rang méri-
> teroit parmi les Maîtres du Théatre une ame à la fois
> grande, simple, forte et sensible, qui se seroit pénétrée de
> tous les principes de la Morale, qui auroit fouillé dans tous
> les replis de la nature, et qui mêlant aux charmes de la
> plus tendre éloquence le coloris du Poëte et les lumières du
> Philosophe, aimeroit assez la vertu et l'humanité pour
> peindre l'une, et instruire l'autre, par l'organe du senti-
> ment.

D'Alembert also admired the philosophical content of the
tragedies, being careful to distinguish it from cold reasoning.
Voltaire succeeded, he says, in introducing 'non pas de la
philosophie froide et *parlière*, mais de la philosophie en
action' (Best. 9325). J. M. B. Clément stressed Voltaire's
originality in this regard: 'Jusques-là, on s'était borné à
rendre les grands crimes odieux; M. de Voltaire fait plus, il
rend la vertu aimable: chacun de ses drames est le pané-
gyrique de l'humanité. Il en est peu, s'il est permis de le
dire, dont on ne sorte plus honnête-homme qu'on n'y était
entré.'[52] Mistelet, in a book on sensibility published in 1777,
paid much the same kind of tribute: '*M. de Voltaire* est
peut-être le premier des Poëtes dramatiques qui ait répandu

---

51. Art. 'Tragédie' in the *Supplément de l'Encyclopédie*.
52. *Anecdotes dramatiques*, III, 488.

le plus de morale & de philosophie dans ses Pieces de Théâtre; & c'est pour cela, sur-tout, qu'elles sont tant suivies.'[53] Voltaire is hailed by this enthusiastic admirer of the literature of sentiment as one of the very few authors to succeed in infusing tragedy with the kind of sensibility more characteristic of the *drame*.[54]

Even hostile critics were forced to concede that from the point of view of moral and philosophical content, Voltaire's plays were unequalled. 'Nous ne dissimulons pas', wrote Sabatier, 'que du côté de la morale, et d'un certain ton d'humanité, qui respire dans toutes ses Tragédies, l'Auteur de *Zaïre* l'emporte sur les autres Poëtes tragiques'.[55] Similarly, Chaudon, in a book defending the 'great men' who happened to be Voltaire's enemies, saw the tragedies as the work of an authentic *philosophe sensible*.[56]

Critics were also aware that the mixture of sensibility, philosophy, and heightened drama represented a radical departure from tradition. In Sabatier's words, 'On sait qu'il s'est fait un genre qui paraît lui être propre':[57] a genre which was imitated by such writers as La Harpe, Fontanelle, Leblanc, and Lemierre and which exerted an obvious influence on the development of the sentimental *drame bourgeois* and on the elevation to literary respectability of the emerging *mélodrame*. 'N'est-ce pas après avoir vu applaudir ces tragédies, qu'on a mis sur la scène d'autres pièces à spectacle, telles que Gaston et Bayard, Guillaume Tell, Hypermnestre? Ne sont-ce pas ces pièces qui ont donné naissance aux mélodrames? Voilà ce qui a fait dire à Palissot: "C'est à Voltaire que les vrais connaisseurs assigneront l'époque de la décadence de l'art".'[58]

---

53. *De la Sensibilité*, p. 21.

54. Servières made a similar observation in his *Mémoires pour servir à l'histoire de M. de Voltaire*, II, 235.

55. *Les Trois siècles*, III, 471.

56. L. M. Chaudon, *Les Grands hommes vengés* (Amsterdam, 1769), I, 2.

57. *Les Trois siècles*, III, 470.

58. E. M. J. Lepan, *Commentaires sur les tragédies et les comédies de Voltaire* (Paris, 1826), I, 7.

# CHAPTER 7

# *Tearful Comedy*

If Voltaire's tragedies must now be considered obsolete, at least a few of them lingered long enough to give the illusion of possible survival. They are still the subject of critical comment. The comedies seem to have disappeared without trace.[1] Of the many paradoxes of Voltaire's literary career, not the least extraordinary is the fact that one of the wittiest and most amusing of all writers, and one moreover who was an accomplished actor, director, and playwright, failed dismally in comedy. Notwithstanding his specific declaration that 'Il faut *vis comica* pour la comédie, et *vis tragica* pour la tragédie; sans cela toutes les beautés sont perdues' (Best. 12160), his comedies are even less comic than his tragedies are tragic. The discrepancy between promise and performance was noted by Linguet:

> Sans doute, on pouvoit espérer que l'homme de son siècle qui a le mieux connu la plaisanterie, & même la satyre; celui qui a peint avec le plus de force, d'énergie, & d'agrément quand il l'a voulu, en style direct, soit les vices, soit les ridicules, ne réussiroit pas moins à les rendre en les personnifiant pour ainsi dire, en joignant la vivacité de l'action à celle du discours; d'autant plus qu'il s'est livré à ce travail sur-tout à l'âge où son goût avoit reçu toute sa perfection; où il étoit le plus maître de son style & du choix des sujets; où l'expérience devoit l'avoir plus complettement initié aux travers de la société, & où il les frondoit en effet de la manière la plus forte & la plus piquante dans ses autres écrits.[2]

1. There is no recent published study of Voltaire's comedies and very little in the way of critical comment on individual plays.
2. *Examen des ouvrages de M. de Voltaire*, pp. 130–131.

Moreover, Voltaire's description in the Prologue to *L'Echange* (1747) of the ideal comedy as a combination of subtle ridicule, finely sketched portraits, amusing rather than farcical incidents, and an 'easy, gay, lively and graceful style' free from tedious moralizing, seems promisingly Voltairean in the best sense (M. III, 254–255). The first law of comedy, as he frequently stated, is that it must be comic. 'Sans guaieté point de salut' (Best. 8203). A comedy which does not provoke laughter is an 'infamy' (Best. 10088), a 'stupid monster' (Best. 9493), a sure sign of the author's lack of genius and of the general decadence of literature in the eighteenth century (Best. 9509). As soon as Zadig attained a position of influence in Babylon, 'il faisait représenter des tragédies où l'on pleurait, et des comédies où l'on riait; ce qui était passé de mode depuis longtemps, et ce qu'il fit renaître parce qu'il avait du goût.'[3] Voltaire was prepared to be liberal in his interpretation of the rules, particularly 'ces petites misères qu'on appelle en France bienséances' (Best. 8311), and on the question of whether prose or verse should be used, but on this point he was adamant. Comedy and tragedy are separate genres; their respective territories may overlap to some extent—for example in the treatment of love (M. V, 9)—but can never coincide.

Voltaire was therefore in theory opposed to 'ce misérable goût de Tragédies bourgeoises, qui est le recours des auteurs sans génie' (Best. 9493). He is referring, of course, to the appearance of a new kind of serious comedy, variously known as 'comédie larmoyante', 'tragédie bourgeoise', or 'drame'. Although it is possible to draw fine distinctions between them, in practice the differences are so slight that Lanson's definition will cover all three: 'La comédie larmoyante est un genre intermédiaire entre la comédie et la tragédie, qui introduit des personnages de condition privée, vertueux ou tout près de l'être, dans une action sérieuse, grave, parfois pathétique, et qui nous excite à la vertu en nous attendrissant sur ses infortunes et en nous faisant applaudir à son triomphe.'[4]

3. *Zadig*, M. XXI, 49.
4. Gustave Lanson, *Nivelle de La Chaussée et la comédie larmoyante* (Paris, 1887), p. 81.

This kind of play existed long before Diderot gave it a name and a comprehensive theory. Several influences and trends, including sentimental English novels and plays, sensationalist philosophy, the desire for more realism, and above all the growing public demand for edifying theatre appealing strongly and directly to the emotions, converged in the 1730s to produce what Lanson called 'the great fact in the history of eighteenth-century comedy', the transition from classical to modern theatre.

La Chaussée is usually credited with the invention of the new genre. Following a tendency already discernible in the comedies of Destouches, who had adopted a serious, didactic tone in contrast to the gaiety of the immediate successors of Molière,[5] he abandoned traditional comedy in favour of a serious and sentimental type of play with a message. *La Fausse antipathie* (1733) was the first example, followed by *Le Préjugé à la mode* (1735), in which bourgeois morality is shown to be superior to the aristocratic notion that it is bad form to show affection for one's wife. Subsequent plays, the most notable being *Mélanide* (1741), established the *comédie larmoyante* as a definite genre, independent of both tragedy and comedy but combining features taken from each. The characters are ordinary citizens, as in comedy, but they are placed in harrowing situations, often resulting from improbable misadventures. As the name indicates, the aim is identical with that of Voltairean tragedy: to bring out the audience's handkerchiefs. Instead of castigating vice, La Chaussée presents the touching spectacle of virtue under severe stress but ultimately triumphant. In short, his plays show the effects of the invasion of sensibility.

By the fourth decade of the century, in spite of resistance from actors and critics, it was obvious that tearful comedy

5. This didacticism is particularly evident in *Le Glorieux* (1732). Destouches would have nothing to do with the *comédie larmoyante*, however, and remained in the tradition of 'pure' comedy. Voltaire considered that his comedies lacked the vigour and gaiety of those of Regnard, but praised him for not exceeding the limits: 'Il a du moins évité le genre de la comédie qui n'est que langoureuse, de cette espèce de tragédie bourgeoise, qui n'est ni tragique ni comique, monstre né de l'impuissance des auteurs et de la satiété du public après les beaux jours du siècle de Louis XIV' (M. XIV, 65).

was more than an interesting experiment or a curiosity of the moment.[6] In the theatre, the attitude of the public is a vital factor and the eighteenth-century public wanted to be moved more than it wanted to be amused.

Lanson's contention that Voltaire was jealous of La Chaussée for having boldly carried out the revolution which he was too timidly conservative to initiate gives a somewhat misleading impression.[7] Voltaire's inclinations and his conception of what constitutes dramatic interest would in any case have led him to similar experiments. His early sentimental tragedies, *Mariamne* (1724) and *Zaïre* (1732), predate La Chaussée's influence. If not the inventor, he was certainly one of the earliest pioneers in the field of tearful comedy. *L'Enfant prodigue* (1736) was the first overwhelming and durable success in the new genre.[8] *Les Originaux*, performed privately in 1732, was the model for La Chaussée's *Le Préjugé à la mode*.[9] This three-act prose comedy, enlivened by the droll interventions of an old sea-dog, M. du Cap-Vert, contains more humour than sensibility, but the bourgeois moral[10] and the recognition scene of the final act, in which Mme du Cap-Vert sheds tears of 'tendresse' and the voice of the heart is mentioned, clearly foreshadow elements of the *comédie larmoyante*.

Voltaire's private opinion of La Chaussée as an insipid

6. Two particularly successful *comédies larmoyantes* were Landois' *Sylvie* (1741) and Mme de Graffigny's *Cénie* (1750).

7. *Nivelle de La Chaussée*, p. 141: 'Voltaire ne pardonne pas à La Chaussée d'avoir deviné ce que lui-même ne pressentait pas: combien le public était mûr pour le romanesque sentimental; il lui en veut d'avoir eu plus de flair ou d'audace, et d'avoir pris ce rôle d'inventeur dont il n'avait pas voulu lui-même.'

8. *L'Enfant prodigue* was given a total of 295 performances in the eighteenth century. La Chaussée's *La Fausse antipathie* was performed 26 times and *Le Préjugé à la mode* 141.

9. See Beuchot's comment (M. II, 393). According to Mme de Graffigny, Voltaire showed the manuscript to Mlle Quinault, who passed on the idea to La Chaussée. The appearance of *Le Préjugé à la mode* prevented Voltaire from having his play performed at the Comédie Française: 'Il l'aurait donnée si Lachaussée n'avait pas fait le *Préjugé*' (Best. D1708). It is unlikely that the resemblances between the two plays were accidental. *Les Originaux* received its first public performance at the Odéon in 1862.

10. 'Contentez-vous d'être le fils de votre père, gendre de votre beau-père, et mari de votre femme' (M. II, 447).

writer who had recourse to a serious form of comedy to make
up for his lack of comic genius (Best. 9491, 14639) did not
prevent him from publicly recognizing the merits of the
author of *Mélanide*. 'Il y a du mérite', he admitted, 'à
savoir toucher, à bien traiter la morale, à faire des vers bien
tournés et purement écrits: c'est le mérite de cet auteur. . . .
On lui a reproché que ce qui approche du tragique dans ses
pièces n'est pas toujours assez intéressant, et que ce qui est
du ton de la comédie n'est pas plaisant. L'alliage de ces
deux métaux est difficile à trouver. On croit que Lachaussée
est un des premiers après ceux qui ont eu du génie' (M.
XIV, 111).

Voltaire's views on the new developments in comedy are
in fact much less conservative than would appear from his
statements flatly denying the validity of 'bourgeois tragedy',
a term which could only horrify a man of taste. He was not so
much opposed to the creation of an entirely new mixed genre
as afraid that it would sever itself completely from comedy
and thus compete with, or even replace, tragedy. As long as
tearful comedy retained some element of the comic, he was
prepared to accept it: 'La comédie, encore une fois, peut donc
se passionner, s'emporter, attendrir, pourvu qu'ensuite elle
fasse rire les honnêtes gens. Si elle manquait du comique, si
elle n'était que larmoyante, c'est alors qu'elle serait un
genre très-vicieux et très-désagréable' (M. V, 10).

His argument against bourgeois tragedy, which he defined
as 'une intrigue tragique entre des hommes du commun',
was that if low-born characters speak in the style of high
tragedy the effect is incongruous; if they use a more natural,
informal style, it is no longer suited to the tragic subject; the
result, in either case, is a 'bastard' form, neither tragic nor
comic. For Voltaire, the very name, 'bourgeois tragedy', was
a contradiction in terms. He found it impossible to imagine
the spectator taking the same kind of interest in the assassination of a bourgeois as in the death of Pompey (M. XXXII, 83).
On the other hand, providing the absolute limits between the
genres are respected, there is no reason why 'la comédie
attendrissante', as he preferred to call it, should not coexist
with traditional comedy. After all, in real life, tears are

quite frequently accompanied by laughter and we regard this mixture as perfectly natural. Why should we not accept it on the stage? (M. V, 10). Moreover, there is no denying that pathetic situations add 'interest' to comedy as much as to tragedy. Whatever one may legitimately object to in tearful comedy, 'cette espèce cependant avait un mérite, celui d'intéresser, et dès qu'on intéresse, on est sûr du succès' (M. XVII, 419).

All these arguments are summed up in the important preface to *L'Enfant prodigue*. Voltaire concludes, 'Nous n'inférons pas de là que toute comédie doive avoir des scènes de bouffonnerie et des scènes attendrissantes. Il y a beaucoup de très-bonnes pièces où il ne règne que de la gaieté; d'autres toutes sérieuses, d'autres mélangées, d'autres où l'attendrissement va jusqu'aux larmes. Il ne faut donner l'exclusion à aucun genre, et si l'on me demandait quel genre est le meilleur, je répondrais: "Celui qui est le mieux traité"' (M. III, 443). Thus the supposed last-ditch defender of classicism is compelled by his own logic to adopt the most liberal position possible: 'Tous les genres sont bons, hors le genre ennuyeux' (M. III, 445).

On the question of moral purpose, Voltaire saw no real difference between comedy and tragedy. Comedy should avoid 'moralités', that is, overt and tedious didacticism, but it should nevertheless be a school of virtue. 'Qu'est-ce en effet que la vraie comédie? C'est l'art d'enseigner la vertu & les bienséances en action & en dialogues. Que l'éloquence du monologue est froide en comparaison! A-t-on jamais retenu une seule phrase de trente ou quarante mille discours moraux? & ne sait-on pas par cœur ces sentences admirables, placées avec art dans des dialogues intéressants?' (Best. 8722).

Excluding simple 'divertissements', Voltaire wrote some fifteen plays which might be called comedies or *comédies larmoyantes*. Of these, only five were performed at the Comédie Française: *L'Enfant prodigue*, *Nanine*, *L'Ecossaise*, *L'Indiscret*, and *Le Droit du seigneur*. The first three mentioned were eminently successful and are by far the most important. Significantly, all three are outstanding examples of tearful comedy.

The other two were comparative failures. The one-act verse comedy, *L'Indiscret* (1725), was apparently well enough received (Best. D246, n.), but lasted for only six performances. It relates, in mildly amusing fashion, the unmasking of a fop who loses his chance of marrying a rich widow because he insists on boasting about his conquest. Voltaire ascribed its failure to hold the stage to his refusal to satisfy public taste for low comedy (M. II, 243), but later admitted that it was 'un peu froide' (Best. 8487). He had a higher regard for *Le Droit du seigneur*[11] and defended it vigorously against the criticisms of d'Argental (Best. 9300). In this case, however, d'Argental was the better judge of what would please the public; while not an outright failure, the play was performed only eight times.

The plot is a version of the Cinderella story. Acanthe, a young lady of great beauty and noble manners, brought up by commoners and persecuted by a cruel stepmother, finally marries her Prince Charming, the 'seigneur' of the title. Before this happy outcome, she is subjected to the unwelcome advances of a wealthy farmer and abducted by an impetuous young nobleman. The twin themes of misalliance and persecuted innocence led some contemporary critics to believe that *Le Droit du seigneur* was simply a repetition of the formula which had proved so successful in *Nanine*. Voltaire retorted, with reason, that the two plays were quite different (Best. 8682). In fact, the egalitarian tendencies of *Nanine* are noticeably absent.[12] The 'droit du seigneur' turns out to be nothing more sinister than a fifteen-minute interview and the question of misalliance is side-stepped by the convenient revelation that Acanthe is the daughter of an impoverished noblewoman.

11. Verse comedy in three acts, performed in five acts in 1762.
12. The farmer, Mathurin, would like to see feudal privileges abolished, but not the class distinctions between himself and his servants (M. VI, 11). Voltaire makes fun of the *noblesse parlementaire* (M. VI, 16). The spirit of the play is more accurately reflected, however, in the following verses:

> Les gens d'un certain nom
> . . . . . . . . . . . . . . . . . . . . . . . . . . . . . . . .
> En savent plus, ont l'âme autrement faite,
> Ont de l'esprit, des sentiments plus grands,
> Meilleurs que nous (M. VI, 21).

Voltaire was evidently attempting to return to his original conception of comedy as a play which provokes laughter as well as emotion. The fairy-tale atmosphere is quite unlike the uniform seriousness of *Nanine*. The scene between Colette and the bailiff, a part played by Voltaire himself, sets a tone of light-hearted gaiety. Yet the play frequently hints at tragedy. We are led to believe that rape and incest could have been committed. Acanthe is the typical suffering heroine of melodrama. There are tears of separation as the worthy Dignant says farewell to the girl he regards as his daughter. And inevitably the repentant libertine reappears, 'confus, soumis, pénétré de remords' (M. VI, 62). While avoiding the worst excesses of sentimentality, Voltaire fails to blend the scattered elements of comedy, fantasy, and pathos into a coherent whole. The public unhesitatingly gave its preference to the undiluted sensibility of *Nanine*.

The other minor comedies consist of *pièces de société*, light-weight dramatic entertainments intended for private performance, or plays with unusual features which made them unsuitable for the stage. The former category includes *L'Echange*, *La Prude*, *La Femme qui a raison*, *Charlot*, and *Le Dépositaire*. Since they were written primarily to amuse a select group of friends, their importance in the development of sensibility and of the theatre in general is minimal. They undoubtedly fulfilled their purpose of satisfying the insatiable appetite for dramatic novelty in the circles frequented by Voltaire, but apart from an occasional effective scene and a few witty lines they have little to offer posterity. Informality does not seem to have had the same happy effect on Voltaire's inspiration in his casual theatre as in his casual poetry.

*L'Echange*[13] concerns a younger son with no money who quarrels with his elder brother, the well-named comte de Fatenville. Assisted by an amusing rogue, Trigaudin, he impersonates his brother in order to marry the latter's

---

13. Prose comedy in three acts, performed privately in 1734 and against Voltaire's will at the Comédie Italienne in 1761 as *Quand est-ce qu'on me marie?*

fiancée. In spite of a few good lines, the humour is rather laboured and the plot peters out unsatisfactorily. Unlike the *comédie larmoyante*, in which everyone is a model of righteousness, the play suffers from the absence of any character with whom one can sympathize. It is difficult to disagree with Voltaire's own assessment of it as 'une farce qui n'est pas digne du public' (Best. D1033).

*La Prude*,[14] an emasculated version of Wycherly's *The Plain Dealer*, is notable only for the moral:

> Je crois encor, dussé-je être en erreur,
> Qu'on peut unir les plaisirs et l'honneur;
> Je crois aussi, soit dit sans vous déplaire,
> Que femme prude, en sa vertu sévère,
> Peut en public faire beaucoup de bien,
> Mais en secret souvent ne valoir rien. (M. IV, 411)

Hypocrisy is also satirized in *Le Dépositaire*,[15] based on an incident in the life of Voltaire's benefactress, Ninon de Lenclos. Not a man to forget a kindness, Voltaire uses the play as an opportunity to pay tribute to the honesty and *bienfaisance* of the notorious Ninon. These qualities are contrasted with the duplicity of Gourville, a character obviously modelled on Tartuffe. Unfortunately, Voltaire is no Molière; his characters bustle about the stage, but this rather pointless activity is merely an ineffective substitute for genuine comic invention.

*Charlot*[16] is the most interesting of the *pièces de société* from the point of view of dramatic innovation. It is an amalgam of just about everything that can be put into one play: 'Il y a un peu de chant et de danse, du comique, du

14. Verse comedy in five acts, composed in 1740 and performed at the théâtre de Sceaux in 1747.

15. Verse comedy in five acts, described in the Kehl edition as a 'comédie de société, jouée à la campagne en 1767' (M. VI, 392). Voltaire considered it unsuitable for public performance (M. VI, 394). In 1770 it was read to the committee of the Comédie Française; unaware of the identity of the author, they rejected it.

16. Described as a 'pièce dramatique', in three acts and verse. It was performed at Ferney in 1767 and was given three performances at the Comédie Italienne in 1782.

tragique, de la morale, et de la plaisanterie. Cette nouveauté n'a point du tout été destinée aux théâtres publics' (M. VI, 343). Of all these features, the 'tragic', more accurately the melodramatic, is the most prominent. The three principal characters are the familiar black and white figures of senti-mental drama. Julie, 'âme honnête et tendre', is to be married to the marquis, a hard-hearted libertine solely pre-occupied with his own selfish pleasures. His virtuous 'frère de lait', Charlot, is the exact opposite, as the other characters rather unnecessarily keep pointing out. Charlot kills the marquis in a duel, but is forgiven when it is discovered that he is the true son of the comtesse de Givry. We are intended to infer from these events that

Les vices de l'esprit peuvent se corriger;
Quand le cœur est mauvais, rien ne peut le changer.

(M. VI, 349)

It would be unfair to judge Voltaire as a writer of comedy on the basis of these hastily concocted theatrical diversions. The same observation applies to the other minor comedies. *L'Envieux*[17] was never performed and was not even published until long after Voltaire's death. Like the later tragedy, *Les Scythes*, it is a *pièce à clef*, the key to which is not very difficult to discover.[18] It is also a *comédie larmoyante*, with Voltaire himself representing virtue in distress. The obliging Ariston, whose 'passion' is friendship, is betrayed by Zoïlin (Voltaire's arch-enemy of the moment, the abbé Desfontaines), but remains steadfastly *bienfaisant* in disgrace and misfortune. Confronted with this noble example, the naïve young Nicodon (Linant) realizes that he has been the dupe of Zoïlin in his scheme to blacken Ariston's character and sheds tears of repentance (M. III, 564). There follows an even more pathetic scene as Ariston is about to be incar-cerated without being permitted to see his wife, children, or

17. Verse comedy in three acts, composed in 1738 for Voltaire's protégé, La Marre, and another young man, who were to share the profits (Best. D1536).
18. Voltaire (Ariston), M. Du Châtelet (Cléon), Mme Du Châtelet (Hortense), Desfontaines (Zoïlin), and Linant (Nicodon), all appear in it.

dying father (M. III, 565). All ends well, however. His innocence established, Ariston magnanimously forgives Zoïlin, who is nevertheless led off to prison. Thus virtue is triumphant, vice is punished, but the man of feeling remains aloof from any petty thoughts of vengeance.

Voltaire never succeeded in finding a satisfactory solution to the problem of blending sensibility and satire in dramatic form. The satirical and sentimental elements are equally clumsy and contrived. Like all Voltaire's stage villains, Zoïlin is unconvincing because he insists on complacently detailing his villainy (e.g. M. III, 527). The simple device of self-condemnation can be amusingly effective in a short polemical piece where all that matters is the expression of a point of view; in the theatre it destroys what is left of dramatic credibility.

Nothing remains of *Thérèse*, composed in 1743, except a few fragments. To judge from these and from d'Argental's shocked reaction—'Le genre auquel vous êtes descendu est tel que, quand vous réussiriez (ce que je n'espère assurément pas), on aurait de la peine à vous pardonner de l'avoir entrepris' (Best. D2790)—it was a sentimental prose drama with 'low' characters involved in tragic events. Voltaire apparently had some hopes of getting it performed (Best. D2790).

The strangest of all these dramatic creations, *Socrate*[19] and *Saül*,[20] can hardly be classified as comedy, or even theatre. It is difficult to imagine that Voltaire was thinking of the stage when he wrote *Saül*;[21] yet it was given at least one private performance, at the court of Frederick. 'On l'a jouée devant un grand Roi. On y frémissait et on y pâmait de rire, car tout y est pris mot pour mot de la sainte écriture'

---

19. In three acts and prose; published in 1759.
20. In five acts and prose; published in 1763.
21. His own tongue-in-cheek description clearly indicates that there was no question of performance: 'On n'a pas observé, dans cette espèce de tragi-comédie, l'unité d'action, de lieu et de temps. On a cru, avec l'illustre Lamotte, devoir se soustraire à ces règles. Tout se passe dans l'intervalle de deux ou trois générations, pour rendre l'action plus tragique par le nombre des morts selon l'esprit juif' (M. V, 575). A character is dismembered on the stage (M. V, 580).

(Best. 14821). Apart from the fact that it is in the form of dialogue and divided into acts and scenes, it contains no element of genuine drama and obviously belongs to the group of miscellaneous commentaries on the Bible usually classified under 'Mélanges'.

*Socrate* is much more coherent and stageworthy than *Saül*,[22] but it too properly belongs to satire. It was intended as a contribution to the decisive battle then being fought between the *philosophes* and their enemies over the publication of the *Encyclopédie*.[23] The allegory is transparent: Anitus (Omer Joly de Fleury), supported by a team of hack writers with barely disguised names, succeeds in having Socrates condemned for 'corrupting youth'. Socrates, 'cet homme dangereux qui ne prêche que la vertu et la divinité', is an idealized portrait of a benevolent *philosophe* which bears more resemblance to Voltaire himself than to the beleaguered Diderot.[24] As in *L'Envieux*, satire is mixed with sentiment. Viewed as drama, *Socrate* is not much more impressive. The sensibility evident in the portrait of Socrates and in the death scene never quite degenerates into *sensiblerie*,[25] but the satire is blunted by the excessive use of the

---

22. There was even some question of public performance and Voltaire was willing (Best. 8192).

23. The *philosophes* are referred to in the play by their opponent, Anitus, as 'ces sobres et sérieux extravagants, qui ont d'autres mœurs que les nôtres, qui sont d'un autre siècle et d'une autre patrie ... qui pensent avoir rempli tous leurs devoirs quand ils ont adoré la divinité, secouru l'humanité, cultivé l'amitié, et étudié la philosophie' (M. V, 367). As La Harpe remarked, Voltaire frequently forgets that the action is taking place in Athens, not Paris.

24. Voltaire's code name for Diderot was 'Platon'. His own identification with Socrates would therefore be appropriate. It is interesting to note that Diderot's reaction to the play was decidedly unfavourable (*Correspondance*, ed. Roth, II, 241–242).

25. If Favart's opinion is any guide, *Socrate* might well have been successful as a sentimental drama. Apparently unaware that Voltaire was the author, he comments: 'Si le premier acte de la *Mort de Socrate* est répréhensible par cet endroit [i.e. anticlericalism], il n'en est point de même des autres, dont, en bonne politique, on devroit ordonner la représentation. Il y a des morceaux si frappans sur l'existence de Dieu, sur son unité, sur l'immortalité de notre âme, que c'est un catéchisme mis en action. Il n'y a pas un grand mouvement dans ce drame; cependant il y a de l'intérêt et du pathétique' (*Mémoires et Correspondance littéraires, dramatiques et anecdotiques* [Paris, 1808], II, 2–3).

familiar technique of self-denunciation and grotesque exaggeration.[26]

None of these minor comedies is of any great importance; they merit comment only insofar as they reveal something of Voltaire the man and the dramatist. They show that he was continually experimenting with different combinations of humour, pathos, satire, and allegory. These experiments extend over an astonishingly wide range of orthodox and unorthodox dramatic forms, including tearful comedy, tragicomedy, 'high' and 'low' comedy, allegorical melodrama, and even the final abomination, prose tragedy with comic relief and bourgeois characters. They show also that Voltaire's comic genius was not suited to the stage. It was not a question of finding the right genre. A 'pure' comedy, such as *L'Indiscret*, is no more successful than the heterogeneous *Charlot*. Nor was Voltaire prevented from writing viable comedy by the constraining influence of classical tradition or by the necessity of satisfying public taste. He was able to express himself in perfect freedom in plays not intended for public performance, but these productions fail to rise above the general level of mediocrity.

Voltaire wrote three comedies which met with public favour: *L'Enfant prodigue*, *Nanine*, and *L'Ecossaise*. Their case is different, not because they are markedly better, but because they were phenomenally successful in the eighteenth century and undoubtedly played an important role in the development of the theatre and of the literature of sensibility in general. Since the comedies have attracted so little attention, it is worth insisting on this point. During the period when sensibility was most fashionable, from 1760 to 1780, *L'Enfant prodigue* and *Nanine* were the most popular of all Voltaire's plays with the single exception of *Tancrède*. *L'Ecossaise* was some way behind, yet it was performed as frequently as *Zaïre*. Bearing in mind that Voltaire was by far the most successful writer of tragedies in the eighteenth century, the figures indicating the number of performances

---

26. e.g. M. V, 382. As René Pomeau has noted, the accuser of Socrates is not even a fanatic. He persecutes Socrates simply because the latter has refused to force his pupil, Aglaé, to marry him and hand over her dowry.

for the three comedies compared with those for the five outstanding tragedies are conclusive evidence that he struck exactly the right note:[27]

|  |  |
|---|---|
| *L'Enfant prodigue* . . . . . | 157 |
| *Nanine* . . . . . . . . . . . . . | 148 |
| *L'Ecossaise* . . . . . . . . . . | 114 |
|  |  |
| *Tancrède* . . . . . . . . . . . . | 173 |
| *Alzire* . . . . . . . . . . . . . | 136 |
| *Sémiramis* . . . . . . . . . . . | 118 |
| *Mérope* . . . . . . . . . . . . | 116 |
| *Zaïre* . . . . . . . . . . . . . . | 114 |

The now-forgotten *L'Enfant prodigue*[28] was one of Voltaire's best-known works. Its continued prosperity is even more remarkable when one considers that it was a very early *comédie larmoyante*. It was given an unusually long initial run of twenty-two performances, interrupted only by the illness of one of the actresses (Best. D1220), and became even more of a favourite with the public in succeeding decades.

The subject was suggested by the actress, Mlle Quinault, a pioneer of the cult of sensibility.[29] Voltaire was duly grateful and apologized to her for the ridiculous role of Mme Croupillac which she played, adding that the tender scenes in the play and its impeccable morality more than made up for the intrusion of burlesque comedy: 'Ce qui me console, c'est que le langage du cœur, que vous entendez si bien, le ton de l'honnête homme, les mœurs, ont réussi. Le fonds de vertu qui est dans cet ouvrage devait vous plaire, et a subjugué le public' (Best. D1167). He insisted on retaining

27. The statistics are taken from Joannidès, *La Comédie-Française de 1680 à 1920*. In order to make the comparison exact, the figures are those indicated for the years 1761–1800 inclusive. During the same period, La Chaussée's most popular *comédies larmoyantes* were given the following number of performances: *La Gouvernante* (124), *Mélanide* (98), *L'Ecole des mères* (81), *Le Préjugé à la mode* (52).

28. Verse comedy in five acts, first performed in 1736. Voltaire told Mme de Graffigny that he composed it 'dans un accès de fièvre sans le corriger' (Best. D1677). Before the identity of the author was revealed, it was variously attributed to Piron, Destouches, and La Chaussée.

29. She also provided La Chaussée with the theme of *Le Préjugé à la mode* and inspired Piron's *La Métromanie*.

the comic characters, however, since he wanted to prove that
'la comédie pouvoit très bien réunir L'intéressant et le
plaisant' (Best. D1220), in accordance with the theory outlined in the preface.

*L'Enfant prodigue*, true to its title, is an updating of the
New Testament parable. Euphémon, the prodigal's father,
decides to disinherit him in favour of his unattractive but
outwardly respectable younger brother, appropriately named
Fierenfat. Rondon's daughter, Lise, originally promised to
the prodigal, is asked to transfer her affections to Fierenfat,
whom she despises. Euphémon is deeply disturbed by the
rumour that the prodigal is dead, but the latter appears, converted by suffering and remorse, to ask his father's forgiveness. Meanwhile Mme Croupillac tries to enlist his assistance
in her attempt to win back Fierenfat. A touching scene of
reconciliation between Lise and the prodigal is interrupted
by Fierenfat, who quarrels with both, accusing Lise of infidelity. Lise finally persuades Euphémon to see his repentant
son. Tears flow freely as the prodigal is forgiven and permitted to marry Lise, while Mme Croupillac triumphantly
claims Fierenfat.

The moral is that of the Christian parable transferred to
the human plane. Voltaire could fully endorse it because it
coincided with his conception of 'true' Christianity. *L'Enfant
prodigue* is in fact a dramatic illustration of the doctrine pro-
pounded in the *Poème sur la loi naturelle* and elsewhere.
Euphémon, Lise, and the prodigal achieve happiness by
heeding the voice of nature. It speaks to Lise through her
love for the prodigal. In the case of Euphémon, it is parental
affection: a father's natural feelings for his son will lead him
to forgive the worst excesses providing a core of virtue
remains. 'Si la vertu règne enfin dans ton âme', he exclaims, 'Je suis ton père' (M. III, 515). For the prodigal,
'nature' is a heavenly voice inspiring remorse in a *sensible*
and therefore receptive soul, enlightened by suffering. He
cries out to Lise in his despair,

Le ciel, ce ciel qui doit nous désunir,
Me laisse un cœur, et c'est pour me punir. (M. III, 488)

At the same time, the plight of the prodigal is an example of what can happen to a young man who allows a legitimate enjoyment of pleasure to become an exclusive and degrading passion. *Le Mondain*, published during the same year, shows one side of the medal, *L'Enfant prodigue* the reverse. Some lines in the play criticize the hypocrisy, frivolity, and dishonesty of 'le beau monde' (M. III, 480) and suggest that honest toil on the land offers a better prospect of happiness (M. III, 479). That Voltaire took his dramatized sermon seriously is indicated by his claim to be able to cite the cases of 'plus de six fils de famille que la comédie de l'Enfant prodigue a corrigés' (Best. 8722).

In conformity with his theory of the proper limits of comedy, Voltaire does his best to maintain the balance between laughter and tears. The characters divide neatly into two equal groups: the 'sensibles' (Euphémon, Lise, and the prodigal) and the 'grotesques' (Rondon, Fierenfat, and Mme Croupillac). Fierenfat is an incredibly pompous fop, 'le roi des pédants fades', whose self-importance and miserliness are exaggerated to the point of burlesque. He has no natural feelings whatsoever and would cheerfully send his brother to the galleys (M. III, 469). Unfortunately, he is neither believable nor particularly funny. In his anxiety to provide comic relief, Voltaire falls between two stools; the clown does not make a convincing villain. The same might be said of the absurdly overdrawn Rondon, who believes that he can command not only his daughter's obedience, but her affections as well. Mme Croupillac is a more successful comic figure, whose droll turns of phrase occasionally enliven the dialogue, but she is an unnecessary addition to the plot.

In spite of these concessions to the orthodox conception of humorous comedy, the dominant tone, especially in the final scenes, is that of melodrama bordering on sentimental tragedy.[30] As in the tragedies, Voltaire depends on theatrical pathos for his main effects; it appears after the premature announcement of the prodigal's death, in the scene between

30. There is a hint of tragedy in the reported death of the prodigal and his desire to die in battle (M. III, 499). Lise, like the heroine of *Tancrède*, is unjustly accused of infidelity.

Lise and the prodigal, and reaches a tearful climax in the meeting of father and son.

The critics, not a particularly adventurous race in the early eighteenth century, had strong reservations about such a radical departure from normal practice.[31] Audiences, on the other hand, were less impressed by the comic scenes, as Voltaire admitted: 'Le public est donc bien rafiné! Il trouve mauvais qu'il y ait du plaisant dans l'enfant prod. et s'il n'y en avoit point eu, il auroit dit, c'est une tragédie' (Best. D1177). They flocked to the theatre to enjoy the novel sensation of being moved to tears by the misfortunes and goodness of heart of people of ordinary rank, like themselves, endlessly repeating words such as 'vertu', 'cœur', 'nature', 'tendresse', which strike the modern reader as trite and conventional, but which then seemed fresh and daring in the context of comedy.

*Nanine*[32] is an even more typical example of sentimental drama. Comedy has almost entirely disappeared.[33] The moralizing tendency, already abundantly evident in *L'Enfant prodigue*, has been accentuated to the point where the play could justifiably be called a sermon. Moreover, *L'Enfant prodigue*, for all its up-to-date emphasis on sensibility, had been firmly based on Christian tradition; *Nanine* had the advantage of being inspired by one of the most fashionably popular of all eighteenth-century sentimental novels, Richardson's *Pamela*.[34]

31. The account in the *Mercure* (December 1736) was highly critical. Contant d'Orville, in his *Lettre critique sur la comédie intitulée l'Enfant prodigue* (Paris, 1737), described the play as 'une Piéce qui n'a d'autre avantage que celui de la nouveauté' (p. 6), and went on to question whether a good comedy can be based on pathos, 'qui ne convient qu'au seul Tragique' (p. 6). He admitted, however, that the public did not share his view and that the play's 'astonishing success' would probably encourage imitation (p. 10). Cf. the more favourable later judgments of Servières (*Mémoires pour servir à l'histoire de M. de Voltaire*, II, 193–194) and Gazon Dourxigné (*Ami de la vérité*, pp. 33–34). According to the latter, *L'Enfant prodigue* reconciled him to 'Thalie la pleureuse'.
32. In three acts and verse; first performed in 1749, it had an initial run of 12 performances.
33. The only trace of it is Blaise's expression of astonishment when he sees Nanine writing: 'Le grand génie! elle écrit tout courant' (M. V, 41).
34. An 'English novel', presumably *Pamela*, is even mentioned in the play (M. V, 23). Two comedies on a similar theme had already been performed: Boissy's *Paméla ou la vertu mieux éprouvée* (1743) and La

The stereotype Voltaire seems a most improbable channel for the diffusion of Richardsonian sensibility in France, a role usually assigned to Prévost, Diderot, and Rousseau. It is certainly true that his comments on Richardson are far from complimentary: 'Je n'aime pas assurément les longs et insupportables romans de Paméla et de Clarice. Ils ont réussi parce qu'ils ont excité la curiosité du lecteur, à travers un fatras d'inutilités, mais si l'auteur avait été assez malavisé pour annoncer dès le commencement que Clarice et Paméla aimaient leurs persécuteurs, tout était perdu, le lecteur aurait jeté le livre.'[35] He saw Richardson as a clever but tedious writer whose one great asset was his ability to keep the reader in suspense. Yet he was sufficiently impressed to consider writing an epistolary novel in the style of *Pamela* based on his correspondence with Mme Denis (Best. 4976). Whether it was actually completed or whether it was ever anything more than a project is not known, since no trace of it survives.[36] There is nothing improbable, however, in the idea that Voltaire, while reproving Richardson's heavy treatment, found the theme and moral of *Pamela* to his taste. Not only *Nanine*, but his whole theatre, is concerned, like Richardson's novels, with the misfortunes of virtue.

The particular misfortunes related in the play are those of a young lady of low birth who has been brought up in the château of the comte d'Alban. The count is infatuated with her in spite of the difference in rank, but Nanine is torn between her love for the count and her awareness of the impossibility of bridging the social gap. The 'rock-hearted' baronne de l'Orme, who wishes to marry the count, tries to

Chaussée's *Paméla* (1743). The English novel in general, and Richardson's novels in particular, have long been recognized as one of the most important influences on the development of sensibility in France. Daniel Mornet noted in *Le Romantisme en France au 18e siècle* (Paris, 1912), p. 21, 'Nous avons trouvé, dans cinq cents bibliothèques du 18e siècle, 1.698 volumes de romans anglais contre 497 de romans français.'

35. Best. 13285. See also Best. 8108 and M. XXIX, 498.

36. Voltaire said that he completed it (Best. 4988). According to Dr. Besterman, he merely invented the project to flatter his niece's vanity and persuade her to hand over his papers (Best. 4890, n.). Alexandre Jovicevich considers that he completed the work and published it in modified form as *Les Lettres d'Amabed* ('A propos d'une Paméla de Voltaire', *FR*, 36 [1962–1963], 276–283).

get rid of Nanine, first by offering to provide her with a dowry to marry the gardener, Blaise, then by encouraging her to take refuge in a convent. The count decides that his love for Nanine is more important than class prejudice, orders her carriage to be turned back, and proposes. On the verge of attaining happiness, Nanine becomes the victim of a misunderstanding reminiscent of *Zaïre* and *Tancrède*. The baronne intercepts an affectionate letter from Nanine to a certain Philippe Hombert. Confronted with the evidence of betrayal, the count sends Nanine away, to the tearful dismay of everyone in the château except the baronne. Philippe Hombert finally makes his appearance. He is, of course, Nanine's father. The repentant count immediately recalls Nanine and marries her with the approval of his equally enlightened mother.

The play is so deeply immersed in sensibility as to be almost a caricature of the *comédie larmoyante*. No opportunity of drawing a tear or extolling a virtuous feeling is missed. Exclamation marks abound:

> O douleur! ô tendresse!
> Des deux côtés quel excès de vertu! (M. V, 64)

Some verses are so earnestly trite as to be amusing, including the notorious line, 'Non, il n'est rien que Nanine n'honore' (M. V, 67).

Nanine represents 'la simple nature' as seen by the eighteenth-century man of feeling. She is modest, submissive, and tirelessly eloquent on the subject of virtue and duty. There is not the slightest trace of selfishness in her character. Every word and act is dictated by her desire to prevent disharmony by the willing sacrifice of her own happiness. She refuses to believe in equality because this would be to her advantage and when she loses the count's favour she leaves without a murmur. She is, in a word, the very image of virtue.

The count is only slightly more complex. In his case, there is no internal conflict between love and social prejudice. As a 'philosophe sensible' (M. V, 45) who believes that 'l'homme doit agir d'après son cœur' (M. V, 18), he has never been swayed by considerations of rank. His one fault is a Voltairean impetuosity which makes him momentarily unjust, but 'dans le fond c'est un cœur généreux' (M. V, 65) and anger quickly yields to remorse.

Perhaps the most striking feature of the play is the extraordinary frankness of Voltaire's approach to questions of social equality and misalliance. The message is quite clear and constantly repeated:

> vous mettez la grandeur
> Dans les blasons: je la veux dans le cœur.
> L'homme de bien, modeste avec courage,
> Et la beauté spirituelle, sage,
> Sans bien, sans nom, sans tous ces titres vains,
> Sont à mes yeux les premiers des humains.[37]

A good heart is the only mark of true, that is, 'natural', nobility. Distinctions of rank, prestige, and wealth are mere 'prejudices' (M. V, 17, 34), awarded on the basis of chance, not merit (M. V, 31). Moreover, for once, the question of misalliance is squarely faced. Nanine does not turn out to be the daughter of a person of quality; she is 'une servante, une fille des champs', whose father is a former soldier, now a peasant. Voltaire emphasizes the disproportion of rank still further by making the count the rival of his gardener. Yet the count refuses to be deterred by the possibility of ridicule. His heart tells him that all men are equal and that the only acceptable distinction is that of virtue:

> Eh quoi! rival de Blaise! Pourquoi non?
> Blaise est un homme; il l'aime, il a raison. (M. V, 32)

A far more subversive play than *Le Mariage de Figaro*, *Nanine* was understandably popular during the early years

---

37. M. V, 17. See also V, 67:
> C'est pour des cœurs par eux-mêmes ennoblis,
> Et distingués par ce grand caractère,
> Qu'il faut passer sur la règle ordinaire:
> Et leur naissance, avec tant de vertus,
> Dans ma maison n'est qu'un titre de plus.

of the Revolution. It undoubtedly helped to create the state of mind which led, forty years after its first performance, to the 'nuit du quatre août', when the French nobility renounced its privileges in an effusion of sensibility.

The real reasons for the popularity of the last of the major comedies, *L'Ecossaise*,[38] have been somewhat obscured by a false interpretation of the play as a mere vehicle for Voltaire's personal attack on Fréron. Voltaire certainly had vengeance in mind when he created the character of a malicious hack and named him Frélon. The well-publicized story of how Fréron insisted on attending the first performance accompanied by his wife and stoically witnessed his own 'public execution' has far more human interest than the play itself and has consequently attracted more attention. The truth is, however, that Frélon is a minor character who plays a very limited role in the events and disappears before the final dramatic scenes. Voltaire seems to have regretted having introduced him at all: 'Le caractère de Frélon est si lâche et si odieux, que nous avons voulu épargner aux lecteurs la vue trop fréquente de ce personnage, plus dégoûtant que comique.'[39] The critics, in general, agreed; the satirical content was regarded as the play's weakest point.[40]

Voltaire emphasized in the Preface what he considered to be the most important features of *L'Ecossaise*: its novelty, its unusual characters, and the purity of its moral:

> La comédie intitulée *l'Ecossaise* nous parut un de ces ouvrages qui peuvent réussir dans toutes les langues, parce que l'auteur peint la nature, qui est partout la même: il a la naïveté et la vérité de l'estimable Goldoni,

38. In five acts and prose; first performed in 1760, when it was given sixteen consecutive performances.

39. M. V, 410. See also M. V, 418 and Best. 8357. In spite of his own practice, Voltaire considered that such characters are generally misplaced in comedy: 'Un malhonnête homme ne fera jamais rire, parce que dans le rire il entre toujours de la gaieté, incompatible avec le mépris et l'indignation' (M. III, 444).

40. Gazon Dourxigné, *Ami de la vérité*, p. 100; G. F. Coyer, *Discours sur la satyre contre les philosophes* (Paris, 1760), p. 87; *Correspondance littéraire*, IV, 299.

avec peut-être plus d'intrigue, de force, et d'intérêt. Le dénoûment, le caractère de l'héroïne, et celui de Freeport, ne ressemblent à rien de ce que nous connaissons sur les théâtres de France; et cependant c'est la nature pure. Cette pièce paraît un peu dans le goût de ces romans anglais qui ont fait tant de fortune; ce sont des touches semblables, la même peinture des mœurs, rien de recherché, nulle envie d'avoir de l'esprit.[41]

The mention of Goldoni and 'English novels' again points to Richardson as the ultimate source of inspiration. Goldoni's *Pamela Nubile*, one of the better dramatic adaptations of Richardson's novel, provided some of the details of the plot. As in *Nanine*, the theme is virtue in distress.[42]

*L'Ecossaise* was one of the century's great 'succès de sensibilité', acclaimed both in Paris and the provinces. At the first performance, according to Marmontel, the audience wept 'comme à Zaïre' and applauded with hands and feet.[43] Even such a severe critic as the abbé Coyer admitted that the play contained 'de l'action, de la chaleur et de l'intérêt', adding that the public knew it by heart before it was staged.[44]

This extraordinary reception was obviously due to other factors besides the attack on Fréron. The fact that the principal characters are Scottish at a time when Scotland was beginning to be thought of as a land of mystery and romance possibly had something to do with it. But the banal and unimaginative plot, which spreads over five acts the discovery that the two guests staying at the coffee-house are Lord Monrose and his long-lost daughter, adds nothing really new. Recognition scenes, fortuitous encounters of fathers and

41. M. V, 409. 'Ce qui est beaucoup plus important, c'est que cette comédie est d'une excellente morale' (M. V, 411).
42. Voltaire's debt to Goldoni and Richardson is discussed by K. M. Lynch, '*Pamela Nubile, L'Ecossaise,* and *The English Merchant*', *MLN*, 47 (Feb. 1932), 94–96. *L'Ecossaise* was immediately translated into English as *The Coffee-House or Fair Fugitive*. In 1767, George Colman produced a successful adaptation entitled *The English Merchant*.
43. Best. 8360. Coyer confirms this (*Discours*, p. 86). See also d'Argental's account in Best. 8339.
44. *Discours*, p. 86.

daughters, generous actions of noble young men, the plight and final triumph of virtue, are the staple features of Voltaire's theatre.

What sets the play apart from the others is the character of Freeport. Rough and abrupt in manner, this English merchant is a man of feeling who disguises his true nature by adopting an air of cynicism. Men, he says, are mostly rogues and fools. Nothing is worth shedding tears over: 'Je n'ai pleuré de ma vie: fi! que cela est sot de pleurer! les yeux n'ont point été donnés à l'homme pour cette besogne' (M. V, 472). His refreshing lack of sentimentality is belied, however, by his incredible generosity. Voltaire obviously has a special affection for him; he represents the true 'homme bienfaisant', the man who acts, whose *bienfaisance* is more than talk and good intentions. 'Il n'est pas complimenteur, mais il oblige en moins de temps que les autres ne font des protestations des services' (M. V, 456). In the latter respect, at least, he is not unlike his creator. Freeport is a close relative of that other Voltairean hero, the good Quaker, but he was sufficiently original to be recognized at once as a valuable addition to the limited stock characters of tearful comedy.

The rest of the play follows the pattern of the conventional *comédie larmoyante*. One knows exactly what to expect when the heroine is continually referred to as 'vertueuse' and 'respectable'. Lindane, like Nanine, is the very model of unhappy innocence. She sums up her situation in characteristically ingenuous fashion: 'Chère Polly, tu le sais, je suis une infortunée dont le père fut proscrit dans les derniers troubles, dont la famille est détruite; il ne me reste que mon courage' (M. V, 430). She is 'un prodige de malheur, de noblesse et de vertu' (M. V, 440). Voltaire places her in much the same situation as Zaïre. Torn between love and filial duty, she gives the same answer: 'La nature doit l'emporter sur l'amour' (M. V, 471). Inevitably, her courage and devotion are suitably rewarded before the final curtain and she is able to satisfy both 'nature' and love, but not before a great many tears have been shed over the apparent infidelity of her suitor and the near-duel between the young man and her father. Her maidservant accurately conveys the dramatic content of *L'Ecossaise*, and indeed of the other comedies, in a few lines: 'Voilà d'étranges aventures! je vois que ce monde-ci n'est qu'un combat perpétuel des méchants contre les bons et qu'on en veut toujours aux pauvres filles!' (M. V, 467).

Thanks largely to the invention of Freeport, Voltaire is more successful than usual in providing a leaven of humour. As an eminently 'respectable' figure, Freeport is perfectly at home in sentimental drama; at the same time, his eccentricities and the perpetual contrast between appearances and behaviour are amusing enough to add a few smiles to the tears of the audience and thus appease the author's artistic conscience.

There is no real relief, however, from the oppressively sentimental atmosphere. Much of the dialogue between the principal characters consists of pious exclamations and protestations of virtue.[45] The spectator is constantly reminded, by the liberal use of abstractions, that the highest moral principles are involved: 'Hélas! ma famille a fait tous les malheurs de la sienne: le ciel, la fortune, mon amour, l'équité, la raison, allaient tout réparer; la vertu m'inspirait; le crime s'oppose à tout ce que je tente: il ne triomphera pas' (M. V, 467). And what passed in the eighteenth century for 'pure nature' tends to find emotional expression in a string of overcharged adjectives, as in the following exchange:

MONROSE

Allons, ma chère fille, seul soutien, unique
consolation de ma déplorable vie! partons.

LINDANE

Malheureux père d'une infortunée! je ne vous
abandonnerai jamais. . . . (M. V, 476)

The reasons for the contemporary triumph and subsequent total eclipse of Voltaire's comedies are obvious enough. Their faults are those which marred all but a small fraction of the literature inspired by the invasion of sensibility. Even more

45. e.g. Lord Murray's appeal to the divinity: 'Grand Dieu, protecteur de l'innocence, je t'implore pour elle! daigne te servir de moi pour rendre justice à la vertu, et pour tirer d'oppression les infortunés!' (M. V, 463).

than the tragedies, they are inseparable from the moral and philosophical climate in which they flourished. Removed from this context, they quickly evaporate. Voltaire's comic genius was not, in any case, well suited to the theatre; it found its ideal medium in the philosophical tale, where fantasy blends perfectly with caricature and satire and where puppets activated by a powerful personality are acceptable substitutes for well-rounded characters. La Harpe was right: 'En fait d'esprit, il était trop *lui* pour devenir un *autre*'.[46] And as Voltaire himself said, 'Il y a, comme on sait, une prodigieuse différence entre raconter plaisamment et intriguer une comédie supérieurement' (M. VI, 393).

It is possible to argue that Voltaire was responsible, as much as anyone, for the change in the direction of the French theatre during the first half of the century. La Chaussée's *La Fausse antipathie* was indisputably the first *comédie larmoyante* to be publicly performed. On the other hand, *Zaïre* was already tearful melodrama in all but name, and it seems likely that the outstanding success of *L'Enfant prodigue*, *Nanine*, and *L'Ecossaise* contributed more than any other factor to the growing popularity of the new genre and its acceptance as a respectable form of drama. Such, at any rate, was the view of contemporary critics. 'Vous venez de fixer par votre Piéce', wrote Guiard de Servigné in his review of *Nanine*, 'le destin du comique larmoyant au théâtre. Vous aviez essayé ce genre dans votre *Enfant prodigue*; on crut alors que c'étoit pour n'y plus revenir; il parut à vos partisans que vous aviez simplement voulu faire une incursion sur les terres de M. de la Chaussée. . . . Votre goût vous ramene dans la même carriere: que M. de la Chaussée se console, & vous cède un bien qui vous appartient *à droit de conquête*.'[47]

---

46. *Commentaire sur le théâtre de Voltaire*, p. 396.

47. Guiard de Servigné, *Lettre à l'auteur de Nanine* (1749), p. 1. Hostile critics, such as J. M. B. Clément, made the same point while blaming Voltaire for the new licence in the theatre: 'Vous aviez pris la défense de la Comédie larmoyante, où vous aviez eu quelque succès: vous aviez dit que *tous les genres sont bons, hors le genre ennuyeux*. Comme personne ne se croit né pour ennuyer, chacun inventa son genre qu'il soutint fort bon, puisqu'on y avoit pleuré; & qu'on ne s'ennuie point à la Comédie, quand on y pleure' (*Première Lettre à M. de Voltaire*, I, 30).

# CHAPTER 8

# *Prose*

It is one of the peculiarities of the age of the Enlightenment that so many of its masterworks were barely recognized at the time as belonging to the realm of literature. In an epoch when very little was sacred and anything resembling dogma was anathema, when literature itself was far from static, the rigid classical division of genres, each with its own prescribed style and function, survived virtually intact, with the result that most formal writing consisted of either sterile imitations or unsuccessful attempts to pour new wine into old bottles. Vitality and originality appeared in works outside the narrow limits of what was considered 'belles lettres': in the novel, in the *conte*, in miscellaneous and usually anonymous pamphlets and *facéties*.

This is particularly true of Voltaire, who was always careful to distinguish between the two aspects of his literary activity. On the one hand poetry, especially epic and dramatic poetry, was intended to establish his reputation as a writer worthy of immortality. It was on these works, the least of which he found more difficult to write than the most ambitious piece of prose (Best. 14541), that he lavished most of his time and energy, endlessly discussing points of detail with friends whose literary judgment he valued. The more formal prose works, such as the histories or the *Traité sur la tolérance*, belong essentially to the same group, although their function is of course different, since they deal with fact and with ideas based on fact, whereas poetry appeals directly to the imagination and feelings. Both formal poetry and formal prose are concerned with ideals and with a view of man; they are governed by the same stylistic principles, namely simplicity, naturalness, freedom from affectation and from gratuitous displays of wit. On the other hand, the philosophical tales, the satires, the innumerable brochures and pamphlets which poured from the presses during the Ferney period, had little to do with 'literature'. They were generally conceived as means of action. They obeyed no rules, needed no esthetic justification and were officially unacknowledged. Providing they achieved their limited aim, they were artistically expendable.

There is no doubt that Voltaire enjoyed this kind of literary infighting. He learned very early that life is a battle and was not a man to suffer too long in silence or to retreat in the face of obstacles. It is difficult to imagine that he was unaware of his own exceptional gifts. In spite of his protests to the contrary, one has the impression that he was not altogether displeased when the public quickly recognized his inimitable style. But the last thing he wanted was to achieve fame as a satirist. All his references to satire, whether in the published work or in the correspondence, are strongly condemnatory. It is the 'poison of literature' (Best. 13128), a 'detestable form of writing' (Best. D415; M. X, 76, n.), which dishonours the literary profession (M. III, 376), corrects no-one, annoys fools, and merely makes them worse.[1] He severely chastised Boileau for indulging in it (M. X, 398–399; XXIII, 53) and publicly regretted having tarnished his own good reputation in the same way (M. X, 76, n., 78, n.). Boileau himself, he said, came to realize 'qu'à la longue l'art d'instruire quand il est parfait, réussit mieux que l'art de médire, parce que la satire meurt avec ceux qui en sont les victimes, et que la raison et la vertu sont éternelles' (M. XXIII, 212). Satire is not only morally wrong, it can have no artistic value beyond the immediate achievement of its goal.

It is not surprising therefore that Voltaire generally considered his satirical works from the point of view of their usefulness as regrettable but necessary pieces of philosophical weaponry and never confused them with what he considered to be his serious and permanent contribution

1. M. XXI, 480–481. The references to the *contes* throughout this chapter are to vol. XXI of the Moland edition.

to literature. His condemnation of satire, however, applies chiefly to attacks on individuals. While it is no doubt equally unfortunate to have to resort to a debased genre in the conflict of ideas, here the ends may arguably be said to justify the means. Moreover, he makes one important concession by invoking the principle of self-defence:

La défense est de droit; et d'un coup d'aiguillon
L'abeille en tous les temps repoussa le frelon.
La guerre est au Parnasse, au conseil, en Sorbonne:
Allons, défendons-nous, mais n'attaquons personne.

(M. X, 428)

During the late 1750s and early 1760s, the *philosophes* were in fact under heavy fire, with the *Encyclopédie* as the main target. It was about this time that Voltaire began to shift the bulk of his effort from *belles lettres* to his campaign against the forces of reaction. He did not, of course, suddenly change from poet to aggressive *philosophe*; Voltaire was a life-long campaigner. Nor did he cease writing plays and poetry after 1760. But propaganda now became a primary consideration.

Voltaire was aware that more than any of the other *philosophes* he possessed the secret of how to destroy oppressors by ridicule. Given the urgency of the situation, the importance of the cause and his own privileged position, he felt that he was not only justified in using it, but morally obliged to do so: 'Quelle comparaison bon dieu des lumières et des connaissances des Dalembert et des Diderot avec mes faibles lueurs! ce que j'ay au dessus d'eux est de rire et de faire rire aux dépends de leurs ennemis' (Best. 8243). He was prepared to use every instrument at his command, including tragedy. The ideal weapon for this type of combat, however, was the *facétie*, which he perfected. It was brief, easily distributed, easily denied, certain to be popularized by official condemnation and offered a total freedom of expression impossible in the formal genres.[2]

2. Diana Guiragossian, *Voltaire's 'Facéties'* (Geneva, 1963), pp. 27–28.

The contrast between some of Voltaire's 'literary' works and his satires is so complete that one is tempted to think in terms of split personality. The common factor is emotional intensity. Voltaire was quickly moved to extreme compassion by the spectacle of suffering, even if the suffering was imaginary, as in the theatre. Compassion was frequently replaced by indignation, followed by action; or the same emotion found release in ironic detachment and laughter. According to Horace Walpole's dictum, 'This world is a comedy to those that think, a tragedy to those that feel.' Voltaire was a highly emotional thinker to whom life was a perpetual tragicomedy.

The rare conjunction of irony and extreme sensibility is surely one of the keys to Voltaire's unique qualities as a writer. In the best satires, as in many passages of the correspondence, one is constantly aware of what Paul Chaponnière has excellently described as 'cette humanité passionnée et douloureuse qui vibre dans l'âpreté de ses sarcasmes'.[3] Jeanne Monty has noted it in her analysis of the style of the *Dictionnaire philosophique*:

> Il serait bon de renverser l'image pour chercher ce que ces différents procédés nous révèlent de l'écrivain lui-même. Et d'abord l'extrême tension affective qui enveloppe toute la polémique. Les invectives directes, les exclamations, les interpellations en témoignent ouvertement. Mais c'est ce que révèlent aussi à des niveaux différents les hyperboles, les superlatifs, les affirmations tranchantes et catégoriques, les accumulations qui font figure de charges contre l'adversaire. L'élimination de tout élément superflu, la rareté des expressions disjonctives, le rythme martelé des phrases accusatrices sont encore le reflet de l'intensité de l'émotion vibrante de Voltaire. Malgré sa réputation de froid intellectuel, il tremble de passion, de rage parfois, d'horreur et de mépris le plus souvent, et communique sa passion au lecteur.[4]

3. Paul Chaponnière, *Voltaire chez les calvinistes* (Geneva, 1932), p. 175.
4. Jeanne R. Monty, *Etude sur le style polémique de Voltaire: Le Dictionnaire philosophique* (Geneva, 1966), *SV*, XLIV, 195.

Many of Voltaire's would-be masterpieces express his
emotion directly or filtered through the conventional style
of eighteenth-century sensibility; occasionally they lapse into
something perilously close to *sensiblerie*. In his real masterpieces, notably the best of the *contes*, there is a constant
tension between humour and compassion, irony and indignation. Their polished surface never quite conceals the
passionate impulse which gives them the kind of vitality and
depth to which wit in itself, however brilliantly deployed,
can never aspire. Their disturbing quality, still vividly
present after two centuries, is not the result of cleverness,
but of what Flaubert saw as disciplined fanaticism.

Thus satire, in Voltaire's case, is not as remote from
sensibility as might appear. True satire, as Basil Willey has
pointed out, implies the condemnation of society by reference
to an ideal and can perfectly well coexist with an optimistic
view of man.[5] The cynic, the sceptic, and the pessimist are
content to demonstrate man's wretchedness and the futility
of expecting anything better; Voltaire, like his great pre-
decessor, Swift, is angry precisely because he is aware of the
gulf between life as it could be if men would only follow
'nature' and the monstrous world in which they live. He
uses the satirist's technique of jolting the reader into seeing
things as they are, stripped of the usual clothing of familiarity, not in order to reconcile him to reality, but on the
contrary to spur him into action. Even at his most pessimistic, he never loses sight of the fact that all men have a
natural instinct for good which is not always suppressed and
which can be developed by example. Eldorado exists, if only
in the mind.

A similar duality characterizes Voltaire's approach to
history. He had two purposes in writing history. One was to
tell the truth about the past by careful control of sources and
by taking up as objective a viewpoint as possible (Best.
D654). The historian should first ascertain the facts, however
depressing: 'Il faut peindre les choses dans toute leur
vérité, c'est à dire dans toute leur horreur' (Best. 8876).

5. Basil Willey, *The Eighteenth-Century Background* (Harmondsworth, 1965), pp. 99–101.

The other was to present and interpret these facts 'en philosophe'.[6] History is not a random collection of information about events and dignitaries such as one finds in a gazette. It should be concerned with the development of civilization and it should have an aim beyond the satisfaction of curiosity.[7]

Voltaire could see no contradiction in the idea that the historian should at one and the same time scrupulously respect the truth and point a moral. Undeniably, history reveals that the world is full of evil and suffering, some of it inherent in the nature of things, much of it avoidable. Men have always been the victims of natural catastrophes and of their own baser instincts. But it would be equally absurd to deny the existence of a moral law which ensures that certain essential values will survive and that order will eventually emerge from chaos. Great men who have obeyed the urgings of this inner voice, and who have consequently rendered great services to mankind, are to be found in all epochs. The historian's duty is to do what he can to hasten progress and promote the spread of *bienfaisance* by underlining these rare examples.[8]

The unity which Voltaire finds in the vast and varied spectacle of world history is that which dominates his whole philosophy. Customs differ widely, but nature is everywhere the same. 'Il résulte de ce tableau', he says of his most ambitious historical work, 'que tout ce qui tient intimement

6. 'Je pense comme mr l'abbé de St Pierre, qu'il faut écrire l'histoire en philosofe' (Best. D1644); 'il n'appartient qu'aux philosophes d'écrire l'histoire' (Best. 2877).

7. 'L'histoire ordinaire, qui n'est qu'un amas de faits opérés par des hommes, et par conséquent de crimes, n'a guère d'utilité, et celui qui lit la gazette aurait même en cela plus d'avantage que celui qui saurait toute l'histoire ancienne. La curiosité seule est satisfaite' (*Sottisier*, pp. 8–9). See also Best. D1334, D2280, 10354 and the Introduction to the *Siècle de Louis XIV*.

8. 'Mon but [in writing the *Siècle de Louis XIV*] n'est pas d'écrire tout ce qui s'est fait; mais seulement ce qu'on a fait de grand, d'utile & d'agréable. C'est le progrès des arts & de l'esprit humain que je veux faire voir, & non l'histoire des intrigues de cour & des méchancetés des hommes' (Best. D1993). Voltaire regretted having devoted too much space to battles in the *Histoire de Charles XII*: 'J'aurais bien mieux fait d'éviter tous ces détails de combats donnés chez des Sarmates, et d'entrer plus profondément dans le détail de ce qu'a fait le czar pour le bien de l'humanité' (Best. D1334).

à la nature humaine se ressemble d'un bout de l'univers à l'autre; que tout ce qui peut dépendre de la coutume est différent, et que c'est un hasard s'il se ressemble. L'empire de la coutume est bien plus vaste que celui de la nature; il s'étend sur les mœurs, sur tous les usages; il répand la variété sur la scène de l'univers: la nature y répand l'unité; elle établit partout un petit nombre de principes invariables: ainsi le fonds est partout le même, et la culture produit des fruits divers' (M. XIII, 182).

The *Essai sur les mœurs* is an astonishing tour de force: a survey of world civilization, remarkably modern in spirit, carefully documented, and written in a lively narrative style. A few well-defined themes constantly emerge, as in a symphony, from the mass of detail. The most immediately striking is the theme of tragic failure: the endless cruelty, the bloody and futile conflicts, the ignorance and superstition of the masses easily converted into murderous fanaticism, the persistent misuse of reason, and the domination of destructive passion. Highly civilized nations relapse into savagery; republics promise a better life for the average citizen, but are no more conducive to happiness than monarchies; tyranny, war, and injustice are the rule, dignity, peace, and freedom the exception. All this is deliberately emphasized as part of the hard lesson to be learned from experience, and also because Voltaire's particular kind of sensibility, his profound humanitarianism, combined with a despairing sense of futility and waste, forces him to dwell with fascinated horror on the darker aspects of humanity.

Yet the other, more optimistic, side of his sensibility is also present. If man has allowed himself too frequently to become the slave of his passions, he is nevertheless animated by a 'secret love of order' which is the source of all law and legitimate authority.[9] His industry is even more impressive than his destructiveness. He is not basically wicked; even fanatics are dupes rather than monsters. Voltaire consistently refuses to believe that it is possible to indulge in wickedness for its own sake: 'En vain quelques

9. *Essai sur les mœurs*, ed. R. Pomeau, II, 808. All subsequent references in this chapter are to this edition.

voyageurs et quelques missionnaires nous ont représenté les prêtres d'Orient comme des prédicateurs de l'iniquité; c'est calomnier la nature humaine: il n'est pas possible qu'il y ait jamais une société religieuse instituée pour inviter au crime' (II, 809). One of the striking features of the *Essai* in fact is a tendency to question extreme examples of debased and cruel conduct. They are unnatural and therefore improbable: 'Les hommes sanguinaires ne le sont que dans la fureur de la vengeance, ou dans les sévérités de cette politique atroce, qui fait croire la cruauté nécessaire; mais personne ne répand le sang pour son plaisir' (I, 731).

The achievement of liberty and equality before the law is shown as an ideal rather than as a permanent acquisition, but Voltaire dwells with obvious admiration on the few societies which have succeeded from time to time in converting something approaching the ideal into precarious reality: Switzerland, Holland and to some extent England, and various primitive peoples. At the same time, his realism obliges him to express reservations. As elsewhere, Voltaire is both monarchist in practice and ardently 'republican' in spirit.

The major theme, as might be expected, is the necessity for tolerance. Besides specific statements to this effect, the whole trend of the *Essai* is to demonstrate that the human tragedy is to a large extent the result of misdirected enthusiasm in the desire to force others to accept beliefs which are often incomprehensible or absurd. The worst of all scourges is war allied with religion, and in this respect the medieval period deserves its reputation as an era of darkness.

Obviously Voltaire is not a reliable guide to the Middle Ages. His judgments lack the kind of sympathetic understanding one would expect from a twentieth-century historian. Yet, given the context of the time in which he was writing, with its inevitable bias against a Church-centred society, his condemnation is less sweeping than is generally supposed. He vigorously defends some Popes[10] and gives

10. He describes the papacy as 'à la fois le scandale, l'horreur et la divinité de l'Europe catholique'. The greatest man of the Middle Ages, according to Voltaire, was Pope Alexander III, who, by condemning Henry II and doing his best to abolish serfdom, 'ressuscita les droits des peuples et réprima le crime dans les rois' (II, 804).

qualified praise to chivalry. The men of the Middle Ages were indeed inclined to barbarous behaviour and outbursts of fanaticism, but no more so than those of the period following the Renaissance, with its witchcraft trials and calamitous civil wars. Each age has its quota of bright periods and great men.

Since human nature is everywhere and at all times the same, Voltaire see little hope for rapid progress towards the elimination of all causes of conflict. Recent improvements, however, show that the forces of enlightenment are gradually gathering strength. Europe, he concludes, is 'incomparably more populated, more civilized, richer, more enlightened' than it was in Charlemagne's time (II, 811). Thus the *Essai* ends on a distinctly optimistic note, in spite of the famous summary of world history as 'un ramas de crimes, de folies et de malheurs' (II, 804).

Although Voltaire felt that history, if it is to appeal to a wide public, should have some of the dramatic qualities of good tragedy, he was careful to distinguish between the styles appropriate to each. Emotional fervour is quite out of place in a prose work attempting to present an undistorted account of past events: 'On mêle partout l'entousiasme, et il n'en faut avoir qu'en vers' (Best. D654). Sensibility, in the *Essai* and other historical works, is more a matter of underlying attitudes than of overt expression. One recent commentator has even spoken of 'emotional aridity'.[11] This is not a criticism which would have occurred to Voltaire's contemporaries. Palissot praised him for writing history 'en philosophe éloquent et sensible': 'C'est dans le genre de

11. J. H. Brumfitt, *Voltaire Historian* (London, 1958), p. 164: 'The impersonal, analytical style, which characterizes all Voltaire's historical works, but above all, the *Essai*, has an emotional aridity which is never really compensated for by the human feeling which obviously exists behind his outbursts of moral indignation at the events related, and the rarer expressions of approval when some brighter gleam is descried in the dark picture of human miseries. It is because of this that Voltaire, great as is his contribution to the science of history, cannot rank among the great historical artists.' For a different view, see Raymond Escholier, 'Le premier de nos historiens: Voltaire', *Europe*, no. 361–362 (mai–juin 1959), p. 33: 'Le secret de sa grande réussite, c'est qu'il échappe sans cesse à la froideur, à la monotonie, à l'uniformité. . . . En lui, tout est chaleur, couleur, ardeur.'

l'Histoire, sur-tout, que M. de Voltaire a répandu cet esprit de tolérance & de paix, d'humanité & de bienfaisance, qui le caractérise essentiellement. Les oppresseurs y sont peints sous des couleurs si odieuses, les opprimés y deviennent si intéressans, qu'il est peu d'ames qui n'éprouvent, en le lisant, la douce illusion de se croire meilleures':[12] the same 'illusion', one might add, which attracted spectators to Voltaire's theatre. And it is significant that Michelet, the romantic historian *par excellence*, considered the *Essai* to be one of the masterpieces of humanist history because it is pervaded by Voltaire's sensibility. 'Cette vive sensibilité', he says, referring to Vauvenargues, 'éclate à chaque instant chez son maître Voltaire, le rieur plein de larmes. Elle alla trop loin même dans son *Désastre de Lisbonne*, l'égara, lui fit croire au désordre de la nature, lui en cacha l'ordre profond. Mais elle est admirable dans l'*Essai sur les mœurs*. Sous forme légère et critique, elle anime partout ce beau livre. Partout on est heureux d'y retrouver *le sens humain*.'[13]

History, like philosophy, is concerned with truth, for which the most suitable medium is prose; fiction, according to neoclassical theory, belongs to the epic or the theatre. Even as late as the mid-century, prose fiction was not taken too seriously. Diderot's disdain for the novel is typical. In his *Eloge de Richardson* (1761), he referred to it as 'un tissu d'événements chimériques et frivoles, dont la lecture était dangereuse pour le goût et pour les mœurs'. Because of its reputation, he would have preferred to find another name for the works of Richardson.[14]

Voltaire's attitude was not very different. He condemned the vast majority of novels as worthless productions of feeble minds, 'qui écrivent avec facilité des choses indignes d'être lues par les esprits solides' (M. XIV, 142). The few references to his own ventures in the genre are generally apologetic. Replying to Panckoucke, who had suggested publishing a collection of his novels, he speaks of novel-writing as a kind of weakness, a secret activity which gives pleasure but which cannot be officially acknowledged: 'Vous me mandez,

12. *Eloge de M. de Voltaire*, p. 23.
13. *Histoire de France*, XV, 388–389.
14. *Œuvres complètes*, V, 212–213.

monsieur, que vous imprimez mes romans, et je vous réponds que si j'ai fait des romans j'en demande pardon à dieu; mais tout au moins je n'y ai jamais mis mon nom, pas plus qu'à mes autres sottises.'[15]

If the novel, with few exceptions, was beyond the pale of literature, according to Voltaire and his contemporaries, the fairy-tale type of fantasy from which the *conte philosophique* was derived was even less respectable. Why then did Voltaire turn to this popular form of sub-culture to express ideas which were important to him and to express them with such instinctively consummate skill that some of these despised 'sottises' have become universally acclaimed masterpieces of world literature? His motives can only be guessed at, since Voltaire considered such matters unworthy of serious discussion.[16] Yet there is evidence that the *contes* were not mere improvisations put together on the spur of the moment to amuse a few intimates. Some of them, at least, were carefully composed and revised, and all of them reflect Voltaire's ideas, activities, and feelings at the time of composition. Jacques Van Den Heuvel has shown that their autobiographical content is considerable.[17]

It seems likely that they were, in the first place, a form of therapy. Voltaire often found release in laughter from the conflicts, annoyances, and even tragedies of everyday existence. It has been suggested that the *contes* performed a similar function.[18] In particular, they enabled him to dis-

15. Best. 11051. This scorn for novels, including his own, is frequently expressed in the correspondence. Referring to *L'Ingénu*, he affirms that 'Queste coglionerié se vendent mieux qu'un bon ouvrage' (Best. 13510). In one of the very few letters in which he deigns to mention *Zadig*, he says that he would have sub-titled it *La Providence* instead of *La Destinée*, 'si on osait se servir de ce mot respectable de providence dans un ouvrage de pur amusement' (Best. 3304).

16. As Dr. Besterman notes (*Voltaire Essays and Another* [London, 1962], p. 60), it is remarkable that in the love letters to Mme Denis, although Voltaire discusses at some length the plays he was writing at the time, 'There is not the slightest reference, however, any more here than in his other correspondence, to the most important literary event of the period, the creation of the *conte philosophique*: yet it was at this time that he wrote *Memnon*, the first version of *Zadig*.'

17. Jacques Van Den Heuvel, *Voltaire dans ses contes* (Paris, 1967), p. 142 and *passim*.

18. Laurence Bongie, 'Crisis and the Birth of the Voltairean *conte*', *MLQ*, 23 (1962), p. 61.

solve tensions between his fundamental optimism and a sense of disillusionment born of bitter experience of human frailty and intermittent awareness of the absurdity of existence. They were, moreover, as he quickly realized, an extremely effective instrument of propaganda, appealing to a large public, including the segment unlikely to read the *Essai sur les mœurs* or the *Traité sur la tolérance*. Finally, they offered perfect freedom for the artist to indulge his natural gifts and taste for fantasy with no risk to his reputation.

The form of the *conte philosophique*, as perfected by Voltaire, seems to leave little scope for sensibility. Fantasy, wit, ridicule, and the perpetual confrontation between pretensions and reality are the most obvious ingredients. The characters are generally puppets, constantly jerked from one outrageous situation to another. Above all, the dominant note is irony, the least hospitable environment for outpourings of emotion or exhortations to idealism. If the basic tendency of romanticism is to maintain a self-consistent, idealized world free from intrusions of realism or destructive irony, then obviously the *contes* are antiromantic. Is not the purpose of *Candide* to destroy illusion and reconcile the reader to the mediocre world in which he is obliged to live?

The trouble with this kind of generalization is that it fails to take into account the variety of tone to be found in the philosophical tales, or even within one of them, as for example the marked differences in treatment of certain episodes in *L'Ingénu*, or even in *Candide*. The predominance of irony and the exclusion of sentiment are by no means absolute. In fact the frequent intrusion of various manifestations of sensibility in a genre in which it would seem to be peculiarly inappropriate is surely an indication of the extent of Voltaire's commitment. There is a natural tendency to judge the *conteur* on the basis of his undoubted masterpiece, *Candide*; he was also the author of *L'Ingénu* and *L'Histoire de Jenni*, which are, in their way, almost as typically representative products of the age of sensibility as *Nanine* or *L'Ecossaise*.

Primitivist themes—simplicity contrasted with luxury,

the return to nature, the noble savage—are highlighted in several of the *contes*, with Voltaire's sympathies becoming progressively more evident. One of the earliest, *Le Monde comme il va* (1748), illustrates Mandeville's theory that the vices of great cities can be justified, and is not far removed from the spirit of *Le Mondain*. Yet one is aware of a certain uneasiness, which manifests itself in the criticism of some aspects of city life and in the unenthusiastic conclusion: in Persépolis, 'si tout n'est pas bien, tout est passable'.

The emphasis in *Jeannot et Colin* (1764) is quite different. 'Le bonheur n'est pas dans la vanité', as Jeannot discovers to his cost in the course of an encounter with the superficial brilliance of *le beau monde*, where wit and a good appearance matter more than the solid virtues and where the art of pleasing is cultivated at the expense of genuine knowledge. Abandoned by his high society friends the moment his wealth has disappeared, Jeannot is finally rescued by the good-hearted Colin, who teaches him that true happiness is not to be found in cities. All ends well: 'La bonté d'âme de Colin développa dans le cœur de Jeannot le germe du bon naturel, que le monde n'avait pas encore étouffé' (p. 148). This little parable, with its exaltation of friendship, *bienfaisance*, and simple good nature and its attack on the values of the *mondain* would not be out of place in Rousseau's *Emile*.

*La Princesse de Babylone* (1768), as previously noted,[19] is a further endorsement of primitivist values, or rather of that form of enlightened primitivism consistently advocated by Voltaire which is hostile to the excesses of superficial worldliness but not to the development of knowledge or the arts.

*Zadig* (1747) is usually regarded as a first inconclusive attempt by Voltaire to come to grips with the deist's dilemma of the existence of evil in a universe governed by an all-powerful and beneficent deity. The sub-title, *La Destinée*, by which is meant Providence (Best. 3304), does indeed direct the reader's attention to the question discussed by Zadig and the angel Jesrad in the penultimate chapter.

19. See above, p. 87.

Faced with a choice between honest doubt occasioned by the evident injustice and absurdity of existence viewed from a human standpoint and the pat answers of an angel thoroughly conversant with the theories of Pope and Bolingbroke, the wise Zadig 'adora la Providence et se soumit' (p. 91). While stubbornly clinging to his faith in Providence, Voltaire was obviously finding it progressively more difficult to accept the justifications offered by philosophical optimism. But *Zadig* is much more than a metaphysical disquisition on the mystery of divine justice. It is concerned rather with the questions raised by the related theme of *bienfaisance*. What is virtue? How can it be developed? Does it lead to happiness?

On the whole, as might be expected in a *conte philosophique*, Voltaire views these matters with the cold eye of the realist. Virtue is not automatically rewarded; more often than not it leads to disaster. Evil-doers are not necessarily unhappy. Men are like 'insects devouring each other on a little atom of mud'. The majority seem to be selfish ingrates, dominated by fear, envy, ambition, and superstition. When Zadig becomes prime minister, he is backed by the populace, not because his policies are good, or because he is reasonable and kind, but simply because he holds the reins of power. And Voltaire's long-suffering hero soon discovers that the road to virtue is strewn with well-nigh insuperable obstacles compared with the primrose path to evil: 'L'occasion de faire du mal se trouve cent fois par jour, et celle de faire du bien une fois dans l'année, comme dit Zoroastre' (p. 41).

The overall impression, however, is not one of cynical despair. The central figure, always in the foreground, is a model of *bienfaisance*. Zadig is no simpleton like Candide. We are clearly intended to admire him as a man of good sense, extraordinarily adaptable, willing to bend with the wind, and capable of separating truth from prejudice, superstition, or mere verbiage. At the same time, there is a strong idealistic streak in his character which forces him to continue to do good, whatever the discouragement and whatever the consequences for himself. He forgives the envious Arimaze for having him condemned to death and refuses to accept

Arimaze's property as compensation (p. 43). He is a man of
exceptional courage, who braves the king's wrath by
praising a minister in disgrace (p. 45). His principles of
government are humane, wise, and benevolent: 'C'est de
lui que les nations tiennent ce grand principe: qu'il vaut
mieux hasarder de sauver un coupable que de condamner un
innocent' (p. 46). Zadig combines the practical wisdom of the
enlightened social reformer with the more spectacular
chivalric virtues of the knight who takes it upon himself to
rescue ladies in distress, even when the latter prove ungrateful.

If a lesson is to be drawn from Zadig's long series of misfortunes, it is obviously not a counsel of resignation, but on
the contrary of compassionate *engagement*. Zadig might well
have chosen to keep out of trouble and demonstrate his
intellectual superiority by mocking the follies and weaknesses of mankind. Instead, he plunges into the mêlée and
takes risks. His idealism is stronger than his 'common sense'.
In a world where natural feelings of benevolence are
normally smothered, it is all the more important to set an
example. This point is underlined in the chapter entitled
'Les Généreux', in which Voltaire returns to the idea,
which seems to have had a special fascination for him, of
offering rewards to encourage *bienfaisance*.

It goes without saying that Zadig is a man of feeling. His
one 'weakness', in the sense that it is a principal cause of his
unhappiness, is also one of his most admirable traits: the
constancy of his affection. There is a revealing dialogue
between the hero and an old fisherman on the subject:
'Quoi! Seigneur, s'écria le pêcheur, vous seriez donc aussi
malheureux, vous qui faites du bien?—Plus malheureux que
toi cent fois, répondait Zadig.—Mais comment se peut-il
faire, disait le bonhomme, que celui qui donne soit plus à
plaindre que celui qui reçoit?—C'est que ton plus grand
malheur, reprit Zadig, était le besoin, et que je suis infortuné par le cœur' (p. 76). Extreme sensibility, as Voltaire
was only too well aware, is the source of the greatest misery
as well as of the greatest happiness.

Whereas in the tragedies weeping is invariably equated

with virtue, the tears shed by minor characters in the *contes* are sometimes the preliminary to some particularly selfish or cynical act. A good example occurs in the first chapter of *Zadig*, when the hero is wounded in the eye while defending his fiancée, Sémire, against an attempt by Orcan to carry her off. 'Sémire ne demandait aux dieux que la guérison de son amant. Ses yeux étaient nuit et jour baignés de larmes: elle attendait le moment où ceux de Zadig pourraient jouir de ses regards'. Zadig is cured, but on his way to Sémire 'Il apprit . . . que cette belle dame, ayant déclaré hautement qu'elle avait une aversion insurmontable pour les borgnes, venait de se marier à Orcan la nuit même.'[20]

Nevertheless, with fine disregard for unity of tone, Voltaire does not hesitate to introduce elements of sensibility. Zadig and Astarté have 'les cœurs les plus nobles et les plus passionnés' (p. 81). Zadig constantly sheds tears and behaves at times like the hero of *Manon Lescaut*. Separated from the Queen, 'cet illustre fugitif, arrivé sur le bord d'une colline dont on voyait Babylone, tourna la vue sur le palais de la reine, et s'évanouit; il ne reprit ses sens que pour verser des larmes et pour souhaiter la mort' (p. 54). As for Astarté, she is as tender and passionate as any of Voltaire's tragic heroines.[21]

In the classic *scène de reconnaissance* between the re-united lovers there is an effusion of sensibility worthy of *Zaïre* or *Alzire*. The whole passage should be cited, since it contains many of the hallmarks of the *roman sensible*: passionate exclamations, torrents of tears, mixed emotions, fainting, exaggerated gestures, and the kind of momentary madness which is intended to indicate the reaction of highly sensitive characters to dramatic events:

20. Pp. 34–35. See also pp. 35–36. It may have been this passage which prompted Raynal to remark in the first real critical comment on *Zadig* (*Correspondance littéraire, philosophique et critique par Grimm, Diderot, Raynal, Meister, etc.*, I, 217) that the novel is devoid of feeling ('Point de sentiment; je ne me souviens pas d'avoir guère lu rien d'aussi sec'). But since Raynal also goes on to say that *Zadig* is equally lacking in wit and ideas, his criticism can hardly be taken seriously.

21. 'Et quand, malgré lui, ses regards se tournaient vers Astarté, ils rencontraient ceux de la reine mouillés de pleurs, dont il partait des traits de flammes' (p. 52).

Il demeura quelque temps immobile; enfin, rompant le silence d'une voix entrecoupée: 'O généreuse dame! pardonnez à un étranger, à un infortuné, d'oser vous demander par quelle aventure étonnante je trouve ici le nom de ZADIG tracé de votre main divine'. A cette voix, à ces paroles, la dame releva son voile d'une main tremblante, regarda Zadig, jeta un cri d'attendrissement, de surprise et de joie, et, succombant sous tous les mouvements divers qui assaillaient à la fois son âme, elle tomba évanouie entre ses bras. C'était Astarté elle-même, c'était la reine de Babylone, c'était celle que Zadig adorait, et qu'il se reprochait d'adorer; c'était celle dont il avait tant pleuré et tant craint la destinée. Il fut un moment privé de l'usage de ses sens; et quand il eut attaché ses regards sur les yeux d'Astarté, qui se rouvraient avec une langueur mêlée de confusion et de tendresse: 'O puissances immortelles! s'écria-t-il, qui présidez aux destins des faibles humains, me rendez-vous Astarté? En quel temps, en quels lieux, en quel état la revois-je?' Il se jeta à genoux devant Astarté, et il attacha son front à la poussière de ses pieds. La reine de Babylone le relève, et le fait asseoir auprès d'elle sur le bord de ce ruisseau; elle essuyait à plusieurs reprises ses yeux, dont les larmes recommençaient toujours à couler (p. 78).

In spite of certain obvious similarities—the succession of misfortunes which befall the hero, the unresolved metaphysical dilemma—*Candide* is very different in spirit from *Zadig*. The usual interpretation of the famous finale, 'il faut cultiver notre jardin', as an exhortation to social action would seem to be in keeping with the earlier *conte*. But if it means what it appears to mean in the context of the preceding remarks made by Martin, the Dervish and the old Turk, Candide is suggesting that the best policy for the little band is to mind their own business, work hard to avoid boredom, steer clear of politics, and not think too much. Voltaire's use of the expression in his correspondence indicates beyond doubt that this is in fact the intended meaning.[22]

Two points should, however, be made. First, Candide is not Voltaire. The latter was not noted for his ignorance, innocence, and simple-mindedness. Nor do Candide and the little band represent the whole of mankind, although perhaps the large majority. Given their situation, their experiences, and the average man's desire for a modest share of peace and security, their conclusion is sound. Secondly, Voltaire himself was frequently tempted to adopt the same attitude, but only temporarily and in moments of depression or exhaustion. As Norman Torrey says, 'His letters from this period on show very definitely that the exhortation at the end of *Candide* meant literally what it said, but this was meant only for those periods when he had reached the bottom of his emotional curve.'[23] Far from containing the quintessence of Voltairean wisdom, *Candide* is the expression of a mood.

Like all masterpieces, *Candide* has a core of mystery which defies all attempts at analysis, however subtle and informed. In many ways, it is entirely untypical of its author. Artistically, it is as far removed as possible from the 'literary' productions by which Voltaire was judged, and wished to be judged, in his own time. It would be difficult to imagine anything less like *Candide* than, say, *Nanine* or *Tancrède*. The moral is not a particularly noble or generous one; practically the whole of Voltaire's career is a denial of it. Philosophically, it is full of inconsistencies. Voltaire is no nearer to finding an answer to the nagging question of the

22. See Norman Torrey, *The Spirit of Voltaire* (New York, 1938), p. 51; R. A. Brooks, *Voltaire and Leibniz* (Geneva, 1964), p. 106; R. Mauzi, *L'Idée du bonheur au XVIII^e siècle*, pp. 64–69. The following are a few examples taken from the correspondence: 'Ma chère nièce, tout ceci est un naufrage. *Sauve qui peut* est la devise de chaque pauvre particulier. Cultivons notre jardin comme Candide' (Best. 9013); 'Mes anges je suis épuisé, rebuté, je renifle sur cette Olimpie. Il faut attendre le moment de la grâce et cultiver le jardin de Candide' (Best. 10447); 'Mon cœur est desséché quand je songe qu'il y a dans Paris une foule de gens d'esprit qui pensent comme nous, et qu'aucun d'eux ne sent la cause commune. Il faudra donc finir comme Candide par cultiver son jardin' (Best. 10969); 'Je ne sais rien, je ne vois le monde que par un trou, de fort loin et avec de très mauvaises lunettes; je cultive mon jardin comme Candide' (Best. 11030).

23. *Spirit of Voltaire*, p. 51.

existence of evil than he is in *Zadig*. As Professor Wade has pointed out, it is not even a convincing attack on optimism.[24] If there is a Providence, then the 'best of all *possible* worlds' theory is a necessary corollary; yet Voltaire retains his belief in the former while making fun of the latter. Pangloss is more logical.

*Candide* is nevertheless profoundly and eternally Voltairean. So much so that one can now hardly think of Voltaire without associating him immediately with his most durable work and with a view of life which is at one and the same time funny and sad, superficial and profound, wise and frivolous, dynamic and resigned. Successive generations have recognized in it a truth which is far more important than mere logic. The fact that it is free from both the paralyzing conventions of neoclassicism and those of sensibility is certainly one of the reasons for its lasting appeal. The kind of feeling which underlies *Candide* is of a much rarer quality. J. G. Weightman perhaps comes as close as one can to explaining its secret when he says that 'Its driving force is an intellectual bewilderment, which is felt as a strong emotion.'[25]

Even in *Candide* there is one bastion of Voltairean idealism: Eldorado. It is significant that in the exact centre of a tale of horror and stupidity, Voltaire should describe a 'primitivist Utopia'[26] which offers a glimpse of life as it might be if men obeyed the laws of nature, worshipped God without superstition, and practised tolerance and *bienfaisance*. Eldorado is remote, but not entirely inaccessible. The fact that Candide and Cacambo find its atmosphere too rarified does not necessarily relegate to it the realm of illusion. It remains as a source of inspiration and an ideal

24. Ira O. Wade, *Voltaire and Candide. A Study in the Fusion of History, Art, and Philosophy* (Princeton, 1959), p. 317: 'It would not take a very skillful lawyer to prove that Voltaire's treatment of optimism is quite as optimistic as the treatment of the optimists themselves, that he says no more for or against it than Leibnitz, Pope, King, and hundreds of others.'

25. J. G. Weightman, 'The Quality of Candide', in *Essays Presented to C. M. Girdlestone* (Durham, 1960), p. 340.

26. Rita Falke, 'Eldorado: le meilleur des mondes possibles', *SV*, II, 37.

which could one day be approximated, if not realized. Its presence in a work such as *Candide* is sufficient refutation of the view that Voltaire was a cynical pessimist.

*L'Ingénu* (1767) has given rise to an even greater variety of interpretations than *Candide*. Since it has usually been regarded primarily as a satire, most critical comment has been directed towards the problem of deciding which particular aspects of the *ancien régime* Voltaire was attacking, although the *sensible* elements of the novel are so blatant that it has not been possible to ignore them altogether.[27] There is no doubt that Voltaire is making a vigorous protest, more often expressed through indignation than irony, against an unjust society. His targets are numerous and include the Jesuits, who come off very badly; religious intolerance, shown to be not only inhumane but economically disastrous; and above all the arbitrary nature of French governmental and legal procedures, particularly the use of *lettres de cachet*, the power enjoyed by ministers and court favourites, and all that is symbolized by the odious Bastille. But it would be a mistake to confuse the theme and substance of the novel with incidental satire. For *L'Ingénu* is not only, in many important respects, a *roman sensible*, but a tract in favour of sensibility and one more appeal for a return, if not to nature, at least to the principles of natural law.

It is impossible to read the novel without being aware, sometimes embarrassingly so, of the author's frequent resort to techniques developed and exploited to the full in his theatre. While he never abandons irony completely, the light satirical touch rapidly gives way to 'torrents of tears'. Sometimes irony and sentiment are oddly combined, as in the description of Mlle de St.-Yves as the 'généreuse et respectable infidèle' (p. 294). More often, the novel tends to

27. For a discussion of the various interpretations of *L'Ingénu*, see J. Van Den Heuvel, *Voltaire dans ses contes*, p. 297, and S. S. B. Taylor, 'Voltaire's *L'Ingénu*, the Huguenots and Choiseul' in *The Age of Enlightenment* (Edinburgh, 1967), p. 113. Two recent critical assessments which start from the position that *L'Ingénu* is what it seems to be, namely a *roman sensible* on a primitivist theme, are Haydn T. Mason, 'The Unity of Voltaire's *L'Ingénu*' in *The Age of Enlightenment* (Edinburgh, 1967), pp. 93–106, and J. Van Den Heuvel, *Voltaire dans ses contes*, pp. 295–317.

become a narrated *comédie larmoyante*, complete with virtuous and unfortunate heroine, a succession of touching tableaux in the manner of Greuze, contrasting emotions, a death scene calculated to bring tears to the eyes of the most insensitive contemporary reader, a 'vieillard sensible et vertueux', and characters with a remarkable propensity for weeping. Tears are shed at almost every event in the narrative: tears of recognition, of grief, of happiness, of compassion, and occasionally of self-pity.

Voltaire stated that he preferred *L'Ingénu* to *Candide* because it is 'infiniment plus vraisemblable' (Best. 13360). This is certainly true of the principal characters, who are depicted as complex individuals capable of real feelings and quite unlike the cartoon figures of most of the *contes*. We are obviously intended to admire their sensibility. Whatever their faults or errors of judgment, their hearts are in the right place. They are granted compassion, generosity, and *grandeur d'âme* and therefore achieve salvation. The Ingénu is quick to anger and given to violence; Gordon has allowed himself to be misled by Jansenism; even Mlle de St.-Yves makes the fatal mistake of overemphasizing the importance of what the world mistakenly takes for 'virtue'. But none could possibly be guilty of a base or ignoble action. Gordon, who resembles the 'bon prêtre' of Voltairean tragedy, is the ideal Mentor for the Ingénu, not primarily because of his wisdom, which, in a Jansenist, is naturally suspect—and in fact he is converted by his pupil—but because 'il n'était pas de ces malheureux philosophes qui s'efforcent d'être insensibles' (p. 300).

The Ingénu himself is an excellent example of *l'homme sensible*, even to his faults, which resemble those of his creator: pride, a passionate impulsiveness, and an immediate and exaggerated reaction to provocation. In spite of them, his behaviour is always chivalrous, compassionate, and honest. He listens to the voice of 'simple nature' (p. 278) and thus attains true reason; in other words, he sees things as they really are (p. 284). Uninhibited by prejudice or sophisticated nonsense, he says what he thinks (p. 250), or rather, as he corrects himself, what he feels (p. 280). Consequently his religion of nature is that of all reasonable men not blinkered by a defective education and he becomes an appropriate mouthpiece for Voltaire's deistic beliefs (p. 274). But the dominating characteristic of both the Ingénu and Gordon is their *bienfaisance*; they both possess that impulse towards altruism which is the true mark of the man of feeling.

Mlle de St.-Yves, 'tendre, vive et sage', is a typical Voltairean heroine: virtuous, self-sacrificing, entirely devoted to the man she loves, self-effacing yet capable of great courage when the occasion demands, and above all *sensible*. It would be difficult to imagine a scene more appropriate to tearful melodrama than her death, which results from a morbid obsession with the sacrifice of her 'honour'. Voltaire braves the risk of ribald comment, which is not lacking in the first part of the novel, to squeeze from it every ounce of pathos.

Critics generally have been strangely reluctant to accept the idea that the story of a Huron's adventures in France by the author of *Alzire* could be a Voltairean version of the noble savage. The hero, it is pointed out, is not a savage at all, since he turns out to be of good Breton stock. Further, he is by no means the idealized primitive of European legend. Voltaire is careful to show the disadvantages as well as the virtues of a Huron upbringing. The Ingénu's direct approach to courtship and total ignorance of the conventions of polite society are harmless enough; the impulse to burn down a convent because Mlle de St.-Yves is imprisoned there is another matter. Obviously, the philosophy of saying what one thinks and doing what one wishes, however appropriate to life in the wilds of Huronia, cannot be tolerated in eighteenth-century France. Finally, the Ingénu is 'converted' to a more civilized way of life during his stay in the Bastille, thanks to an ample supply of suitable books and the presence of an 'enlightened friend'. He is changed from a brute to a man: 'Le jeune Ingénu ressemblait à un de ces arbres vigoureux qui, nés dans un sol ingrat, étendent en peu de temps leurs racines et leurs branches quand ils sont transplantés dans un terrain favorable' (p. 279).

All this is true; but to conclude that *L'Ingénu* has little to do with primitivism, or even that it constitutes an attack on the doctrines of Rousseau,[28] is surely to miss Voltaire's point. *L'Ingénu* was not his first, or last, treatment of the noble savage theme. *Les Scythes*, a play which has some affinity with the novel, and which Voltaire described as 'en quelque sorte l'état de nature mis en opposition avec l'état de l'homme artificiel, tel qu'il est dans les grandes villes' (M. VI, 267), was performed in the same year. The revelation of the Ingénu's identity has very little relevance, since Voltaire nowhere implies that Europeans are inherently superior. Environment, not heredity, is the key factor, and the hero is to all intents and purposes a Huron, as the title of the Paris edition, *Le Huron ou l'Ingénu*, suggests.[29] Whatever the defects of his character—and Voltaire would hardly consider impulsiveness to be a capital sin—the Ingénu is a veritable paragon compared with the majority of Frenchmen portrayed in the novel. His integrity, his courage, his 'cordialité noble et fière' (p. 250), his 'bon sens naturel', which so astonished the learned Gordon, and above all his *bienfaisance*, more than make up for his gauche behaviour.

By making the Ingénu a living embodiment of natural law, Voltaire is simply reaffirming what he had often stated: that the simpler life is more conducive to genuine feeling, and therefore to 'humanity'. In civilized society, says the abbé de St.-Yves, natural law, without the necessary reinforcement of positive laws, 'ne serait presque jamais qu'un brigandage naturel'; but he admits that there are more rogues in the cities of Europe than among the Hurons (p. 264). As the Ingénu puts it, 'Mes compatriotes d'Amérique ne m'auraient jamais traité avec la barbarie que j'éprouve; ils n'en ont pas d'idée. On les appelle sauvages; ce sont des

28. There is one almost certain reference to Rousseau in the description of the death of Mlle de St.-Yves (p. 302), which is probably being compared with that of Julie in *La Nouvelle Héloïse*: 'Que d'autres cherchent à louer les morts fastueuses de ceux qui entrent dans la destruction avec insensibilité.' Voltaire's point is not that Rousseau overplays sensibility, but that he is not *sensible* enough. It is reinforced by the remark on p. 285: '[L'Ingénu] lut quelques romans nouveaux; il en trouva peu qui lui peignissent la situation de son âme. Il sentait que son cœur allait toujours au delà de ce qu'il lisait. "Ah! disait-il, presque tous ces auteurs-là n'ont que de l'esprit et de l'art".'

29. Marmontel's dramatic adaptation was also called *Le Huron*.

gens bien grossiers, et les hommes de ce pays-ci sont des coquins raffinés' (p. 272).

There is in fact a perpetual contrast in the novel between the crude but compassionate savage and the hypocrisy which characterizes the 'coquins raffinés' of Paris. The Ingénu, having enjoyed the benefits of Rousseau's 'negative education' (p. 256), has never acquired the superstitions, prejudices, and penchant for frivolity which are only too evident in the city-dwellers he encounters. The reader is clearly intended to compare his generous attitude with the callous indifference of Paris and Versailles, where men are treated like monkeys: 'On les bat et on les fait danser' (p. 301). If the savages of Huronia sometimes avenge themselves on their enemies, at least they do not oppress their friends (p. 285).

St.-Pouange is a typical product of this over-refined environment. His natural goodness has been stifled by the endless pursuit of pleasure: 'St.-Pouange n'était point né méchant; le torrent des affaires et des amusements avait emporté son âme, qui ne se connaissait pas encore' (p. 303). Consequently, he is incapable of the kind of concern for his fellow-man which is reserved for the man of feeling. On seeing Mlle de St.-Yves' coffin, he turns way, 'avec ce simple dégoût d'un homme nourri dans les plaisirs, qui pense qu'on doit lui épargner tout spectacle qui pourrait le ramener à la contemplation de la misère humaine' (p. 303).

L'Ingénu is a good example of Voltaire's moderate primitivism. Without endorsing every facet of noble savagery and without abandoning the real values of civilization—notably cultivation of knowledge, of the arts, and of good manners—Voltaire is clearly sympathetic to the 'man of nature', with his greater capacity for emotion, and implacably hostile to the 'petit-maître' outlook which dominated the upper echelons of Parisian society.

The novel represents something of a departure in the Voltairean *conte*, although certain features are foreshadowed in *Zadig*. Voltaire was experimenting, not altogether successfully, with a combination of his well-developed satirical techniques and those of the *roman sensible*. *L'Ingénu* is a flawed masterpiece, not because the two elements are completely incompatible—on the contrary, the satire of inhumane or indifferent behaviour complements the positive thesis in favour of sensibility, and Voltaire passes from one to the other with considerable skill—but for the same reasons which have led to the disappearance of so many eighteenth-century works. The faults of *L'Ingénu* which make it, contrary to the author's opinion, greatly inferior to *Candide*, are those which mar the tragedies and comedies: melodramatic exaggeration and an overemphasis on the externals of emotion.

These faults are much more in evidence in *L'Histoire de Jenni* (1775), which is also a mixture of satire, sensibility, and a touch of ribaldry, but in which sensibility degenerates very quickly into sentimental rhetoric. The noble savage makes yet another appearance, in a more conventional and less complex form. He plays a comparatively minor part, however, since the subject of *Jenni* is religion rather than primitivism. His role is to emphasize the connection between them by proclaiming, with appropriate gesture, the superiority of the religion of the heart: '"Vous avez donc, lui dis-je, votre Dieu et votre loi?—Oui, nous répondit-il, avec une assurance qui n'avait rien de la fierté; mon dieu est là", et il montra le ciel; "ma loi est là dedans", et il mit la main sur son cœur' (p. 546).

*Jenni* is a fable illustrating the necessity for Voltairean deism, whose credo is announced by the principal character, Freind: 'Je crois, avec Jésus-Christ, qu'il faut aimer Dieu et son prochain, pardonner les injures et réparer ses torts. Croyez-moi: adorez Dieu, soyez juste et bienfaisant: voilà tout l'homme' (p. 532). Three years before his death, at the end of the long and bitter campaign against *l'Infâme*, Voltaire is still the high priest of 'true Christianity'. If he is no nearer to a satisfactory solution of the eternal problem of evil, he appears to have dispelled whatever doubts he may have had about the ultimately benevolent nature of Providence. *Jenni* is a veritable 'justification of the ways of God to man', somewhat similar to Rousseau's *Lettre sur la Providence*. Reading it, one can understand why Voltaire was an enthusiastic admirer of the *Vicaire savoyard*. Physical evil, according to the author's spokesman, can be explained by the fact that the universe is governed by general laws; in any case, natural catastrophes have been exaggerated; moral evil results from man's abuse of his God-given liberty: 'Il est impossible qu'un Dieu ne soit pas bon; mais les hommes sont pervers' (p. 564).

This is a surprising attitude, since Voltaire had been expressing very different views on the question of free will.[30] The important thing, however, is not theology, but morality, and virtue lies in avoiding two opposite extremes: 'L'athéisme et le fanatisme sont les deux pôles d'un univers de confusion et d'horreur. La petite zone de la vertu est entre ces deux pôles' (p. 574). Hence the structure of *Jenni*, which has a debate on fanaticism with a fanatic at the beginning and ends with a debate on atheism with an atheist. In both cases, the extremist is vanquished by the arguments of the saintly figure who dominates the novel and whose beliefs and actions represent the restricted middle ground occupied by virtue.

Freind is a typical father figure of the literature of sensibility. His name suggests both his affinity with the good Quaker[31] and his naturally benevolent character. A man of 'astonishing virtues', he is a kind of French Squire Allworthy: modest, firm but forgiving, generous, and compassionate. His conduct towards others is governed by the principle enunciated by Alvarez in *Alzire* that 'La douceur peut tout'.[32] When his son is corrupted by bad company, he refuses to 'force nature', or even to reprimand him. One can only teach morality effectively by example, and this eloquent exponent of benevolent deism is an embodiment of Voltaire's creed, 'Adore dieu et sois juste et bienfaisant'. Freind does not claim that obedience to it guarantees happiness, but that true happiness is otherwise unattainable: 'Il n'y a point de bonheur sans la vertu' (p. 541). He is not merely a person of impeccable morals; like Cicero, he is a man

30. e.g. M. XXVIII, 530: 'Nous sommes des machines produites de tout temps les unes après les autres par l'Eternel géomètre.'
31. He is a grandson of Penn (p. 547).
32. *Alzire*, M. III, 419.

of action, a politician, and an eloquent debater.[33] Finally, he is, of course, a man of deep feeling, although he has learned to remain in control of his passions: 'Sa raison commande à son cœur comme un bon maître à un bon domestique' (p. 539).

*L'Histoire de Jenni* belongs very clearly to the age of sensibility, which was reaching its apogee at about the time the novel was published. Apart from a few sallies in the debate on fanaticism, the wit and irony which provide the essential contrast in *L'Ingénu* are drowned in a flood of tears. The characters, ranging from the 'belle, vertueuse et tendre' Miss Primerose, whose near-fatal illness leads to a pathetic scene reminiscent of the death of Mlle de St.-Yves, to the unfeeling Lady Clive-Hart, follow the pattern of the *comédie larmoyante*. Jenni himself is 'né sensible' and sheds tears;[34] we are certain therefore that in spite of his bad behaviour under the influence of his atheist friends, he is capable of repentance and ultimate salvation.

The style of this sentimental moral fable is in keeping with the content. Terms such as 'le respectable Freind', 'torrent de larmes', 'tendresse', 'sensible', 'frémissement' recur frequently. The narrator himself is so overcome by this feast of emotion that at one critical point in the story he is unable to proceed: 'Ici, le souvenir de ce que j'ai vu me suffoque. Mes pleurs mouillent mon papier. Quand j'aurai repris mes sens, je reprendrai le fil de mon histoire' (p. 542). As one commentator has remarked, even Rousseau could not have asked for more.[35]

33. Freind is a member of the House of Commons (p. 536).
34. '[Jenni] se détourna un moment pour verser quelques larmes. J'en augurai bien; je conçus une grande espérance que Jenni pourrait être un jour très honnête homme' (p. 540).
35. Clifton Cherpack, 'Voltaire's *Histoire de Jenni*: a synthetic creed', *MP*, 54 (August 1956), p. 27.

# EPILOGUE

# *Voltaire and the Romantics*

'Romantic' is a term invented in the seventeenth century which has acquired a number of definitions, not all of them compatible. Its original meaning was quite precise: suggestive of old romances, and therefore highly imaginative and unrealistic. In the eighteenth century, it was at first generally used to describe landscapes which had unusually picturesque features. Later, the emphasis shifted from the scene itself to the quality of the emotion felt by the observer. As it passed into the vocabulary of literary criticism, 'romantic' was most often applied to something which aroused a strong but undefinable feeling, peculiar to a particular individual at a particular moment.

One aspect of that first wave of romanticism, eighteenth-century sensibility, which has hardly been touched upon because it has little to do with Voltaire, is the tendency to introspection, evident in Prévost, Diderot, and particularly Rousseau. It is in this sense, rather than in his supposed exaltation of reason at the expense of feeling, that Voltaire may be said to be antiromantic. The other great exponents of the literature of sensibility were to a large extent subjective writers, fascinated by the uniqueness of their own personalities. Voltaire was very definitely an extrovert, who was far more interested in the social effect of ideas and actions or in the artificially contrived emotions of the theatre than in probing his own innermost thoughts and feelings. He has very little to say about these, even in his *Mémoires*, and would certainly have been incapable of the kind of self-analysis perfected by Rousseau. As one who knew him put it,

'Satisfait de lui-même, il se repose dans une noble confiance de sa force; il jouit trop de sa pensée pour sentir le besoin continuel d'une puérile vanité: c'est par des choses utiles aux hommes qu'il les attache à son souvenir.'[1]

For the same reason, Voltaire contributed little to pre-romantic melancholy, apart from a few touches in his more sombre tragedies. In the words of another contemporary, 'Sa sensibilité plus vive que douce, qui se passionnoit vivement pour tous les objets, s'allioit peu à la mélancolie qui se recueille dans elle-même et se plaît à reposer sur les mêmes impressions. Voltaire en général n'est pas le poëte de l'homme solitaire. Il veut être lu dans le fracas des grandes villes, dans la pompe des cours, au milieu de toutes les décorations de la société perfectionnée et corrompue.'[2] Young's *Night Thoughts* and its many imitations presented a Pascalian view of life as a vale of tears which is foreign to Voltaire's philosophy of active reform.

It would be absurd therefore to pretend that Voltaire was a romantic *avant la lettre*. He was too much of a meliorist to spend valuable time probing his own emotions or soliloquizing on death and decay in graveyards, even if he had not been handicapped by a lively sense of humour. It is not absurd, however, to suggest that he was one of the central figures in the transition from enlightenment to nineteenth-century romanticism, a transition which, as Jean Fabre and others have pointed out, was never the complete break that so many critics would have us believe.[3] One has only to recall some of the points made in the preceding chapters. It was Voltaire who introduced Shakespeare and Milton to France, who imposed the view of Shakespeare as an untaught genius, and who was most responsible for the wave of *Anglomanie*. He was the prophet of a new, purified religion and of the cult of *bienfaisance*. As a playwright, he furnished the most success-

1. Mme Suard in *Lettres de Mme de Graffigny*, p. 398.
2. Fontanes, quoted by Métra, *Correspondance littéraire secrète*, 14 (11 juin 1783), 372.
3. Jean Fabre, *Lumières et romantisme*, p. vii: 'Mais le romantisme, cette vibration ou crispation des lumières, ne pourra jamais en être isolé, même quand il prétend s'en dissocier par un anathème ou un refus.'

ful examples of tearful tragedy and comedy, and dominated the theatre for over half a century with plays which were often romantic melodramas in all but name. As a critic, he insisted on the primacy of feeling, fostered cosmopolitanism, and helped to popularize the idea that genius is more important than taste. He stimulated a new interest in history, and did much to focus attention on the more colourful aspects of the Middle Ages. A legend in his own lifetime, he was an outstanding example of the romantic ideal of universal genius, and the story of his life and career is of such improbably epic proportions that it required all the eloquence of a Victor Hugo to do it justice.

The importance of Voltaire in the development, not only of sensibility, but of romanticism proper, can hardly be denied. A glance at Victor Hugo's dramas, which Emile Faguet picturesquely and aptly called 'des tragédies de Voltaire enluminées de métaphores',[4] would be enough to establish it. But Voltaire's influence is visible everywhere: in ethical and religious ideas, in the esthetic theories of Mme de Staël, in the poetry of Byron and Lamartine, in the novels of Chateaubriand and Vigny. It would be instructive therefore to learn something of the views of the romantics and their immediate predecessors on this aspect of the Voltairean heritage. Unfortunately, there is no comprehensive work on the subject. Obviously, an extended treatment would require another book and is far beyond the scope of a concluding chapter. What follows is an incomplete and tentative outline.

The 'father of romanticism', as all the textbooks tell us, was Jean-Jacques Rousseau. And Rousseau, according to his own statements, was the disciple of Voltaire, whom he referred to as 'maître', 'chef', and 'frère'. Even at the tensest moments of their quarrel, Rousseau's admiration for the works, if not always for the person, of the man who is often supposed to be his opposite, was never in question. He addressed him as 'celui de mes contemporains dont j'honore le plus les talens et dont les écrits parlent le mieux à mon

4. Emile Faguet, *Dix-huitième siècle* (Paris, 1890), p. 272.

cœur'.[5] In 1750, on the threshold of fame, he made the following pledge, which he kept: 'Je ne renoncerai jamais à mon admiration pour vos Ouvrages. Vous avez peint l'Amitié et touttes les vertus en homme qui les connoit et les aime. J'ai entendu murmurer l'envie; j'ai méprisé ses clameurs et j'ai dit sans crainte de me tromper, ces Ecrits qui m'élèvent l'âme et m'enflamment le courage ne sont point les productions d'un homme indifférent pour la vertu' (Leigh 149). Much later, Mme de Genlis noted in her account of a conversation with Rousseau that he was still expressing the same view: 'Il rendit une entière justice aux talents de M. de Voltaire; il disait même qu'il était impossible que l'auteur de *Zaïre* et de *Mérope* ne fût pas né avec une âme très-sensible; il ajoutait que l'orgueil et la flatterie l'avaient corrompu.'[6]

There is little to be gained by recounting yet again the well-known details of the quarrel between the two writers or by repeating the charges and counter-charges of their respective partisans. The history of their relationship is a sad one which does no credit to either of two great men. Their mutual hostility seems to have originated partly in Rousseau's jealousy of Voltaire's growing prestige and influence in his beloved Geneva and partly in Voltaire's annoyance at the personal inconvenience he experienced as a result of Rousseau's attack on the theatre.[7] In 1760, Rousseau ended an otherwise courteous letter with an unprovoked verbal assault: 'Je ne vous aime point, Monsieur; vous m'avez fait les maux qui pouvoient m'être les plus

5. *Lettre à Voltaire* (1756), *Œuvres complètes*, Bibliothèque de la Pléiade (Paris, 1961–), IV, 1074. (All subsequent references to the works of Rousseau are to this edition. Quotations from Rousseau's correspondence, identified as 'Leigh' followed by a number, refer to the *Correspondance complète*, ed. R. A. Leigh [Geneva, 1965–]). In the same work, Rousseau asserts that all his friends are aware of his love for Voltaire's writings (p. 1059), and goes on to say that he is 'encore attendri d'une première lecture [of the *Poème sur la loi naturelle* and the *Poème sur le désastre de Lisbonne*], où mon cœur écoutoit avidement le vôtre, vous aimant comme mon frere, vous honorant comme mon Maître' (p. 1059).

6. Mme de Genlis, *Mémoires*, I, 99.

7. This is the complaint mentioned most frequently in the correspondence. The first hostile references to Rousseau date, however, from August 1757 (Best. 6663).

sensibles, à moi votre disciple et vôtre enthousiaste. . . . Je vous hais, enfin, puisque vous l'avez voulu; mais je vous hais en homme encore plus digne de vous aimer si vous l'aviez voulu. De tous les sentimens dont mon cœur étoit pénétré pour vous, il n'y reste que l'admiration que l'on ne peut refuser à vôtre beau génie et l'amour de vos écrits' (Best. 8238). The strangest feature of this strange letter is that Rousseau continues to insist that he is a fervent disciple,[8] even as he declares his 'hatred'. There could hardly be a more convincing proof of his idolatry, although in the circumstances the idol might be excused for not noticing it.

After the publication of the *Lettres écrites de la montagne* (1764), revealing Voltaire as the author of the *Sermon des cinquante*, open war was inevitable. Voltaire retaliated with understandable but regrettable ferocity. Yet the two 'frères ennemis' retained a strange kind of affection for each other. Voltaire was probably expressing his true feelings when he wrote to Damilaville: 'Oh! comme nous aurions chéri ce fou, s'il n'avait pas été faux frère! et qu'il a été un grand sot d'injurier les seuls hommes qui pouvaient lui pardonner!'[9] He several times offered to shelter Rousseau and, if the anecdotes are true, would have welcomed him with all the forgiving compassion and benevolent sensibility of the true man of feeling. The following incident, according to a reliable witness, occurred in 1762:

On était à déjeuner; M. de Végobre, assis près de Mme Denis, prenait paisiblement sa tasse de café. Les lettres de Paris, les papiers publics arrivent; M. de Voltaire ouvre et lit; sa physionomie s'altère et devient sombre; on l'interroge; il donne ses lettres à sa nièce et les papiers à M. de Végobre, en lui disant d'en faire tout haut la lecture. On y racontait tout au long l'histoire de la persécution qu'éprouvait alors le célèbre et malheureux auteur de la *Profession de foi du vicaire savoyard*, le décret de prise de

8. 'Enthousiaste', in the eighteenth century, was normally used to describe a fanatic. Rousseau is expressing his admiration in the strongest possible terms.

9. Best. 9812. 'Rousseau Jean Jacques, que j'aurais pu aimer s'il n'était pas né ingrat' (Best. 8915).

corps, lancé contre lui, sa fuite; M. de Voltaire n'y tint plus, il se mit à fondre en larmes, et de ce ton de voix, moitié solennel, moitié sépulcral, qui lui était propre, il s'écria à diverses reprises: 'Qu'il vienne, qu'il vienne! Je le recevrai à bras ouverts, il sera ici plus maître que moi; je le traiterai comme mon propre fils.'[10]

It is a pity that this great scene of reconciliation, worthy of the author of *l'Enfant prodigue*, did not actually take place.

As for Rousseau, he was too proud to take the necessary first step, but he was so far from harbouring feelings of implacable hatred that we find him defending Voltaire's character in conversation with his disciple, Bernardin de Saint-Pierre: 'On sait combien Voltaire l'avait maltraité, et cependant il ne parlait jamais de lui qu'avec estime. Personne à son gré ne tournait mieux un compliment; mais il ne le trouvait pathétique qu'en vers. Il disait de lui: Son premier mouvement est d'être bon; c'est la réflexion qui le rend méchant. Il aimait d'ailleurs à parler de Voltaire'[11] This testimony is confirmed by that of Dussaulx. In the last years of his life, Rousseau often spoke admiringly of Voltaire's talents; 'Quant à son caractère, il n'en disait que ces mots: "Je ne sache pas d'homme dont les premiers mouvements aient été plus beaux que les siens, mais la réflexion le rend méchant".'[12]

According to the *Confessions* (I, 214), Rousseau first became interested in serious study after reading Voltaire's *Lettres philosophiques*, 'quoiqu'elles ne soient assurément pas son meilleur ouvrage'. But it was surely Voltaire's early contributions to the literature of sensibility which fired his enthusiasm for their author, whom he addressed as 'touchant

10. Quoted by Gaston Maugras, *Querelles de philosophes: Voltaire et J.-J. Rousseau* (Paris, 1886), pp. 216–217. Desnoiresterres (*Voltaire et la société au XVIII*e *siècle*, VI, 320) relates the same anecdote and states that there can be no doubt about its authenticity. For a similar account, see Grimm, *Correspondance littéraire*, VI, 459–460.

11. Bernardin de Saint-Pierre, *Œuvres* (Paris, 1818), XII, 95–96. See also p. 116.

12. Quoted by Maugras, *Querelles de philosophes*, p. 567. A similar judgment was confided to Kirchberger in 1763: 'C'est un homme né bon, il a foncièrement le caractère le plus aimable' (Best. 10117, n.).

Voltaire'.[13] Rousseau repeated so often that Voltaire's verses spoke directly to his heart, that there is no reason why he should not be taken at his word.

Moreover, there is ample evidence that he was deeply affected by Voltairean sensibility in the theatre; so much so, that an indifferent performance of *Alzire* in 1737 gave him palpitations:

> On représenta Alzire, mal à la vérité; mais je ne laissai pas d'y être ému, jusqu'à perdre la respiration; mes palpitations augmenterent étonnamment et je crains de m'en sentir quelque temps.
>
> Pourquoi, Madame, y a-t-il des cœurs sensibles au grand, au sublime, au pathétique, pendant que d'autres ne semblent faits que pour ramper dans la bassesse de leurs sentimens? (Leigh 16)

Apart from the generous tributes to Voltaire's talents as a playwright in the *Lettre à d'Alembert sur les spectacles*, there are clear indications of the sincerest form of flattery in Rousseau's own plays, especially *La Découverte du nouveau monde* (c. 1740) and *La Mort de Lucrèce* (1754).

The former is similar in plot and message to *Alzire*. It contains a contrast between conquering Spaniards and native Americans, emphasizing the courage and virtue of the latter, yet not entirely condemning the civilizing influence of the European invaders. The theme of jealousy is combined with philosophical propaganda directed against clericalism and in favour of human values. As in *Alzire*, the Spanish leader magnanimously pardons the youthful hero of the Americans. It is worth noting that as an affirmation of primitivism, Rousseau's play, considerably weakened by the intrusion of rather conventional *galanterie*, is less forceful than *Alzire*, and that Voltaire places much greater stress on the equation of virtue with sensibility. *La Mort de Lucrèce* is a political tragedy with a republican bias which resembles *Brutus* and *La Mort de César*, not only in its eloquent pleas for liberty, but also in a certain note of caution. Like

13. 'et toi, touchant Voltaire, / Ta lecture à mon cœur restera toujours chère' (*Le Verger de Madame de Warens*, published in 1739 [II, 1129]).

Voltaire, Rousseau presents opposing arguments and implies that the overthrow of a tyrant may be followed by an even worse tyranny of the multitude.

Voltaire's views on Rousseau's writings are conspicuously less enthusiastic, as might be expected in view of their relative positions of master and wayward disciple. In general, he seems to have regarded him as a *philosophe* and writer of undoubted talent, albeit over-inclined to paradox, who unfortunately went mad and deserted the cause. He never realized, or could never bring himself to admit, that Rousseau was a genius and one of his few equals.

Curiously enough, whereas Rousseau paid homage to Voltaire's sensibility, Voltaire criticized Rousseau, 'ce Diogène sans cœur' (Best. 9707), 'cet ennemi de la nature humaine' (M. IX, 533), for his misanthropy and lack of feeling. The portrait of Rousseau inserted in *La Guerre civile de Genève* (1768) is particularly revealing:

D'un vrai Rousseau tel est le caractère;
Il n'est ami, parent, époux, ni père;
Il est de roche; et quiconque, en un mot,
Naquit sensible, est fait pour être un sot.[14]

Obviously Voltaire's unjust assessment of Rousseau as a person reflects the bitterness of their quarrel. The same might be said of his literary criticism. The terse rejections of *Emile* ('un fatras d'une sotte nourrice en quatre tomes'), *La Nouvelle Héloïse* ('un mélange monstrueux de débauche et de lieux communs de morale, sans intrigue, sans événements, sans génie, sans intérêt'), and the other works of Rousseau are well known. One wonders, however, whether he would have expressed himself in this way had there been

14. M. IX, 538. There is a more violent diatribe in *Les Trois Manières*, 1763 (M. X, 30):
>Malheur aux esprits faux dont la sotte rigueur
>Condamne parmi nous les jeux de Melpomène!
>Quand le ciel eut formé cette engeance inhumaine,
>La nature oublia de lui donner un cœur.

Lack of sensibility was one of the most telling charges a *philosophe* could bring against another. Diderot made the same accusation: 'Homme insensible et dur! deux larmes versées dans mon sein m'eussent mieux valu que le trône du monde' (*Correspondance*, I, 243).

no personal feud and no question of 'betrayal' on the part of Rousseau. Voltaire was certainly deeply impressed by Rousseau's affirmation of sentimental deism, *La Profession de foi du vicaire savoyard*, since he took the trouble to edit and publish long extracts from it along with works of his own.[15]

It is by no means certain that the sarcasms of the *Lettres sur la Nouvelle Héloïse* represent Voltaire's real opinion. An anonymous citizen of Geneva, annoyed by the insulting tone of this pamphlet, supposedly by the marquis de Ximenès, wrote a 'fifth letter', which claims to report what Voltaire had said about Rousseau's novel in private, and which may well represent a more accurate reflection of his views:

Que ne puis-je vous peindre la douceur, la candeur et la noblesse avec laquelle il applaudit aux bons endroits! Que ne puis-je vous rendre avec la même éloquence les éloges qu'il donna aux Lettres sur les Duels, sur le Suicide, sur l'Education, et à tout ce qu'il y a de vraiment philosophique!

Pour achever d'éclairer ceux qui l'écoutaient, il critiqua avec la même générosité. Il désapprouva sans aigreur l'affectation du style de plusieurs endroits. Il condamna avec douceur ce qu'il y avait de trop libre. Il fit sentir que M. Rousseau ne connaissait point assez le cœur humain, et il le plaignit avec charité sur son goût pour les paradoxes et pour les singularités. Il porta la lumière la plus vive sur cet ouvrage, sans en obscurcir l'auteur. L'envie et la

---

15. In the *Recueil nécessaire* (1766). See R. Naves, 'Voltaire éditeur de Rousseau', *RHL*, 44 (1937), 245–247. Voltaire wrote to Mme Du Deffand, 26 July 1764: 'J'aimerai toujours l'auteur du vicaire savoiard, quoi qu'il ait fait, et quoi qu'il puisse faire. Il est vrai qu'il n'y a point en Savoie de pareils vicaires, mais il faudrait qu'il y en eut dans toute l'Europe' (Best. 11177). Voltaire was delighted that the 'représentants' supported Rousseau against the intolerant Council of Geneva: 'Il est bon que nos frères sachent, qu'hier, six cent personnes vinrent pour la troisième fois, protester en faveur de Jean Jaques contre le conseil de Genêve, qui a osé condamner le vicaire savoiard. . . . Je ne serais pas fâché de voir une guerre civile pour le vicaire savoiard. Je ne crois pas qu'il y en ait dans Paris pour Saül et David' (to Damilaville, 21 August 1763, Best. 10553).

jalousie, que l'humanité laisse quelquefois entrer dans le cœur des grands hommes, étaient loin du sien et de sa bouche. L'homme de génie, l'homme universel, l'homme supérieur, rendait justice au Philosophe: on adorait le premier, et on plaignait le second en l'admirant.[16]

The notes which Voltaire jotted in the margin of Rousseau's works in his library are particularly enlightening, providing they are used with all due caution. As the editor correctly points out, 'It is a natural human tendency to note points of disagreement more frequently than the opposite, and emphasis upon Voltaire's critical notations might easily give a false impression.'[17] Voltaire is often simply searching for faults, as when he indignantly exclaims, 'tu adheres formellement à la pure et sainte relligion du deisme et tu feins d'etre cretien!'[18] Had he not done the same? Real divergences, of course, exist. Voltaire was completely opposed to many of Rousseau's political and social ideas, especially his attack on private property and the proposal to establish 'civic dogmas'. He had no time for 'chimerical' projects of perpetual peace and felt that Rousseau was making an unwarranted claim to omniscience by proclaiming the soul's immortality as a fact. Like many other readers, then and since, he was misled by Rousseau's rhetorical turn of phrase into believing that he favoured a return to a sub-human 'state of nature'.

In reality, if one ignores the stereotypes and the clash of personalities, the fundamental resemblances between their philosophies are more striking than the differences.[19] Rousseau did not favour blind emotionalism; nor was Voltaire an arid rationalist; like the other *philosophes*, both attempted to reconcile the claims of the heart and the mind. They are united in condemning the two extremes of fanaticism and atheism. Their religious views are very similar. As

16. Quoted by Eugène Ritter, 'Le Marquis de Ximenez, Voltaire et Rousseau', *RHL*, 4 (1897), 579.
17. George R. Havens, *Voltaire's Marginalia on the Pages of Rousseau*, p. 70.
18. *Voltaire's Marginalia*, p. 173.
19. For a more extensive discussion of this question, see John Pappas, 'Le Rousseauisme de Voltaire', *SV*, LVII, 1169–1181.

Voltaire noted, quite correctly, Rousseau's profession of faith is an elaboration of his own views on natural religion.[20] It was Voltaire who said that the true religion is the religion of the heart (Best. 14412; M. XXVI, 440) and who tried to live accordingly. What divides them is not a different conception of Providence,[21] or of the goodness of human nature, or of the role of conscience,[22] but the emphasis, in Rousseau's case on the search for personal salvation, and in Voltaire's on *bienfaisance*. The well-known passage in the *Lettre à Voltaire* in which Rousseau compares their respective destinies, representing Voltaire as famous, wealthy, and free and yet complaining of Providence, is in reality an involuntary tribute to a man who was incapable of placing his personal well-being before the plight of suffering mankind.

One can understand why the names of Voltaire and Rousseau were so often linked at the end of the eighteenth century and during the Revolution. They were generally considered to have preached the same message and to have attacked the same targets. There was no question of contrasting Voltaire's scepticism with Rousseau's sensibility; both were regarded as men of feeling and champions of free thought. As late as 1817 they were still linked as enemies of the Church and dangerous radicals by the abbé Clausel de Montals, who refers to them as 'the two leaders of modern incredulity'. After castigating Voltaire, this stalwart defender of orthodoxy continues, 'Pour ce qui regarde Rousseau, on connaît assez le but d'un fameux épisode de son Emile, les attaques qu'il a livrées à notre foi avec autant de

20. 'Tout ce discours', he wrote on his copy of the *Vicaire savoyard*, 'se trouve mot à mot dans le poème de la *Religion naturelle* et dans l'*Epître à Uranie*' (Naves, 'Voltaire éditeur de Rousseau', p. 247). See also R. Pomeau, *La Religion de Voltaire*, p. 279.

21. See R. A. Leigh, 'From the *Inégalité* to *Candide*: notes on a desultory dialogue between Rousseau and Voltaire (1755–1759)' in *The Age of Enlightenment*, pp. 87–88: 'Whether Voltaire thought he was refuting Rousseau or not, or whether Rousseau thought he was being refuted in *Candide* or not, it is clear that their views about the role of Providence in human affairs coincide to a great extent.'

22. Both were faced with the same problem: how to reconcile the theory of a spontaneous and instinctive conscience with the rejection of innate ideas. See the note by Masson in his critical edition of the *Profession de foi du vicaire savoyard* (Paris, 1914), pp. 265–266.

malignité, et même plus de vigueur que Voltaire.'[23] The reconciliation of the two *philosophes* in the Elysian Fields became a
popular subject of poems, pamphlets[24] and engravings. M. J.
Chénier's verses aptly sum up the views of the men of the
Revolution:

O Voltaire! son nom n'a plus rien qui te blesse:
Un moment divisés par l'humaine faiblesse,
Vous recevez tous deux l'encens qui vous est dû:
Réunis désormais, vous avez entendu,
Sur les rives du fleuve où la haine s'oublie,
La voix du genre humain qui vous réconcilie![25]

Some of the more fanatical followers of Rousseau were
less inclined to forgive and forget. Undoubtedly Voltaire's
noisy quarrels, not only with Jean Jacques but with Jean
Baptiste Rousseau, with Desfontaines, Maupertuis, Fréron,
and many others, damaged his reputation. Not that he was
accused, even by his enemies, of any lack of sensibility; on
the contrary, it was recognized that this was the source of his
irascible behaviour;[26] but the air of scandal and intrigue
which constantly surrounded him seemed inconsistent with
the dignity of a *philosophe*.[27]

Typical of this attitude is the comparison between
Voltaire and Rousseau by Loaisel de Tréogate, devout

23. C. H. Clausel de Montals, *Questions importantes sur les nouvelles
éditions des Œuvres complètes de Voltaire et de J.-J. Rousseau* (Paris,
1817), p. 18.

24. e.g. the anonymous pamphlet published in 1778 entitled *Dialogue
entre Voltaire et J.-J. Rousseau après leur passage du Styx*, in which
Voltaire says, 'Il me semble que vous avez dit à-peu-près comme moi.
Nous sommes tous d'accord, nous autres; et vous n'avez paru différent
d'avec nous, que par la bizarrerie de vos paradoxes, la singularité de vos
pensées, & le caractère original de vos expressions' (p. 5).

25. *Epître à Voltaire*, p. 11.

26. Sabatier de Castres said of Voltaire, 'Il eût été le premier homme
de son siècle, s'il n'eût pas été peut-être le plus sensible, le plus emporté,
le plus intolérant contre tout ce qui a osé contredire ses prétentions'
(*Tableau philosophique de l'esprit de M. de Voltaire* [Geneva, 1771],
p. x).

27. See Billard-Dumonceau's remark in his comedy, *Voltaire apprécié*
(1779), p. 57:

Vous qui prêchez, sans fin, la paix, l'humanité,
Non pas d'un cœur fervent, mais d'un ton qui dénote
Que vous étrangleriez le malheureux *Nonotte*.

Rousseauist and author of a collection of elegies entitled *Aux âmes sensibles*. In his novel, *Dolbreuse* (1783), while paying homage to the 'inimitable magic' of Voltaire's style and the 'astonishing variety of his genius', he says that pleasure in reading him is poisoned by the memory of Voltaire's malicious attacks on his critics: 'Nous étions fâchés de voir cet homme si extraordinaire, si au-dessus des autres hommes, afficher quelquefois l'envie et la haine des petites ames.'[28] Other admirers of Rousseau were less disturbed by this aspect of Voltaire's reputation. Restif de la Bretonne, for example, found Voltaire so far above him that 'il étouffait en moi jusqu'à la velléité d'écrire'.[29]

Another important figure among the preromantics, L. S. Mercier, referred to Voltaire as 'cette âme sensible'. There is nothing, he says, in the French theatre more touching than *Zaïre*, *Mérope*, *Adélaïde*, and *Tancrède*. He attributes Voltaire's success as a playwright to the fact that he has 'au-dessus de ses prédécesseurs cette morale touchante, ces principes de vertu et d'humanité qui attendrissent et parlent à toutes les âmes'.[30]

Mercier's Utopian novel, *L'An 2440* (1771), is both typical of late eighteenth-century sensibility and full of reminiscences of Voltaire. The author's guiding principle is a love of humanity (p. 52), accompanied by a hatred of superstition, fanaticism, and tyranny. In the ideal state of the future, a thoroughly Voltairean religion has been established,[31] with lay saints and a 'Temple of God' (p. 113), where a simple cult is celebrated. Theology has disappeared, replaced by the universal doctrine of *bienfaisance* (p. 129). The narrator admires a statue to Humanity, one of whose figures represents France kneeling to implore 'le pardon de la nuit horrible de la S. Barthélémy, de la dure révocation de

28. *Dolbreuse*, 2ᵉ partie, pp. 111–112.
29. Quoted by Charles A. Porter, *Restif's Novels, or an Autobiography in Search of an Author* (New Haven, 1967), p. 26.
30. Léon Béclard, *Sébastien Mercier, sa vie, son œuvre, son temps, d'après des documents inédits* (Paris, 1903), I, 415.
31. Mercier defines its credo as follows: 'Adorer Dieu, respecter son prochain, écouter cette conscience, ce juge qui toujours veille assis au dedans de nous, n'étouffer jamais cette voix céleste & secrette, tout le reste est imposture, fourberie, mensonge' (p. 121).

l'Edit de Nantes, & de la persécution des sages qui naquirent dans son sein' (pp. 143–144). Torture has been banished and justice is solidly based on reason and humanity (p. 81). Theatres are now state-supported, 'car on en a fait une école publique de morale & de goût. On a compris toute l'influence que l'ascendant du génie peut avoir sur des ames sensibles' (pp. 168–169). The narrator is invited to the performance of a play, which turns out to be the story of the Calas family (p. 172). Even the political system is Voltairean, being neither monarchic nor aristocratic nor democratic but 'raisonnable & fait pour les hommes' (p. 297). Thanks to a revolution which was the work of a philosopher-king, the good of the state and the rights of the individual have finally been reconciled (p. 310).

Mme Roland's case is interesting, according to Gita May, because it offers 'un exemple frappant d'un esprit de femme façonné par Voltaire et les Encyclopédistes, mais converti au rousseauisme et subjugué par la vogue préromantique'.[32] 'Conversion' is perhaps not the most appropriate term, since Mme Roland, like Mme de Staël, exemplifies the coexistence of enlightenment and sensibility. It seems probable that not only her scepticism but her humanitarian fervour were stimulated by the reading of Voltaire, whose plays, she said, left a 'religious impression'.

Undoubtedly the two most important figures in the transitional period between the age of sensibility and the full flowering of romanticism were Mme de Staël and Chateaubriand, both of whom owed a considerable debt to Voltaire. Mme de Staël advocated the substitution for classicism of a national, popular, Christian, and chivalric literature and further suggested that foreign influences should be welcomed, even if the rules had to be disregarded. This is not, of course, Voltaire's position, but the influence of his critical theory, and even more of the example set by some of his tragedies, is obvious. Mme de Staël herself makes the point: 'Voltaire est celui de nos grands tragiques qui a le plus souvent traité des sujets modernes. Il s'est servi, pour

32. Gita May, *De Jean-Jacques Rousseau à Madame Roland: Essai sur la sensibilité préromantique et révolutionnaire* (Geneva, 1964), p. 22.

émouvoir, du christianisme et de la chevalerie; et si l'on est de bonne foi, l'on conviendra, ce me semble, qu'*Alzire*, *Zaïre* et *Tancrède* font verser plus de larmes que tous les chefs-d'œuvre grecs et romains de notre théâtre.'[33]

It is true that Mme de Staël was one of those most responsible for perpetuating the idea that Voltaire is a rationalist whereas Rousseau speaks to the heart. She accused him, along with his century, of 'frivolity', totally misreading *Candide*, which she calls 'cet ouvrage d'une gaîté infernale; car il semble être écrit par un être d'une autre nature que nous, indifférent à notre sort, content de nos souffrances, et riant comme un démon, ou comme un singe, des misères de cette espèce humaine avec laquelle il n'a rien de commun'. But she goes on to say, 'Le plus grand poète du siècle, l'auteur d'*Alzire*, de *Tancrède*, de *Mérope*, de *Zaïre* et de *Brutus*, méconnut dans cet écrit toutes les grandeurs morales qu'il avait si dignement célébrées'.[34]

She leaves the impression that in her view Voltaire would have been *the* great romantic dramatist, if only he had not been inhibited by his respect for the rules. He depicted grief more vividly than any of his predecessors and his tragedies have a stronger emotional effect than those of Racine. Above all, Voltaire is *modern*: 'Les sentiments, les situations, les caractères que Voltaire nous présente, tiennent de plus près à nos souvenirs. Il importe au perfectionnement de la morale elle-même que le théâtre nous offre toujours quelques modèles au-dessus de nous; mais l'attendrissement est d'autant plus profond que l'auteur sait mieux retracer nos propres affections à notre pensée.'[35]

Chateaubriand's attitude to Voltaire was equally ambivalent. He obviously admired the author of the histories and the tragedies particularly, yet saw his influence, on the whole, as pernicious.[36] Ironically, in view of Voltaire's own

33. Mme de Staël, *De l'Allemagne* (Paris, 1968), I, 222.
34. *De l'Allemagne*, II, 134–135.
35. *Œuvres complètes*, I, 285.
36. Chateaubriand insisted, however, that the majority of Voltaire's works were not harmful. 'Dans les Œuvres complètes de Voltaire, quand vous aurez retranché une douzaine de volumes, et c'est beaucoup, le reste ne pourrait-il pas être mis entre les mains de tout le monde?' (*Œuvres complètes*, VII, 472).

comments on Shakespeare, Corneille, and the Greeks, Chateaubriand placed the chief blame for his faults on the 'mediocrity' of the age in which he lived. He had really nothing in common with Diderot, d'Alembert, and the Encyclopaedists and would have realized the full measure of his genius had he lived in the seventeenth century.[37] Even so, there is no doubt whatsoever as to his importance: 'La grande existence de ce siècle est celle de Voltaire.' He accomplished a revolution in religious ideas which would ultimately be beneficial: 'Si l'irréligion était poussée jusqu'à l'outrage, si elle prenait un caractère sophistique et étroit, elle menait néanmoins à ce dégagement des préjugés qui devait faire revenir au véritable christianisme.'[38]

Chateaubriand seems to have regarded Voltaire as a fore-runner *malgré lui*, whose attacks on Christianity are all the more deplorable because his best work is Christian in inspiration. He returns again and again to the same point, that Voltaire 'poursuit à travers soixante-dix volumes, ce qu'il appelle l'*infâme*; et les morceaux les plus beaux de ses écrits sont inspirés par la *religion*.'[39] If the author of *Le Génie du christianisme* is to be believed, the moment Voltaire touches on religion in *La Henriade*, he becomes a true poet: 'L'auteur de *La Henriade* doit au culte même qu'il a persécuté les points frappants de son poëme épique, comme il lui doit les plus belles scènes de ses tragédies.'[40] And the same is true of the histories: 'Il lui est arrivé en histoire ce qui lui arrive toujours en poésie: c'est qu'en déclamant contre la religion, ses plus belles pages sont des pages chrétiennes.'[41]

Not surprisingly, Chateaubriand takes Voltaire seriously as a Christian dramatist and quotes with approval his statement that he was attempting to introduce into *Zaïre* everything that was most moving and interesting in the Christian

37. *Œuvres complètes*, II, 159–160.
38. *Œuvres complètes*, X, 343.
39. *Œuvres complètes*, II, 160. 'Voltaire est bien ingrat d'avoir calomnié un culte qui lui a fourni ses plus beaux titres à l'immortalité' (II, 179).
40. *Œuvres complètes*, II, 157. See also VIII, 578.
41. *Œuvres complètes*, II, 329.

religion. In particular, the recognition scene between Zaïre and Lusignan, 'dont le ressort gît tout entier dans la morale évangélique et dans les sentiments chrétiens', is 'marvellous'.[42] *Alzire*, 'malgré le peu de vraisemblance des mœurs, est une tragédie attachante; on y plane au milieu de ces régions de la morale chrétienne, qui, s'élevant au-dessus de la morale vulgaire, est d'elle-même une divine poésie.'[43] Paradoxical as it may appear, it is possible that Chateaubriand's sentimental approach to Christianity owed something to Voltaire's example.

Nor was this his only debt. There are traces of Voltairean primitivism in the *Essai sur les révolutions*, notably the contrast between Scythians and Greeks and the eulogy of Swiss peasants, and Jean Pommier has shown that Chateaubriand had *L'Ingénu* in mind when he wrote *René* and *Atala*.[44]

If the negative aspects of the criticism of Voltaire by Chateaubriand and Mme de Staël have been exaggerated, this is even more true of the romantics in general. It has long been assumed that they were unanimous in detesting the writer who acquired the reputation, in the early nineteenth century, of being the very spirit of irreverent mockery.[45] The truth is that many of the greatest among them—Goethe, Byron, Lamartine, Michelet, Hugo, Delacroix—admired Voltaire only just short of idolatry. Their admiration is understandable if one considers that Voltaire played a leading role in the two eighteenth-century movements which shaped romanticism; that he posed some of the fundamental questions which were to preoccupy the romantic poets, such as the problem of Providence and the existence of evil, the need for a purified, universal religion, the relation between conscience and moral values, the reconciliation of reason and feeling, of faith and scepticism;

---

42. *Œuvres complètes*, II, 173.
43. *Œuvres complètes*, II, 177.
44. Jean Pommier, 'Le Cycle de Chactas', *RLC*, 18 (1938), 604–629.
45. According to A. Adam, 'L'un des traits caractéristiques du romantisme, au même titre que les couchers du soleil, les vierges en pleurs et les cimetières sous la lune, c'est la haine de Voltaire' ('Voltaire et les lumières', p. 18).

that his histories, especially the *Essai sur les mœurs*, were a mine of subjects;[46] that he was the first universal genius to attempt to excel, like the romantics themselves, in all genres; and that his career as prophet, legislator, patriarch, man of letters, and man of action was remarkably similar to the romantic conception of the poet as 'mage'.

It was in any case extremely difficult to ignore Voltaire in the early nineteenth century. His works enjoyed an astounding popularity. During the period 1817–1824, twelve editions of his complete works were published and sold out, comprising something over one and a half million volumes, not counting editions of works published separately.[47] In the words of Desnoiresterres, 'Ce fut comme un déluge qui envahit, inonda le pays.'[48]

Romanticism was, of course, a European movement, which developed comparatively late in France. The two towering figures of Goethe and Byron had absorbed Voltaire's influence long before Lamartine and Victor Hugo. Goethe, who could recite whole speeches from *La Mort de César* from memory,[49] and who translated *Mahomet* and *Tancrède* into iambic verse, said of him that he was the greatest man of letters of all time and the most astonishing creation of the author of nature. It would be difficult to find enough superlatives to cap this verdict, but Byron, the very symbol of romanticism in the early nineteenth century, held essentially the same view. He called him 'that great and unequalled genius—the universal Voltaire'.[50] Voltaire's presence can be felt in almost every work he wrote, and not

46. See R. Pomeau's Introduction to his edition, pp. lvi–lvii.

47. During the same period, there were thirteen editions of Rousseau's works, about half a million volumes. See J. Vercruysse, 'C'est la faute à Rousseau, c'est la faute à Voltaire', *SV*, XXIII, 62, and M. Cornu, 'Le Second Voltaire', *Europe*, no. 361–362 (mai–juin 1959), 136–151.

48. *Voltaire et la société au XVIIIᵉ siècle*, VIII, 517.

49. Geneviève Bianquis, 'Goethe et Voltaire', *RLC*, 24 (juillet–septembre 1950), 388.

50. Byron was lashing out against the accusation of superficiality brought against Voltaire by the poets of the Lake School, 'the whole of whose filthy trash of Epics, Excursions, etc., etc., etc., is not worth the two words in Zaïre, "*Vous pleurez*", or a single speech of Tancred' (*The Works of Lord Byron: Letters and Journals*, ed. R. E. Prothero [London, 1922], V, 600).

least in his masterpiece, *Don Juan*. Small wonder then that the Duc de Broglie,[51] Stendhal,[52] and Shelley[53] compared Byron with his favourite author, whom he placed even above Shakespeare, Dante, and Milton.

Another great romantic, the painter Delacroix, had a 'veritable passion' for Voltaire, as revealed in his *Journal*, into which he frequently copied extracts from Voltaire's works, usually with enthusiastic comments.[54] Again, the leader of the Enlightenment is considered incomparable: 'Mais qu'est-ce que Dumas et presque tout ce qui écrit aujourd'hui en comparaison d'un prodige tel que Voltaire, par exemple?... cette merveille de lucidité, d'éclat et de simplicité tout ensemble.'[55] Delacroix' biographer, René Huyghe, says that he was a genuine 'disciple', who recognized in Voltaire exactly that balance between reason and emotion which he was striving to achieve in his own work.[56]

Of the French romantic writers, Lamartine was the most consistent in his admiration for Voltaire. Although there is an obvious influence on the form and content of his poetry,[57] he seems to have been particularly impressed by Voltaire as a man and as a philosopher. The portrait which emerges from the pages of the *Cours familier de littérature* is that of a humane, sensitive apostle of *bienfaisance*: 'Bon, honnête, fidèle de cœur cependant, compatissant pour le malheur, la main large à la bienfaisance et à l'aumône, pitoyable même à l'ingratitude, souvent irrité, jamais méchant. Il y avait en

---

51. *His Very Self and Voice: Collected Conversations of Lord Byron*, ed. J. Lovell, Jr. (N. York, 1954), p. 190.

52. *His Very Self and Voice*, p. 199.

53. 'Shelley used to compare him to Voltaire, to whom he would have thought it the greatest compliment to be compared; for if there was any one writer whom he admired more than another it was the author of *Candide*' (Thomas Medwin, quoted in *His Very Self and Voice*, p. 272). Shelley himself opened *Queen Mab* with Voltaire's war cry, *Ecrasez l'infâme*.

54. Victor Brombert, 'Voltaire dans le Journal de Delacroix', *FR*, 30 (1956-7), 335–341.

55. Eugène Delacroix, *Journal, 1822–1863*, ed. André Joubin (Paris, 1932), II, 94.

56. René Huyghe, *Delacroix* (New York, 1963), p. 238.

57. See Albert Desvoyes, 'Voltaire et Lamartine', *RHL*, 19 (1912), 911–913.

lui du bonhomme dans le grand homme, et de l'enfant dans le vieillard.'[58]

Where religion is concerned, he places Voltaire firmly on the side of the angels. 'Le blasphème ne fut jamais en lui qu'un accident ou une manœuvre, la foi en Dieu était sa nature. . . . Ce fut le dernier ou le premier de nos théistes.'[59] As a deist himself, haunted, as was Voltaire, by the insoluble questions of human destiny, Lamartine is far from dismissing the author of the *Dictionnaire philosophique* as the prince of mockers. In a remarkable passage, he describes him rather as a kind of mystic of the Enlightenment, who 'parvient par les seules forces de sa raison jusqu'à des extases d'adoration et de vertu qui égalent le plus sublime mysticisme de l'Inde ou du christianisme'.[60]

Victor Hugo is even closer in spirit to Voltaire. The striking resemblances between these two literary giants, who dominated their respective centuries, have been noted by several critics. Their 'religion of humanity' is almost identical; both disliked priests but believed in God; both had a strong sense of mission and carried on unending battles for liberty and greater human dignity; both became patriarchs in exile and returned in triumph to Paris; and both combined the role of prophet and man of action with that of universal writer. Even their faults—a fondness for melodramatic gesture and a lack of psychological depth in depicting character—are similar.

The traditional view that Hugo set out from his earliest youth to imitate Chateaubriand is not in accordance with the facts; the greatest single intellectual influence during his

---

58. *Cours familier*, XXVIII, 264.

59. *Cours familier*, XXVIII, 248. Lamartine refers to the famous line, 'Si Dieu n'existait pas, il faudrait l'inventer' as 'le plus beau de vérité de tous les vers' (XXVIII, 250).

60. *Cours familier*, XXVIII, 251. Lamartine is referring particularly to the article on 'Religion'. 'Comment', he adds, 'la calomnie de l'esprit de parti religieux a-t-elle pu taxer d'athéisme l'homme qui a senti, pensé et gravé de pareilles lignes sur la face du firmament?' (XXVIII, 252). Lamartine's admiration for Voltaire's character and ideas should be compared with his violent attack on Rousseau, whom he describes as a magnificent rhetorician, but a detestable thinker.

formative years was Voltaire, not the author of *René*.[61] His first detailed critique of Voltaire, however, dates from 1823, by which time he had temporarily adopted the fashionable 'crown and altar' pose. It is largely an attack on Voltaire as the architect of revolution from a monarchist-Catholic point of view and contains the usual charges of superficiality and immorality. Voltaire's work is 'un bazar élégant et vaste, irrégulier et commode, étalant dans la boue d'innombrables richesses'.[62] Even here, he recognizes Voltaire's genius and praises the tragedies.[63]

In 1840, he was still using Mme de Staël's expression to refer to Voltaire as 'ce singe de génie'. His affinity is evident, however, not only in his work, particularly the theatre, but in the general direction of his philosophy, and one might say of his life; so that when, towards the end of it, he composed a speech for the centenary of Voltaire's death, he found it natural to address Voltaire in the familiar second person as a fellow-campaigner, an intimate friend, and a kindred spirit: 'Alors tu commenças l'épouvantable procès du passé, tu plaidas contre les tyrans et les monstres la cause du genre humain et tu la gagnas. Grand homme, sois à jamais béni!'[64] Among the many remarkable passages in this impassioned eulogy, three are particularly notable: one in which Voltaire is seen as an eighteenth-century Christ, whose task was to speak for the poor and the victims of injustice;[65] another comparing Voltaire with Rousseau ('la fibre civique vibre en Rousseau; ce qui vibre en Voltaire, c'est la fibre universelle');[66] and a clear statement on Voltaire's sensibility: 'Il a eu la tendresse d'une femme et la colère d'un héros. Il a été un grand esprit et un immense cœur.'[67]

61. G. Venzac, *Les Premiers maîtres de Victor Hugo* (Paris, 1955), p. 335: 'Pour Victor Hugo, écolier et collégien, c'est Voltaire qui représente encore la littérature et la poésie vivantes.'

62. Victor Hugo, *Œuvres complètes* (Paris, 1904–), I, 112.

63. Especially *Zaïre*, 'chef d'œuvre ... auquel il ne manque que la couleur du lieu et une certaine sévérité de style. *Zaïre* eut un succès prodigieux et mérité' (*Œuvres*, I, 110).

64. Victor Hugo, *Le Discours pour Voltaire: la lettre à l'évêque d'Orléans* (Paris, 1878), p. 10.

65. *Discours pour Voltaire*, p. 13.

66. *Discours pour Voltaire*, p. 15.

67. *Discours pour Voltaire*, p. 11.

Like Hugo, Alfred de Vigny was introduced to Voltaire's works early and consulted them frequently. Following the fashion set by Mme de Staël, his comments are often hostile,[68] yet the imprint of Voltaire is unmistakeable in his view of history, in the tales in *Stello*, which one critic has described as 'contes voltairiens',[69] in his dream of a pure religion[70] and his revolt against the jealous God of the Old Testament. Even his pessimism seems to have been confirmed by his readings of Voltaire, whom he sees as a writer with anguish in his soul: 'Je n'ai point connu d'écrivain gai. Voltaire qui semble l'être par sa forme est un des plus désespérés. Les autres s'arrêtent à la mélancolie. Voltaire va au-delà jusqu'au désespoir.'[71]

Strangely enough, the writer whose outlook is supposed to have most in common with that of Voltaire, Stendhal, is one of his severest critics. His comments indicate that he saw only the stereotype: a clever but shallow author who over-simplified complex issues, and a heartless cynic, incapable of either feeling or depicting tender emotions; in short, the 'prince des persifleurs'.[72]

Stendhal—and Musset and Baudelaire—notwithstanding, even a brief summary of romantic opinion is sufficient in itself to demonstrate the absurdity of this image. If the stereotype of Voltaire were true, would Rousseau or Byron have been his disciples? Would Mercier have called him 'cette âme sensible' or Hugo 'cet immense cœur'? As Lamartine and Hugo perceived, Voltaire's most important contribution, not merely to romanticism but to the

68. In the *Journal*, for example, Voltaire is described as 'railleur, grossier et cynique' (*Œuvres complètes* [Paris, 1960–1964], p. 1053).

69. Marc Citoleux, *Alfred de Vigny, persistances classiques et affinités étrangères* (Paris, 1924), p. 246.

70. J. Sungolowsky, *Alfred de Vigny et le dix-huitième siècle* (Paris, 1968), p. 61. Sungolowsky also points out the influence of *Zaïre* on Vigny's sensibility (p. 129) and the importance of the theme of 'ennui', which may owe something to *Candide* (p. 164).

71. See the comments of J. Sungolowsky, pp. 164 and 170.

72. Arnold Ages, 'Stendhal and Voltaire: the philosophe as target', *SV*, LXII, 87–89. It is worth noting, however, that Julien Sorel, just before his execution at the end of *Le Rouge et le noir*, turns away from the God of the Old Testament to the 'Dieu de Voltaire, juste, bon, infini'.

sensibility of western man, was the example of his life. Sensibility, for Voltaire, was synonymous with virtue, and he clearly thought of himself as *un homme sensible*.

Is 'virtuous' too incongruous a term to apply to this complex, volatile man, whose motives were not always pure, whose thirst for fame was as proverbial as his irreverence? Perhaps the answer is to be found in the final paragraph of that sum of Voltairean wisdom, the *Dictionnaire philosophique*:

> Quelques théologiens disent que le divin empereur Antonin n'était pas vertueux; que c'était un stoïcien entêté, qui, non content de commander aux hommes, voulait encore être estimé d'eux; qu'il rapportait à lui-même le bien qu'il faisait au genre humain; qu'il fut toute sa vie juste, laborieux, bienfaisant, par vanité, et qu'il ne fit que tromper les hommes par ses vertus; je m'écrie alors: 'Mon Dieu, donnez-nous souvent de pareils fripons!'

# WORKS CITED

ADAM, ANTOINE. *Le Mouvement philosophique dans la première moitié du XVIII^e siècle.* Paris, 1967.

—— 'Voltaire et les lumières', *Europe*, 361–362 (mai–juin 1959), 8–19.

AGES, ARNOLD. 'Stendhal and Voltaire: the *philosophe* as target', *SV*, LXII, 83–99.

ALEMBERT, JEAN LE ROND D'. *Discours préliminaire de l'Encyclopédie*, ed. F. Picavet. Paris, 1899.

ALLIZÉ, F. 'Voltaire à La Haye en 1713', *Revue de Paris*, 22 (15 novembre 1922), 321–324.

AQUIN DE CHÂTEAU-LYON, PIERRE LOUIS D'. *Siècle littéraire de Louis XV, ou Lettres sur les hommes célèbres.* 2 vols. Paris, 1753.

ARGENS, JEAN BAPTISTE DE BOYER, MARQUIS D'. *Lettres juives.* The Hague, 1761.

ARNELLE. *Les Filles de M^me Du Noyer (1663–1720).* Paris, 1920.

ASCOLI, GEORGES. 'Voltaire: L'Œuvre poétique', *RCC*, 25² (15 juin, 15 juillet 1924), 417–428, 616–630.

AUBERTIN, CHARLES. *L'Esprit public au XVIII^e siècle.* Paris, 1873.

BÉCLARD, LÉON. *Sébastien Mercier, sa vie, son œuvre, son temps, d'après des documents inédits.* I. *Avant la Révolution, 1740–1789.* Paris, 1903.

BERNARDIN, N. M. 'Le Théâtre de Voltaire: *Zaïre.* Conférence faite à l'Odéon', *RCC*, 22 (20 juin 1914), 659–672.

BESTERMAN, THEODORE. *Voltaire.* London, 1969.

—— *Voltaire Essays and Another.* London, 1962.

BIANQUIS, GENEVIÈVE. 'Goethe et Voltaire', *RLC*, 24 (juillet-septembre 1950), 385–393.

BILLARD-DUMONCEAU, EDME. *Voltaire apprécié. Comédie.* [Paris, 1779].

BOISMONT, NICOLAS THYREL DE. *Lettres secrettes sur l'état actuel de la religion et du clergé de France.*

BONGIE, LAURENCE L. 'Crisis and the Birth of the Voltairean *Conte*', *MLQ*, 23 (1962), 53–64.

BRAILSFORD, HENRY NOEL. *Voltaire.* London, 1935.

BRENNER, CLARENCE D. *L'Histoire nationale dans la tragédie française du XVIII^e siècle.* Berkeley, 1929.

BROMBERT, VICTOR. 'Voltaire dans le Journal de Delacroix', *FR*, 30 (1956–7), 335–341.

BROOKS, RICHARD A. *Voltaire and Leibniz*. Geneva, 1964.

BRUCE, HAROLD L. 'Period of Greatest Popularity of Voltaire's Plays on the English Stage', *MLN*, 33 (January 1918), 20–33.

BRUMFITT, J. H. *Voltaire Historian*. London, 1958.

BYRON, GEORGE GORDON, LORD. *The Works of Lord Byron. Letters and Journals*, ed. R. E. Prothero. 6 vols. London, 1922.

———. *His Very Self and Voice: Collected Conversations of Lord Byron*, ed. Ernest J. Lovell, Jr. New York, 1954.

CAMERON, MARGARET M. *L'Influence des Saisons de Thomson sur le poésie descriptive en France (1759–1810)*. Paris, 1927.

CARAMASCHI, ENZO. 'Du Bos et Voltaire', *SV*, X, 113–236.

CAUSSY, FERNAND. *Voltaire seigneur de village*. Paris, 1912.

CHABANON, MICHEL PAUL GUI DE. *Vers sur Voltaire*. 1778.

CHAMFORT, SÉBASTIEN. *Maximes et anecdotes*, ed. Jean Mistler. Monaco, 1944.

CHAMPION, EDME. *Voltaire: Etudes critiques*. Paris, 1921.

CHAPONNIÈRE, PAUL. *Voltaire chez les calvinistes*. Geneva, 1932.

CHASTELLUX, FRANÇOIS JEAN DE. *De la félicité publique, ou Considérations sur le sort des hommes*. 2 vols. Amsterdam, 1772.

CHATEAUBRIAND, FRANÇOIS RENÉ DE. *Œuvres complètes de Chateaubriand*. 12 vols. Paris, 1859–61.

CHAUDON, L. M. *Les Grands hommes vengés*. 2 vols. Amsterdam, 1769.

CHÉNIER, MARIE J. B. *Œuvres*. 5 vols. Paris, 1824.

———. *Epître à Voltaire*. Paris, 1806.

———. *Jean Calas: Tragédie en 5 actes*. Paris, 1793.

CHEREL, ALBERT. 'XVIIIᵉ siècle et romantisme', *Revue politique et littéraire*, 71 (1933), 533–537.

CHERPACK, CLIFTON. *The Call of Blood in French Classical Tragedy*. Baltimore, 1958.

———. 'Voltaire's *Histoire de Jenni*: a Synthetic Creed', *MP*, 54 (August 1956), 26–32.

CHINARD, GILBERT. *L'Amérique et le rêve exotique dans la littérature française au XVIIᵉ et au XVIIIᵉ siècles*. Paris, 1913.

CITOLEUX, MARC. *Alfred de Vigny, persistances classiques et affinités étrangères*. Paris, 1924.

CLAUSEL DE MONTALS, CLAUDE HIPPOLYTE. *Questions importantes sur les nouvelles éditions des Œuvres complètes de Voltaire et de J.-J. Rousseau*. Paris, 1817.

CLÉMENT, JEAN MARIE BERNARD. *Anecdotes dramatiques*. Paris, 1775.

——. *Première Lettre à Monsieur de Voltaire*. 3 vols. The Hague, 1773–1776.

CLÉMENT, PIERRE. *Les Cinq Années littéraires, ou Lettres de M. Clément sur les ouvrages de littérature qui ont paru dans les années 1748–1752*. Berlin, 1755.

COLLINI, CÔME ALEXANDRE. *Mon Séjour auprès de Voltaire, et lettres inédites que m'écrivit cet homme célèbre jusqu'à la dernière année de sa vie*. Paris, 1807.

COMPARET, JEAN ANTOINE. *La Vérité, Ode à M. de Voltaire*. London, 1765.

CONTANT D'ORVILLE, A. G. *Lettre critique sur la comédie intitulée l'Enfant prodigue*. Paris, 1737.

CORNU, MARCEL. 'Le Second Voltaire', *Europe*, 361–362 (mai–juin 1959), 136–151.

*Correspondance littéraire, philosophique et critique par Grimm, Diderot, Raynal, Meister, etc*. 16 vols. Paris, 1877–1882.

COYER, GABRIEL FRANÇOIS. *Discours sur la Satyre contre les philosophes*. Paris, 1760.

CROCKER, LESTER G. *Nature and Culture: Ethical Thought in the French Enlightenment*. Baltimore, 1963.

DAGUES DE CLAIRFONTAINE, SIMON ANTOINE CHARLES. *Bienfaisance française, ou Mémoires pour servir à l'histoire de ce siècle*. 2 vols. Paris, 1778.

DARGAN, E. PRESTON. 'The Question of Voltaire's Primacy in Establishing the English Vogue', in *Mélanges offerts à Fernand Baldensperger*. Paris, 1930. II, 187–198.

DEBIDOUR, ANTONIN. 'L'Indianisme de Voltaire', *RLC*, 4 (January–March 1924), 26–40.

DELACROIX, EUGÈNE. *Journal, 1822–1863*, ed. André Joubin. 3 vols. Paris, 1932.

DELATTRE, ANDRÉ. *Voltaire l'impétueux: essai présenté par R. Pomeau*. Paris, 1957.

DELISLE DE SALES, JEAN BAPTISTE CLAUDE IZOUARD. *Essai sur la tragédie*. 1772.

DERATHÉ, ROBERT. *Le Rationalisme de Rousseau*. Paris, 1948.

[DESFONTAINES ET GRANET]. *Veritez littéraires sur la tragédie d'Herode et de Mariamne, adressées à M. de Voltaire*. Paris, 1725.

DESMARAIS, CYPRIEN. *Essai sur les classiques et les romantiques*. Paris, 1824.

DESNOIRESTERRES, G. *Voltaire et la société au XVIIIᵉ siècle*. 8 vols. Paris, 1871–1876.

DESPRÉAUX DE LA CONDAMINE, SIMIEN. *Soirées de Ferney, ou Confidences de Voltaire, recueillies par un ami de ce grand homme*. Paris, 1802.

DESVOYES, ALBERT. 'Voltaire et Lamartine', *RHL*, 19 (1912), 911–913.

DIDEROT, DENIS. *Œuvres complètes*, ed. J. Assézat. Paris, 1875.

——. *Correspondance*, ed. Georges Roth. Paris, 1955–.

DOIGNY DU PONCEAU, RENÉ. *Aux mânes de Voltaire, par un citoyen de l'univers*. Amsterdam, 1779.

DUBOS, JEAN BAPTISTE. *Réflexions critiques sur la poésie et sur la peinture*. 3 vols. Paris, 1770.

DU CHASTEAU. *Epistre à monsieur Voltaire sur la nouvelle tragédie d'Alzire*. Paris, 1736.

DU CHÂTELET, MME. *Lettres inédites de Mme la Marquise du Châtelet à M. le comte d'Argental*. Paris, 1806.

[DUPUY-DEMPORTES]. *Parallèle de la Sémiramis de M. de Voltaire et de celle de M. de Crébillon*. Paris, 1748.

DUVERNET, T. I. *La Vie de Voltaire*. Geneva, 1786.

ESCHOLIER, RAYMOND, 'Le premier de nos historiens: Voltaire', *Europe*, 361–362 (mai–juin 1959), 19–33.

FABRE, JEAN. *Lumières et romantisme, énergie et nostalgie, de Rousseau à Mickiewicz*. Paris, 1963.

FAGUET, EMILE. *Dix-huitième siècle*. Paris, 1890.

——. *Histoire de la poésie française de la renaissance au romantisme*. Vol. VII. *Voltaire (1694–1778)*. Paris, 1934.

FALKE, RITA. 'Eldorado: le meilleur des mondes possibles', *SV*, II, 25–41.

FARGHER, R. 'The Retreat from Voltairianism (1800–1815)', in *The French Mind: Studies in Honour of Gustave Rudler* (Oxford, 1952), pp. 220–237.

FAVART, CHARLES SIMON. *Mémoires et correspondance littéraires, dramatiques et anecdotiques*. Paris, 1808.

FAŸ, BERNARD. *L'Esprit révolutionnaire en France et aux Etats-Unis à la fin du XVIII^e siècle*. Paris, 1925.

FÉNELON, FRANÇOIS DE SALIGNAC DE LA MOTHE-. *Œuvres complètes*. 10 vols. Paris, 1850.

FENGER, H. *Voltaire et le théâtre anglais*. Copenhagen, 1949.

FIELDS, MADELEINE. 'Voltaire et le *Mercure de France*', *SV*, XX, 175–215.

FLAUBERT, GUSTAVE. 'Voltaire jugé par Flaubert', ed. Theodore Besterman. *SV*, I, 133–158.

——. *Le Théâtre de Voltaire,* ed. Theodore Besterman. *SV,* vols. L and LI.

FLETCHER, DENIS J. 'Montesquieu's Conception of Patriotism', *SV,* LVI, 541–555.

FONTAINE, LÉON. *Le Théâtre et la philosophie au XVIII^e siècle.* Paris, 1878.

FONTENELLE, BERNARD LE BOVIER DE. *Œuvres complètes,* ed. G. B. Depping. 3 vols. Paris, 1818.

FORMEY, S. *Souvenirs d'un citoyen.* 2 vols. Berlin, 1789.

FUSIL, C. A. *La Contagion sacrée ou Jean-Jacques Rousseau de 1778–1820.* Paris, 1932.

GAY, PETER. *The Party of Humanity: Essays in the French Enlightenment.* New York, 1964.

GAZON DOURXIGNÉ. *L'Ami de la vérité, ou Lettres impartiales, semées d'anecdotes curieuses, sur toutes les pièces de théâtre de M. de Voltaire.* Amsterdam, 1767.

GENLIS, MME DE. *Mémoires.* 2 vols. Paris, 1928.

GEOFFROY, JULIEN LOUIS. *Cours de littérature dramatique.* 6 vols. Paris, 1825.

GRAFFIGNY, FRANÇOISE DE. *Lettres de Mme de Graffigny . . .,* ed. Eugène Asse. Paris, 1879.

GUIARD DE SERVIGNY, J. B. *Lettre à l'auteur de Nanine.* 1749.

GUIRAGOSSIAN, DIANA. *Voltaire's 'Facéties'.* Geneva, 1963.

HAMPSON, NORMAN. *The Enlightenment.* Harmondsworth, 1968.

HARTLEY, K. H. 'The Sources of Voltaire's *Mariamne*', *AUMLA,* 21 (1964), 5–14.

HAVENS, GEORGE R. 'The Nature Doctrine of Voltaire', *PMLA,* 40 (1925), 852–862.

——. *Voltaire's Marginalia on the Pages of Rousseau.* New York, 1966.

HAZARD, PAUL. *La Pensée européenne au XVIII^e siècle de Montesquieu à Lessing.* 3 vols. Paris, 1946.

——. 'L'Homme du sentiment', *RR,* 28 (December 1937), 318–341.

HELVÉTIUS, CLAUDE ADRIEN. *De l'esprit.* Paris, 1758.

HÉRISSAY, J. *Le Monde des théâtres pendant la Révolution (1789–1800) d'après des documents inédits.* Paris, 1922.

HERVIER, MARCEL. *Les Ecrivains français jugés par leurs contemporains.* Vol. II. *Le XVIII^e siècle.* Paris, 1936.

HUGO, VICTOR. *Œuvres complètes.* Paris, 1904–.

——. *Le Discours pour Voltaire: la lettre à l'évêque d'Orléans.* Paris, 1878.

HUME, DAVID. *A Treatise of Human Nature*, ed. L. A. Selby-Bigge. Oxford, 1896.

HUYGHE, RENÉ. *Delacroix*. New York, 1963.

JACQUART, JEAN. *L'Abbé Trublet critique et moraliste, 1697–1770*. Paris, 1926.

JOANNIDÈS, A. *La Comédie-Française de 1680 à 1920*. Paris, 1921.

JOVICEVICH, ALEXANDRE. 'A propos d'une Paméla de Voltaire'. *FR*, 36 (1962–1963), 276–283.

KENNEDY, JOHN H. *Jesuit and Savage in New France*. New Haven, 1950.

LA CURNE DE SAINTE-PALAYE, JEAN BAPTISTE DE. *Mémoires sur l'ancienne chevalerie, considérée comme un établissement politique et militaire*. 3 vols. Paris, 1759–1781.

LA HARPE, J. F. DE. *Aux mânes de Voltaire . . .* Paris, 1779.

——. *Commentaire sur le théâtre de Voltaire par M. de La Harpe*. Paris, 1814.

——. *Eloge de Voltaire*. Geneva, 1780.

——. *Lycée, ou Cours de littérature ancienne et moderne*. 16 vols. Paris, 1798.

——. *Les Muses rivales, ou l'Apothéose de Voltaire*. Paris, 1779.

LAMARTINE, ALPHONSE DE. *Cours familier de littérature*. 28 vols. Paris, 1856–1869.

LA METTRIE, JULIEN OFFRAY DE. *Œuvres philosophiques*. 2 vols. Amsterdam, 1753.

LANCASTER, HENRY CARRINGTON. *A History of French Dramatic Literature in the Seventeenth Century*. 9 vols. Baltimore, 1929–1942.

LANSON, GUSTAVE. *Nivelle de La Chaussée et la comédie larmoyante*. Paris, 1887.

LAYA, J. L. *Jean Calas, tragédie en 5 actes*. Paris, 1791.

LECLERC DE MONTMERCI. *Voltaire, poème en vers libres*. 1764.

LEIGH, R. A. 'From the *Inégalité* to *Candide*: notes on a desultory dialogue between Rousseau and Voltaire (1755–1759)', in *The Age of Enlightenment* (Edinburgh, 1967), pp. 66–92.

——. 'An anonymous eighteenth-century character-sketch of Voltaire', *SV*, II, 241–272.

LEMIERRE D'ARGY, A. J. *Calas, ou le Fanatisme, drame en 4 actes*. Paris, 1791.

LEPAN, EDOUARD MARIE JOSEPH. *Commentaires sur les tragédies et les comédies de Voltaire*. 2 vols. Paris, 1826.

LEVESQUE DE POUILLY, LOUIS JEAN. *Théorie des sentimens agréables*. Geneva, 1747.

LEZAY-MARNÉSIA, C. F. A. *Le Bonheur dans les campagnes*. Neuchâtel, 1785.

——. *Essai sur la nature champêtre*. Paris, 1787.

LINGUET, SIMON NICOLAS HENRI. *Examen des ouvrages de M. de Voltaire, considéré comme Poète, comme Prosateur, comme Philosophe*. Brussels, 1788.

LOAISEL DE TRÉOGATE, J. M. *Dolbreuse, ou l'homme du siècle, ramené à vérité par le sentiment & par la raison. Histoire philosophique*. Amsterdam, 1783.

LOMBARD, ALFRED. *L'Abbé Dubos, un initiateur de la pensée moderne (1670–1742)*. Paris, 1913.

LONGCHAMP, SÉBASTIEN AND WAGNIÈRE, JEAN LOUIS. *Mémoires sur Voltaire et sur ses ouvrages*. 2 vols. Paris, 1826.

LOVEJOY, ARTHUR O. 'The Supposed Primitivism of Rousseau's Discourse of Inequality', *MP*, 21 (1923), 165–186.

LYNCH, K. M. '*Pamela Nubile, L'Ecossaise*, and *The English Merchant*', *MLN*, 47 (February 1932), 94–96.

MARAIS, MATHIEU. *Journal et mémoires sur la régence et le règne de Louis XV (1715–1737)*. 4 vols. Paris, 1863–1868.

MARMONTEL, JEAN FRANÇOIS. *Œuvres complètes*. Paris, 1787–1806.

MASON, HAYDN T. 'The Unity of Voltaire's *L'Ingénu*', in *The Age of Enlightenment* (Edinburgh, 1967), pp. 93–106.

MAUGRAS, GASTON. *Querelles de philosophes: Voltaire et J.-J. Rousseau*. Paris, 1886.

MAUZI, ROBERT. *L'Idée du bonheur au XVIIIᵉ siècle*. Paris, 1967.

MAY, GEORGES. *Diderot et 'la Religieuse'*. Paris, 1954.

MAY, GITA. *De Jean-Jacques Rousseau à Madame Roland: Essai sur la sensibilité préromantique et révolutionnaire*. Geneva, 1964.

MERCIER, LOUIS SÉBASTIEN. *L'An deux mille quatre cent quarante, rêve s'il en fût jamais*. Amsterdam, 1771.

MERCIER, ROGER. *La Réhabilitation de la nature humaine (1700–1750)*. Villemonble, 1960.

MÉTRA, FRANÇOIS. *Correspondance littéraire secrète*. 19 vols. Neuwied, 1775–1793.

MICHELET, JULES. *Histoire de France*. 16 vols. Paris, 1893–1897.

MISTELET. *De la sensibilité par rapport aux drames, aux romans, et à l'éducation*. Amsterdam, 1777.

MONGLOND, ANDRÉ. *Histoire intérieure du préromantisme français, de l'abbé Prévost à Joubert*. Grenoble, 1929.

——. *Le Préromantisme français*. 2 vols. Grenoble, 1930.

MONTESQUIEU. *Œuvres complètes*, ed. Edouard Laboulaye. 7 vols. Paris, 1879.

MONTY, JEANNE R. *Etude sur le style polémique de Voltaire: Le Dictionnaire philosophique. SV*, vol. XLIV. Geneva, 1966.

MORNET, DANIEL. *Le Romantisme en France au XVIII^e siècle.* Paris, 1912.

MORTIER, ROLAND. 'Unité ou scission des lumières?' *SV*, XXVI, 1207–1221.

MUSSET, ALFRED DE. *Œuvres complètes en prose.* Paris. 1960.

NAVES, RAYMOND. *Le Goût de Voltaire.* Paris, 1938.

——. 'Voltaire éditeur de Rousseau', *RHL*, 44 (1937), 245–247.

——. *Voltaire et l'Encyclopédie.* Paris, 1938.

——. *Voltaire, l'homme et l'œuvre.* Paris, 1942.

NONNOTTE, C. F. *Les Erreurs de Voltaire.* 2 vols. Lyon, 1770.

NOUGARET, P. J. B. *Eloge de Voltaire, Poème* . . . Geneva, 1779.

*Nouveaux Amusements du cœur et de l'esprit.* Paris, 1737–1749.

OLIVIER, JEAN-JACQUES. *Henri-Louis Le Kain de la Comédie-Française.* Paris, 1907.

OULMONT, CHARLES. *Voltaire en robe de chambre.* Paris, 1936.

PALISSOT, CHARLES. *Eloge de M. de Voltaire.* London, 1778.

PAPPAS, JOHN. 'Le Rousseauisme de Voltaire', *SV*, LVII, 1169–1181.

PECQUET, ANTOINE. *Parallèle du cœur, de l'esprit et du bon sens.* Paris, 1740.

PELLEGRIN, S. J. "Dissertation sur l'Œdipe de Corneille, et sur celui de M. de Voltaire', *Mercure* (juin 1729), 1316–1317.

PEREY, LUCIEN AND MAUGRAS, GASTON. *La Vie intime de Voltaire aux Délices et à Ferney 1754–1778.* Paris, 1885.

PEYRE, HENRI. 'Romantic Poetry and Rhetoric', *Yale French Studies*, XIII, 30–41.

PLEKHANOV, G. V. *Art and Social Life.* London, 1953.

POMEAU, RENÉ. *La Religion de Voltaire.* Paris, 1956.

——. 'Voltaire et le héros', *Revue des Sciences Humaines*, 64 (octobre–décembre 1951), 345–351.

——. *Voltaire par lui-même.* Paris, 1955.

POMMIER, JEAN. 'Le Cycle de Chactas', *RLC*, 18 (1938), 604–629.

POMPADOUR, MME DE. *Lettres de Mme la Marquise de Pompadour.* London, 1773.

PORTER, CHARLES A. *Restif's Novels, or an Autobiography in Search of an Author.* New Haven, 1967.

PRÉVOST, ABBÉ ANTOINE FRANÇOIS. *Le Pour et contre.* 20 vols. 1733–1740.

PUJOULX, M. J. B. *La Veuve Calas à Paris ou le Triomphe de Voltaire.* Paris, 1791.

QUÉRARD, JOSEPH MARIE. *Bibliographie voltairienne.* Paris, 1842.

RAYNAL, GUILLAUME THOMAS FRANÇOIS. *Histoire philosophique et politique des Etablissement et du Commerce des Européens dans les deux Indes.* 10 vols. Geneva, 1780.

RIDGWAY, RONALD S. *La Propagande philosophique dans les tragédies de Voltaire.* *SV*, vol. XV. Geneva, 1961.

RITTER, EUGÈNE. 'Le Marquis de Ximenez, Voltaire et Rousseau', *RHL*, 4 (1897), 578–580.

ROBINOVE, PHYLLIS B. 'Voltaire's Theater on the Parisian Stage, 1789–1799', *FR*, 32 (May 1959), 534–538.

ROLLIN, CHARLES. *De la manière d'enseigner et d'étudier les belles lettres par rapport à l'esprit & au cœur.* Paris, 1726–1728.

ROUSSEAU, JEAN JACQUES. *Œuvres complètes.* Paris, 1961–.

——. *Correspondeance complète*, ed. R. A. Leigh. Geneva, 1965–.

——. *La 'Profession de foi du vicaire savoyard'*, ed. Maurice Masson. Fribourg, 1914.

ROWE, CONSTANCE. *Voltaire and the State.* New York, 1955.

SABATIER DE CASTRES, ANTOINE. *Tableau philosophique de l'esprit de M. de Voltaire....* Geneva, 1771.

——. *Les Trois siècles de la littérature française.* Amsterdam, 1774.

SAINTE-BEUVE, CHARLES AUGUSTIN. *Causeries du lundi*, 2ᵉ édition. 15 vols. Paris, 1869.

SAINT-PIERRE, JACQUES HENRI BERNARDIN DE. *Œuvres*, ed. Aimé Martin. 12 vols. Paris, 1818.

SERVIÈRES, BARON DE. *Mémoires pour servir à l'histoire de M. de Voltaire.* 2 vols. Amsterdam, 1785.

SHUVALOV, ANDRÉ PETROVICH, COMTE. *Lettre à Voltaire.* Amsterdam, 1779.

STAËL, MME DE. *Œuvres complètes de Madame la baronne de Staël-Holstein.* 2 vols. Paris, 1836.

——. *De l'Allemagne.* 2 vols. Paris, 1968.

STANISLAS Iᵉʳ, ROI DE POLOGNE. *Œuvres du philosophe bienfaisant.* 4 vols. Paris, 1763.

STEPHEN, LESLIE. *History of English Thought in the Eighteenth Century.* 2 vols. London, 1881.

STERN, JEAN. *Belle et Bonne, une fervente amie de Voltaire (1757–1822).* Paris, 1938.

STRACHEY, GILES LYTTON. *Books and Characters.* London, 1922.

SUNGOLOWSKY, JOSEPH. *Alfred de Vigny et le dix-huitième siècle.* Paris, 1968.

TAYLOR, S. S. B. 'Voltaire's *L'Ingénu*, the Huguenots and Choiseul', in *The Age of Enlightenment* (Edinburgh, 1967), pp. 107–136.

TELLEEN, JOHN MARTIN. *Milton dans la littérature française.* Paris, 1904.

TERRASSON, ABBÉ JEAN. *Dissertation critique sur l'Iliade.* 2 vols. Paris, 1715.

THÉMISEUL DE SAINTE-HYACINTHE. *Recueil de divers écrits.* Paris, 1736.

TIERSOT, JULIEN. *Les Fêtes et les chants de la Révolution française.* Paris, 1908.

TOPAZIO, VIRGIL W. *Voltaire: A Critical Study of his Major Works.* New York, 1967.

TORREY, NORMAN L. *The Spirit of Voltaire.* New York, 1938.

——. 'Voltaire's Reaction to Diderot', *PMLA*, 50 (1935), 1107–1143.

TRUBLET, NICOLAS. *Essais sur divers sujets de littérature et de morale.* 4 vols. Paris, 1749.

VAN DEN HEUVEL, JACQUES. 'Voltaire', in *Histoire des Littératures, Encyclopédie de la Pléiade* (Paris, 1958), III, 711–728.

——. *Voltaire dans ses contes.* Paris, 1967.

VAN TIEGHEM, PAUL. *Le Préromantisme: Etudes d'histoire littéraire européenne.* 3 vols. Paris, 1924–1930.

VAUVENARGUES, LUC DE CLAPIERS, MARQUIS DE. *Œuvres . . . publiées avec une introduction et des notices par Pierre Varillon.* 3 vols. Paris, 1929.

VEAU DE LAUNAY, PIERRE L. A. *Voltaire, Ode et autres poésies.* London, 1780.

VENZAC, G. *Les Premiers maîtres de Victor Hugo.* Paris, 1955.

VERCRUYSSE, J. 'C'est la faute à Rousseau, c'est la faute à Voltaire', *SV*, XXIII, 61–76.

VERNIÈRE, PAUL. 'L'idée de l'humanité au XVIIIᵉ siècle'. *Studium Generale*, 15 (1962), 171–179.

VIGNY, ALFRED DE. *Œuvres complètes.* 2 vols. Paris, 1960–1964.

VILLARET, CLAUDE. *L'Esprit de M. de Voltaire.* Paris, 1759.

VOLTAIRE, FRANÇOIS MARIE AROUET DE. *The Complete Works of Voltaire*, ed. Theodore Besterman and others. Geneva, 1968–.

——. *Œuvres complètes de Voltaire*, nouvelle édition publiée par Louis Moland. 52 vols. Paris, 1877–1882.

——. *Contes de Guillaume Vadé.* Geneva, 1764.

——. *Correspondence, 1704–1778*, ed. Theodore Besterman. 107 vols. Geneva, 1953–1965.

——. *Essai sur les mœurs*, ed. R. Pomeau. Paris, 1963.

——. *La Henriade*, ed. O. R. Taylor. *SV*, vol. XXXIX. Geneva, 1965.

——. *Mélanges*, ed. Jacques Van Den Heuvel. Paris, 1961.

——. *Romans et contes*, ed. René Groos. Paris, 1964.

——. *Le Sottisier de Voltaire*. Paris, 1880.

'Voltaire's British Visitors', ed. Sir Gavin de Beer, *SV*, IV, 7–136; X, 425–438; XVIII, 237–261 (ed. Sir Gavin de Beer and A. M. Rousseau).

WADE, IRA O. 'A Favourite Metaphor of Voltaire', *RR*, 26 (1935), 330–334.

——. *The Search for a New Voltaire; Studies Based upon Material Deposited at the American Philosophical Society*. Philadelphia, 1958.

——. *Voltaire and Candide. A Study in the Fusion of History, Art, and Philosophy*. Princeton, 1959.

——. *Voltaire and Madame Du Châtelet, An Essay on the Intellectual Activity at Cirey*. Princeton, 1941.

WALLAS, MAY. *Luc de Clapiers, Marquis de Vauvenargues*. Cambridge, 1928.

WEIGHTMAN, J. G. 'The Quality of *Candide*', in *Essays Presented to C. M. Girdlestone* (Durham 1960), pp. 335–347.

WELSCHINGER, HENRI. *Le Théâtre de la Révolution 1789–1799*. Geneva (Slatkine Reprints), 1968.

WHITE, FLORENCE. *Voltaire's Essay on Epic Poetry, a Study and an Edition*. New York, 1915.

WILLEMAIN D'ABANCOURT. *La Bienfaisance de Voltaire, pièce dramatique en un acte et en vers*. Paris, 1791.

WILLEY, BASIL. *The Eighteenth-Century Background*. Harmondsworth, 1965.

WILLIAMS, DAVID. 'Voltaire and the Language of the Gods', *SV*, LXII, 57–81.

——. *Voltaire: Literary Critic. SV*, XLVIII. Geneva, 1966.

# INDEX